T0277240

General Peter Muhlenberg

Journal of the American Revolution Books highlight the latest research on new or lesser-known topics of the revolutionary era. The *Journal of the American Revolution* is an online resource and annual volume that provides educational, peer-reviewed articles by professional historians and experts in American Revolution studies.

Other Titles in the Series

Washington's War, 1779
by Benjamin Lee Huggins

John Adams vs. Thomas Paine: Rival Plans for the New Republic
by Jett B. Connor

The Invasion of Virginia, 1781
by Michael Cecere

The Burning of His Majesty's Schooner Gaspee:
An Attack on Crown Rule Before the American Revolution
by Steven Park

Grand Forage 1778: The Battleground Around New York City
by Todd W. Braisted

*The Road to Concord: How Four Stolen Cannon Ignited
the Revolutionary War*
by J. L. Bell

A JOURNAL OF THE AMERICAN REVOLUTION BOOK

GENERAL PETER MUHLENBERG

A VIRGINIA OFFICER OF THE CONTINENTAL LINE

MICHAEL CECERE

WESTHOLME
Yardley

Westholme Publishing, LLC
904 Edgewood Road
Yardley, Pennsylvania 19067
Visit our Web site at www.westholmepublishing.com

ISBN: 978-1-59416-342-5
Also available as an eBook.

Printed in the United States of America.

CONTENTS

Contents

List of Maps

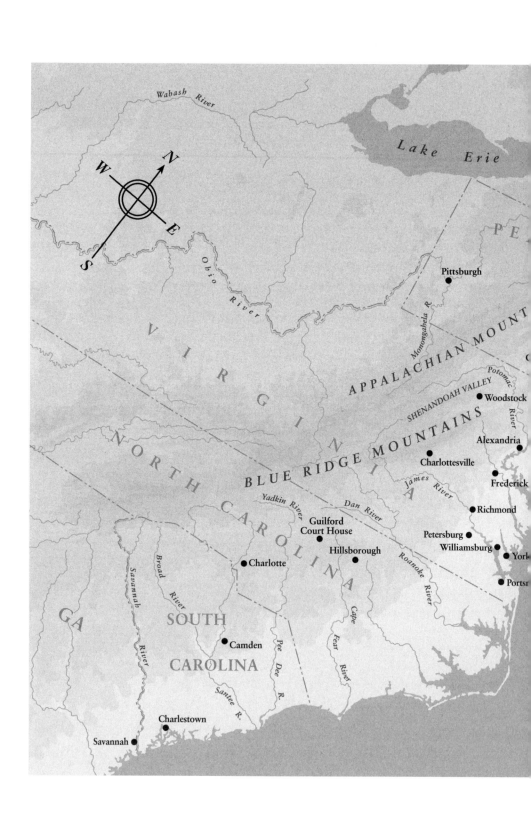

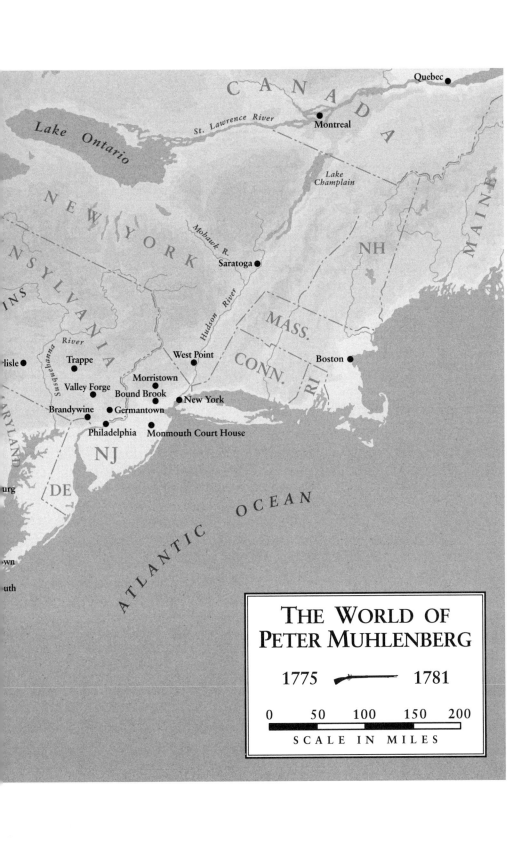

CANADA

Quebec

Lake Ontario

St. Lawrence River

Montreal

NEW YORK

Lake Champlain

Mohawk R.

MAINE

NH

Saratoga

PENNSYLVANIA

INS

Hudson River

MASS.

Susquehanna River

lisle

Trappe

West Point

CONN.

Boston

RI

Morristown

Valley Forge

Bound Brook

New York

MARYLAND

Brandywine

Germantown

Philadelphia

Monmouth Court House

NJ

DE

urg

ATLANTIC OCEAN

wn

uth

THE WORLD OF PETER MUHLENBERG

1775 ⟶ 1781

| 0 | 50 | 100 | 150 | 200 |

SCALE IN MILES

INTRODUCTION

GENERAL JOHN PETER GABRIEL MUHLENBERG IS REMEMBERED by few Americans today outside of those who study the American Revolution. In his own day, Peter Muhlenberg was revered as both a clergyman and American patriot, a Continental officer who served with distinction for nearly the entire Revolutionary War. In 1849, more than forty years after Peter Muhlenberg's death, his great nephew Henry Muhlenberg published the first biography of his ancestor. Filled with his great uncle's correspondence, Muhlenberg's account is a valuable resource. It is also the origin of the most famous incident of Muhlenberg's life, namely, his farewell sermon as the "Fighting Parson."

As told by Henry Muhlenberg, it is an inspiring story of a minister selected to command troops from Virginia's Shenandoah Valley and his farewell address to his many parishioners who had gathered in Woodstock, Virginia, to hear his last sermon. Drawing inspiration from scripture, Reverend Muhlenberg declared to his congregation, "that there was a time for all things, a time to preach and a time to pray, but those times had passed away." After a dramatic pause, Muhlenberg continued, asserting that "there was a time to fight, and that time had now come!" He then reportedly cast off his minister's robe to reveal his Continental colonel's uniform underneath.

This account of the Fighting Parson took on various forms in the years following the publication of Henry Muhlenberg's book. Although the details differed in each telling, there is little doubt that Peter Muhlenberg did indeed address his congregation dressed in his military uniform—possibly a hunting shirt covered by his minister's robe—prior to marching off to war in 1776.

After he left the pulpit that day, Muhlenberg devoted the next seven years of his life to the American army, a commitment that helped gain America's independence from Great Britain. Muhlenberg's service as a regimental and brigade commander took him to South Carolina and Georgia in 1776, to the mid-Atlantic states in 1777 through 1779, and back to Virginia from 1780 to 1783. Few officers or men in the Continental army served as long as Muhlenberg did. He saw action at Charleston (1776), Brandywine and Germantown (1777), Monmouth (1778), and Stony Point (1779). After returning to Virginia, he led the state's militia against the American traitor Benedict Arnold's attack on the state in early 1781. Muhlenberg remained in Virginia, fighting under the command of the Marquis de Lafayette in the spring and summer of 1781, and when Washington arrived at Yorktown in the fall, Muhlenberg commanded the American light infantry troops at the siege of Yorktown. Following the war, he returned to his native Pennsylvania, where he represented the state as a congressman and a senator.

This brief study focuses on the military career of General Muhlenberg. It uses primary sources that were not available to Henry Muhlenberg to get a better idea of how Muhlenberg interacted with both the soldiers he led and his fellow officers during his long, distinguished service for the American cause. What it reveals is a man who fought alongside Charles Lee, Lafayette, Friedrich von Steuben, Nathanael Greene, and others, and whose ability his commander in chief held in high regard.

One

Finding a Calling

J OHN PETER GABRIEL MUHLENBERG WAS BORN ON OCTOBER 1, 1746, in Trappe, Pennsylvania, a largely German settlement about thirty miles northwest of Philadelphia.[1] His father, Henry Melchoir Muhlenberg, had immigrated to Pennsylvania from Germany several years earlier. As an ordained minister of the Lutheran Church, Henry Muhlenberg was well received by the steadily growing German population of Pennsylvania.[2] In 1745 he married Anna Weiser, the daughter of renowned frontiersman and Indian agent Colonel Conrad Weiser, and their first child, John Peter Gabriel, arrived the following year.[3]

John Peter Gabriel (who went by Peter) spent his childhood in Trappe where he reveled in the type of outdoor activities still common to rural settlements, specifically hunting and fishing.[4] When Peter was fourteen, Henry Muhlenberg relocated his family to Philadelphia, in part because of church affairs but also in hopes of providing his children more educational opportunities.[5]

He was evidently disappointed with the result, for within months of moving to Philadelphia, Reverend Muhlenberg wrote to a trusted fellow minister in London, Chaplain Frederick Ziegenhagen, soliciting his assistance in arranging an opportunity for his son Peter to learn a trade in Europe. Muhlenberg explained:

> My oldest son, Peter, is entering his sixteenth year. I have had him taught to read and write German and English, and, after the necessary instruction, he has been confirmed in our Evangelical Church; moreover, since I have been in Philadelphia, I have sent him to the Academy to learn [Latin]. But now I write in great anxiety on account of the corruption among the impudent and emancipated youth of this city, and I am not able to provide for his welfare any longer. It would be a great scandal and offence in my position, and to the ruin of his own soul, if he should fall into wild ways. Is there not an opportunity among the members of your Church for him to learn surgery, or even an honest trade?[6]

Over a year passed before Peter, accompanied by his two younger brothers, Friedrich and Heinrich, was sent to Halle, Germany. The two younger brothers were to attend the Halle Institute (just as their father had done) to improve their education and moral character, but their older brother Peter, who confessed he "had a great fancy for business," eagerly consented to a six-year apprenticeship to learn an honest trade with a grocer and druggist in Lubeck.[7] The agreement between Peter and the grocer, Leonhard Niemeyer, was signed in late September 1763, and all parties, both those in Germany and Peter's parents in Pennsylvania, seemed pleased with the arrangement.[8]

After two years, however, Reverend Muhlenberg became concerned about the treatment of his oldest son and wrote to a friend in London, Lector Pasche, to ask if he would inquire into Peter's situation.[9] Pasche wrote to Peter Muhlenberg, sharing with him his father's specific concerns and instructing Peter to write to his father with answers. Peter Muhlenberg instead wrote back to Pasche with startling details.

> I consented joyfully to the six years, because at the time I had a great fancy for business. But as it has turned out quite differently, I leave it to your Honor's opinion, if six years are not too many.

. . . It is really true that last winter I was obliged to wear one shirt for from four to six weeks, because I only had two and because my clothing was very bad, and we had to stand the whole winter long in an open shop, and I was obliged to suffer from the cold . . . . I begged my mistress to have something mended for me. She answered shortly, she would have nothing else repaired for me, and if my parents did not send any money, I might go naked, and because I troubled nobody with complaints, it was always so. . . . Your Honor knows very well that there is not much to be learned in a grocery store, and I assure you that when I had been here four weeks, I knew as much as I do now, for when I learned how to pour out a glass of brandy and to sell a little tea, sugar, etc., I had learned everything. He [Niemeyer the grocer] himself takes charge of the little drug shop, and, as I have by this time entirely forgotten my Latin, I have no longer any desire to learn medicine. We have nothing at all to do with writing, or reckoning. I assure your Honor that, to please my dear parents, I will willingly stay out my apprenticeship, only it seems to me very hard that I must sacrifice six of the best years of my life without learning anything. If my master would allow me to learn bookkeeping, I could serve him willingly and heartily. . . . If I only had Sunday free, I could practice writing and arithmetic a little, but our shop is open Sundays as well as other days until ten o'clock in the evening.[10]

The observations and accusations in Peter Muhlenberg's letter to Lector Pasche were shared by Pasche with officials in Halle (who were responsible for Peter's well-being) who initially met them with disbelief. However, they were confirmed by a second source, Sebastian Fabricius, who was informed by an acquaintance of Peter and a cousin of Herr Niemeyer that

The youth had gone to the wrong merchant to learn his trade, and had probably cause enough to be discontented with his situation. We wonder greatly that Herr Neimeyer's conscience would allow him to take a young man who had come so far to learn the business, as an apprentice for six years, when the business can be perfectly acquired within a year. We had young Muhlenberg with us yesterday, etc. It is a sin that anyone should want him to stay here with Herr N.; only the worst of the peasant youth from the country, accustomed to rough work from their youth up, are taken into such a business.[11]

Peter Muhlenberg confirmed this sentiment to Herr Fabricius several days later in his own letter:

I can assure your Honor that I have profited very little here, and knew as much in the first four weeks as I know now, and have only lost my precious time. I cannot profit at all by the little drug shop, and take pleasure in nothing but business, as I wrote to my Papa, and my employer has no business by which I can profit. . . . I cannot complain that my employer does not keep me well in food, etc., but it seems very hard to me that I am ruining my health by standing the whole winter and summer in the shop and learning nothing. My dear brothers will be able by the grace of God in the future to point to what they have gained in Europe, but I have nothing to show.[12]

By early May 1766, Peter Muhlenberg had resolved that he would break his agreement and leave the grocery in the fall.[13] His decision triggered efforts to find a reasonable accommodation for both Peter and Herr Niemeyer, the grocer, and unsurprisingly, the solution came down to money. A new contract was agreed to in July releasing Peter of his service to Herr Niemeyer on Easter Day 1767, nearly two and a half years prior to his original agreement. In return, Peter, through his father, would pay the grocer a hundred thalers, which would more than offset the cost of a journeyman replacement for Peter in the shop. Peter even received permission to take four hours a week off for instruction of arithmetic and bookkeeping, albeit at his own expense.[14]

It seemed that all were satisfied with this new arrangement, but early in the morning of August 14, Peter Muhlenberg packed up his few possessions and left the grocery shop for good. A note penned by Muhlenberg and delivered to the grocer that same morning explained his actions:

My dear Herr Niemeyer!

You will be not a little vexed when you hear that I have gone away so unexpectedly, without knowing any cause therefore. You have done your very best for me, and it is not your fault. It is partly owing to my love for my native country, and the other reasons I cannot disclose to you. I have enlisted as [a] cadet among the Englishmen, who are going into garrison in America. I now humbly entreat you not to injure your health by useless anger, because it cannot be changed now. . . . You will receive the money from Madame Neubauer, and if you will come to an amicable agreement with me, I will try to procure fifty thalers for you from my Captain. But if you try to seize me forcibly I will go to Retzeberg. I would willingly offer to remain two or four weeks with you until you are a little in order. But you will hesitate to take me in your shop now. Nevertheless, I can take my oath that I leave you with a clear conscience, without having taken away the slightest thing, although I certainly had opportunities enough. Reassure for me my dear parents, whom I should certainly have not done anything in opposition to, if I had not had weighty reasons which God alone knows. I shall thankfully acknowledge, as long as I live, what you have done for me. Your until now faithful servant, J.P.G.M[15]

Madame Neubauer, who had played a significant role in brokering the new agreement between Muhlenberg and Niemeyer, an agreement now shredded by Muhlenberg's actions, provided additional detail of the events regarding the young apprentice's flight in a letter to Sebastian Fabricius.

The last post day [August 13] I had the honor of forwarding to you the agreement about Monsieur Muhlenberg, assuring you, at the same time, that everything else should be arranged in the best possible way. You will be all the more astonished when I inform you that the aforesaid Monsieur Muhlenberg, on the day after, the 14 of this month, at half past four in the morning, secretly ran away from Herr Niemeyer's house, having his trunk and clothing carried away at the same time, and voluntarily enlisted as a soldier in the English recruiting office of Captain von Fiser, whence he sent a letter to his employer in the course of half an hour. As soon as Herr Niemeyer discovered this, he came to me in not a little consternation. . . to lament over the trouble whereupon we immediately repaired to Monsieur Muhlenberg at the recruiting-office, so as to have a complete understanding; but he only answered that the reason was merely his great longing to return to his native country.[16]

Madame Neubauer reported that Niemeyer pleaded with Muhlenberg to reconsider, but the young man declared,

If two hundred ducats were laid on the table before him, he would not consent to remain here in Germany, since he had now such an excellent opportunity to return home to his native land. M. Muhlenberg said, he well knew that it would not please his father to hear this, but he could not help it. M. Muhlenberg is on the point of becoming Regimental Secretary, as he writes a good hand and has a good appearance, and he told Herr Niemeyer that in this position he was better off than many officers. The young man does not consider the consequences . . . there is no reasoning with him, he holds fast to his intention of returning home.[17]

What accounted for Muhlenberg's sudden change of heart is impossible to say. It very well may have been a combination of homesickness and the sudden opportunity of a quick way home to America with the soon to be departing 60th Royal American Regiment. This unit, which was comprised of riflemen from Germany and other parts of Europe, had distinguished itself in America during the French and Indian War. A portion of the regiment, which was recruiting in the Lubeck region of Germany, was heading back to America for garrison duty, and Peter Muhlenberg jumped at the opportunity to join them. Muhlenberg's assertion in his letter to Niemeyer announcing his departure for "other reasons I cannot disclose" hints of other factors in his decision, but with no evidence to examine, identifying such factors is purely speculative.

What is not speculative is young Muhlenberg's attraction to the military. He expressed his pleasure with his new life in the British army to Herr Niemeyer in mid-September when he visited his former employer just prior to his departure. Niemeyer recalled that Muhlenberg "came to take leave of me, when he thanked me for all the love and kindness shown him."[18] Niemeyer tried one last time to alter Muhlenberg's mind, but his effort was in vain. "A military life," wrote Niemeyer, "appeared to him in this last conversation, to be the most excellent of all."[19]

Despite the likely disappointment and disapproval that Muhlenberg knew Niemeyer held for him, the new recruit of the 60th Regiment audaciously requested money for clothing expenses, assuring the likely dumbfounded grocer that his father would surely be good for the loan. Muhlenberg explained to Niemeyer that "if he supported himself in clothing and washing, he would be able on arriving in America, to get his discharge."[20] Niemeyer graciously agreed to Muhlenberg's request, noting that he held no ill will toward the young man.[21]

Muhlenberg departed by ship with his regiment in late September and after several stops, set sail for the American colonies in October. Word of Peter Muhlenberg's actions reached his father before he did. Mortified by the news of his son's behavior, Henry Muhlenberg wrote to Professor Francke in Halle to express his sincere sorrow and outrage: "I see today, the 9th of December, with sorrow that my eldest boy has allowed himself to be overcome by the world, the flesh, and the devil, and gone headlong into destruction. . . . It mortifies and bows me to the ground with shame."[22]

Concerned that his son's behavior was a reflection upon him, Muhlenberg assured Francke that "If my boy had played me this trick here and enlisted, I would have sold him as a servant until his majority [age 21] or have put him in the House of Correction."[23]

Henry Muhlenberg's anger at his son apparently abated over time, for when Peter reached Philadelphia in mid-January 1767, his father paid a thirty-pound sterling debt to Captain Fiser.[24] With his debt to the British army settled, Peter Muhlenberg, volunteer of the 60th Royal American Regiment, was honorably discharged.[25]

Henry Muhlenberg wrote to his friend Lector Pasche in London in late March 1767 that Peter had been sent to a private English school in Philadelphia "where he is learning bookkeeping, and making some progress. He keeps himself quiet and retired, and yet is popular among friends."[26] Several trades were considered for Peter, but it was the Lutheran Church that ultimately attracted the young man's interest.

In the spring of 1767, a Swedish minister and friend of Reverend Muhlenberg took young Peter into his home to teach him the foundations of theoretical and practical religion. Peter Muhlenberg was also tutored in Latin and Greek, and before year's end, he was delivering catechetical discourse in several of the county churches outside of Philadelphia.[27]

Preaching came naturally to Peter, and large crowds turned out to hear him.[28] Henry Muhlenberg happily wrote to his friends in London and Germany about his eldest son's ecclesiastical abilities: "Impartial, intelligent, and experienced people say that he has a pleasant tenor voice, a clear and distinct delivery, puts emphasis in the right place, is polite, quiet, and guarded in his conversation and will have nothing to do with strong drink."[29]

Reverend Muhlenberg could not have been prouder; his son Peter had found his calling.

Encouraged by his father to preach as often as possible, Peter was appointed a deacon of the Lutheran Church in June 1769.[30] Able to conduct church services in German and English, he was in high demand and preached regularly in both Pennsylvania and New Jersey. In the fall of 1771 twenty-four-year-old Peter Muhlenberg took yet another step toward respectability, marrying Hanna Meyer, the daughter of a successful potter in Philadelphia.[31]

Earlier that same year James Wood Jr. of Frederick County, Virginia, heard of Peter Muhlenberg's abilities in the pulpit while visiting Philadelphia. Wood had been asked by the vestry of a neighboring parish in Virginia to be on the lookout for a qualified minister with the ability to preach in both German and English. In early May 1771 Wood wrote to Muhlenberg with an offer.

> I have been requested by the Vestry of a Vacant Parish in Virginia, to use my Endeavours to find a Person of an unexceptionable

Character, either Ordained or Desirous of Obtaining Ordination of the Clergy of the Church of England; who is capable of Preaching both in the English and German Languages. . . . I am very inclined to Believe you would fully Answer the Expectation of the People of that Parish.[32]

The parish in question was Beckford Parish, which was located in soon to be established Dunmore County in the Shenandoah Valley of Virginia. Intrigued by the offer, Muhlenberg took to the road to visit Virginia and meet the vestry of Beckford Parish. Both he and the vestrymen seemed pleased with each other, but there was one problem; the parish needed a minister that had been ordained by a bishop of the Church of England. This was necessary to allow the minister and vestry to legally enforce the collection of tithes used to maintain the several churches of the parish as well as assist the needy of the parish. If Peter Muhlenberg truly desired the post in Virginia, he needed to sail to England to be formally ordained by a bishop of the Church of England.

Muhlenberg set sail for London on March 2, 1772, and was ordained by the Bishop of London in the King's Chapel on April 25.[33] A month passed before he could secure passage back to Pennsylvania, but upon his return in midsummer he made arrangements to move to Virginia, commencing the two-hundred-mile journey in August. He settled with his wife in the small town of Woodstock, the county seat of newly established Dunmore County, in early September 1772.[34]

Two

Crisis in Virginia

DUNMORE COUNTY, WHICH ENCOMPASSED OVER EIGHT HUNDRED square miles in 1772, was situated just south of Frederick County (from which the former was carved out of by the House of Burgesses in 1772).[1] For years prior to Muhlenberg's arrival, German, Scotch-Irish, and English settlers had followed the Great Wagon Road from Pennsylvania into the Shenandoah Valley. Many continued on past Dunmore County, but hundreds stayed and established farms and settlements. A 1783 census reported that over 1,300 white families lived in Dunmore County (renamed Shenandoah County in 1777), 110 of which held approximately 360 slaves (the largest slave-owning family accounting for seventeen slaves).[2] German settlers outnumbered Scotch-Irish and English settlers, but the significant numbers of the latter groups made the need for a minister with Reverend Muhlenberg's language skills all the more apparent.[3]

Reverend Muhlenberg settled in quickly in his new parish, conducting a marriage within days of his arrival and preaching his first sermon in Woodstock before a month had passed.[4] As there were eight churches scattered throughout the parish, six predominately

German and two predominately English, Muhlenberg felt obliged to vary the location of his services every week. This meant that he was on the road a lot, but he was sure to devote at least one Sunday every month to the parishioners of the Woodstock church.[5]

Within a year of his arrival the vestry made good on its offer of glebe land (two hundred acres), and Muhlenberg took on the added responsibility of managing a small farm with his growing family. Judging from the number of baptisms (463) and marriages (158) he performed from 1772 to 1774, Reverend Muhlenberg clearly did not neglect the spiritual welfare of his parishioners.[6] Such devotion undoubtedly impressed the residents of Dunmore County, so much so that in the fall of 1773 Muhlenberg was nominated to serve as a county magistrate (justice of the peace).[7] He was approved by the royal governor, John Murray, the Earl of Dunmore, and sworn into the position in May 1774.[8]

Less than a month later, when a special meeting of freeholders and other inhabitants assembled in Woodstock on June 16, 1774, to consider the best measures to "secure their liberties and properties" and draft a set of resolves pertaining to the British parliament's harsh measures against Boston for the Tea Party of 1773, Reverend Muhlenberg was selected to moderate the meeting.[9] After much discussion, a committee of six gentlemen, of which Muhlenberg was one, met to draft the actual resolves.[10] Given his rather short time in Virginia, Muhlenberg's selection was a mark of the high esteem the residents of Dunmore County held for their minister.

The resolves approved in Dunmore County that day included a pledge to cheerfully submit to the lawful authority of the king and an assertion that parliamentary taxation of the colonies was unconstitutional and designed to enslave a free and loyal people.[11] The committee also warned that parliament's actions against Boston risked disunion of the empire and potential civil war and that a stoppage of all imports from and exports to Britain was justified until the oppressive policies against Massachusetts were repealed.[12] Lastly, a boycott of all East India products was endorsed and a Committee of Correspondence (comprising Muhlenberg and the others on the committee that drafted the resolutions) was formed to better coordinate efforts with other counties and colonies.[13]

Similar meetings were held through Virginia that summer, and in August delegates from each county in Virginia met in Williamsburg to select representatives for the general congress that was to meet in Philadelphia in September. Interestingly, Reverend Muhlenberg was not selected as a delegate to the First Virginia Convention, but two of his fellow members of the Committee of Correspondence, Francis Slaughter and Abraham Bird, were.[14]

The First Continental Congress met through October and settled on a continent-wide nonimportation association to assist Boston. It was to go into effect in December and be enforced in Virginia by each county. The freeholders of Dunmore County formed a twenty-five-man committee to implement the resolves of congress and Reverend Muhlenberg was once again selected as the chairman of the committee.[15] He wrote to his brother Frederick, no doubt with some sense of pride, about his selection: "The times are getting troublesome with us, and begin to wear a hostile appearance. Independent [militia] companies are forming in every county, and politics engross all conversation. I had thrown up my commission as chairman of the Committee of Correspondence, and of magistrate likewise; but last week we had a general election in the county for a Great Committee, according to the resolves of Congress, and I am again chosen chairman, so that, whether I choose or not, I am to be a politician."[16]

The "Great Committee" was tasked with not only enforcing the boycott on British imports but also with securing all available gunpowder in the county held by merchants.[17]

In the spring of 1775, Muhlenberg, along with Jonathan Clark, the clerk of court for Dunmore County (and brother of George Rogers Clark, future victor at Kaskaskia and Vincennes during the Revolutionary War) were selected by Dunmore County's freeholders as delegates to the Second Virginia Convention in Richmond.[18] Both were likely in attendance to hear Patrick Henry's powerful argument—his "liberty or death" speech—in favor of placing Virginia into a "posture of defense." Reverend Muhlenberg likely voted with the slim majority in favor of the measure. He was not, however, selected to the committee tasked with implementing Henry's resolution. That responsibility fell to the likes of Patrick Henry, George Washington, Thomas Jefferson, Richard Henry Lee, Benjamin Harrison, Edmund Pendleton, and several other delegates with more military and political experience than Muhlenberg.[19]

Less than a month after the Second Virginia Convention adjourned, Patrick Henry's prediction that bloodshed in New England was inevitable proved true when fighting erupted at Lexington and Concord. British troops, who had marched into the Massachusetts countryside to seize gunpowder and arms, were met by determined Massachusetts militia. Scores on both sides were killed and many more wounded.

Virginia's royal governor, John Murray, the Earl of Dunmore, ignited his own crisis in Virginia just two days after Lexington by seizing a supply of the colony's gunpowder from the powder magazine in Williamsburg. This act was met with outrage by Virginians, and the anger teetered on outright rebellion by the end of April when news of Lexington and Concord reached Virginia. It appeared that a coordinated effort to disarm the colonists was in play by royal authorities, and many Virginians reacted by moving closer to armed resistance. Within a few weeks of these incidents, Lord Dunmore fled Williamsburg with his family, taking refuge onboard a British warship in the York River.

Events cascaded toward greater conflict with additional bloodshed in Massachusetts at Bunker (actually Breed's) Hill and a full-on siege of Boston by thousands of New England militia and the appointment of George Washington as commander in chief of a newly formed Continental army.

By the summer of 1775, county delegates in Virginia met for a third convention (in place of the still-suspended House of Burgesses). Peter Muhlenberg was once again selected to serve as a representative from Dunmore County, but for some unknown reason he did not attend.[20] If he had, it is likely he would have supported the convention's decision to raise two regiments of regular troops as well as a committee of safety to oversee governmental functions in place of the missing governor and dissolved House of Burgesses. As it was, Muhlenberg continued with his efforts on the Dunmore County Committee, hosting a meeting at his residence in September and gathering a count of the number of firearms in the county in November.[21]

Bloodshed ultimately came to Virginia in the fall of 1775 with fighting between Dunmore's force (comprised of a small detachment of British regulars and sailors as well as a handful of loyalist Virginians and a growing number of runaway slaves) and the Virginia Convention's force of militia and newly raised regular troops.

In December, with Governor Dunmore's force in control of Norfolk and the surrounding area and with hundreds of runaway slaves joining him in hopes of gaining their freedom, the Fourth Virginia Convention met in Williamsburg. Peter Muhlenberg and Johnathan Clark once again represented Dunmore County and attended the convention for over a month, from early December through early January.[22] It was at this convention that Peter Muhlenberg's life took a dramatic turn toward military affairs when the convention selected him to command one of six new regiments of regulars, the 8th Virginia Regiment.[23]

The 8th Virginia was unique from the other Virginia regiments of regulars in 1776 in that a preponderance of its soldiers were German settlers from the Shenandoah Valley. Colonel Muhlenberg, along with Abraham Bowman and Peter Helphinstone (who were appointed by the Fourth Convention to serve as lieutenant colonel and major of the 8th Regiment, respectively) were, like many of their troops, of German descent and well respected among the German population of the valley.[24]

However, although Muhlenberg's regiment was labeled the German Regiment by the Virginia Convention, a number of its troops were not German but rather of "British extraction," specifically Irish, Scottish, and English.[25] The unifying factor of the 8th Regiment was not so much their ethnicity but their frontier backgrounds. They were all men of the frontier who were accustomed to using long rifles, a weapon very different from the smoothbore muskets and fowlers that most Virginia soldiers carried.

Peter Muhlenberg's appointment as colonel of the 8th Virginia Regiment meant he had to surrender his several civil positions (delegate to the convention, chairman of the committee of Dunmore

County) and devote his attention to recruiting troops for his regiment. The six new authorized regiments were to consist of ten companies of sixty-eight men each along with company officers and noncommissioned officers, so his regiment would number above seven hundred men when completely raised. The convention ordered the counties of Dunmore, Frederick, Augusta, West Augusta, Berkeley, Culpeper, Fincastle, and Hampshire to raise companies for the regiment. Dunmore and Augusta Counties raised two companies each.[26] The respective county committees selected the company officers (captains and lieutenants) who then oversaw recruitment for their companies. Each officer was expected to raise a certain quota of recruits to justify their appointment.[27]

Colonel Muhlenberg and his fellow field officers were to oversee and encourage the recruitment effort. It was in this capacity that the event for which Peter Muhlenberg is perhaps most famous for transpired—an occurrence that earned him the moniker the Fighting Parson.

The traditional version of Peter Muhlenberg's farewell sermon, first shared by his great nephew, Henry A. Muhlenberg, in his 1849 biography of General Muhlenberg, goes as follows. Peter Muhlenberg hurried home to Dunmore County from the Fourth Virginia Convention in mid-January, and upon his return word spread quickly that he was to give a farewell sermon on the next Sabbath. Muhlenberg's parishioners packed the Woodstock church on the appointed day in late January, many standing outside in the cold to hear their beloved minister. When Muhlenberg arrived and took the pulpit he had on his military uniform, covered by his black minister's robe. He began his sermon by recounting the many wrongs inflicted upon the colonists by Great Britain and reminded his parishioners of the worthiness of the cause for which they all struggled and for which he was about to surrender his altar. He then declared, "that, in the language of holy writ, there was a time for all things, a time to preach and a time to pray, but those times had passed away. . . that there was a time to fight, and that time had now come!"[28]

Muhlenberg then removed his robe and stood before the congregation in his military uniform, an inspiration to all. Nearly three hundred men enlisted in Muhlenberg's regiment as a result of his sermon, according to this version, and a legend was thus born.[29]

The author of this account assured his readers in 1849 that "numerous traditionary accounts" of what transpired that day still existed throughout the Woodstock community, although he confessed that "of the matter of the sermon, various accounts remain." Henry Muhlenberg insisted, however, that all concur "in attributing to [the sermon] great potency in arousing the military ardour of the people, and unite in describing its conclusion."[30]

Although this version of events remains by far the most popular and most believed account of what happened at Peter Muhlenberg's farewell sermon, it was not the first account in print. In 1823, Dr. James Thacher, a veteran of the Revolutionary War, published his extensive journal of the war and included a different version of Muhlenberg's farewell sermon. He noted in his journal that

> General Muhlenberg was a minister of a parish in Virginia, but participating in the spirit of the times, exchanged his clerical profession for that of a soldier. Having in his pulpit inculcated the principles of liberty and the cause of his country, he found no difficulty in enlisting a regiment of soldiers, and he was appointed their commander. He entered his pulpit with his sword and cockade, preached his farewell sermon, and the next day marched at the head of his regiment to join the army, and he does honor to the military profession.[31]

Thacher's journal entry is dated November 3, 1778, in Fishkill, New York. Thacher recorded in his journal that on that day he chanced upon an entertainment of forty some officers hosted by Muhlenberg. It is impossible to say from whom Thacher learned the details of Muhlenberg's sermon; perhaps the general himself shared the story, or perhaps he heard it secondhand from another officer, but the fact that he recorded the details in 1778, just two years after they reportedly occurred and nearly seventy-five years before Henry Muhlenberg's much more popular account, gives Thacher's version some credibility.

Both accounts agree that Muhlenberg wore a uniform in the pulpit on the day of his farewell sermon, although the former account claimed the uniform was initially covered by Muhlenberg's church robe. Both accounts also acknowledge that Muhlenberg fiercely defended the American cause in his sermon. Thacher offers no specifics as to what Muhlenberg actually said, while Henry Muhlenberg offers very eloquent words that have been passed down in various forms for nearly two centuries.

Where the accounts differ is over when the sermon was actually delivered and the impact the sermon had on Muhlenberg's parishioners. Thacher's observation that Muhlenberg marched to join the army the day after his farewell sermon means he likely delivered it in mid-March 1776 (probably Sunday, March 17), for Muhlenberg departed Woodstock on March 21 and was in Williamsburg on April 3 to receive his colonel's commission from the Virginia Committee of Safety.[32] The probability that Muhlenberg's farewell sermon occurred in March is also supported by the fact that the Beckford Parish register records that Peter Muhlenberg continued to baptize and marry parishioners up until his departure from the Shenandoah Valley in March.[33] It is not a stretch to assume that if he continued in those activities, he likely continued delivering sermons until his departure as well, which would mean his farewell sermon likely occurred in mid-March. This would thus align more with Thacher's account that he led the troops eastward after his sermon.

Another point that supports Thacher's account is that Muhlenberg's regiment consisted of ten companies from eight different counties and that the company commanders (captains) and their lieutenants were primarily responsible for recruiting the sixty-eight men for each company. When one considers that all of Dunmore County contributed at most 140 troops to the 8th Virginia, it is hard to imagine nearly three hundred troops enlisted on the same day in Woodstock after Muhlenberg's sermon in January (as Henry Muhlenberg contends). What is more likely is that hundreds of troops from several companies of the 8th Virginia assembled in Woodstock in March in preparation for their march east and they were thus there when Peter Muhlenberg delivered his farewell sermon.

We will likely never know with certainty what actually occurred or even what was said on the day that Peter Muhlenberg delivered his farewell sermon. What we do know is that the former minister of Beckford Parish in Dunmore County was now colonel of the 8th Virginia Regiment and that, in late March 1776, he and his troops marched eastward to join the war.

Three

To the Defense of Charleston

THE WAR THAT COLONEL MUHLENBERG AND HIS TROOPS WERE marching toward had erupted in Virginia six months earlier and had turned into a stalemate in the southeastern corner of the colony. Lord Dunmore's initial military success in the fall of 1775 in Princess Anne County was undone by his stunning defeat in early December at the Great Bridge, eleven miles south of Norfolk. The heavy losses his small detachment of British redcoats suffered demoralized Dunmore's supporters, and they, along with the governor, abandoned Norfolk for the safety of numerous vessels anchored in the Elizabeth River.

The victorious Virginians briefly occupied Norfolk and then burned it to the ground on New Year's Day. They could not harm Dunmore and his force in the river, however, because a handful of British warships guarded the governor and his supporters.

As winter settled in, Dunmore used a portion of Portsmouth (which lay across the river from the ruins of Norfolk) to shelter and partially alleviate the misery of his troops and the loyalist refugees that remained with him.

The patriot force of North Carolina and Virginia troops on the Norfolk side of the river, under the command of Brigadier General Robert Howe of North Carolina and Colonel William Woodford of Virginia, grew weary of the standoff and withdrew to Suffolk in early February. Outposts at Kemp's Landing and the Great Bridge (to the east and south of Norfolk) were maintained to prevent Dunmore from straying too far from the river, and both sides essentially disengaged for the winter.

Suffolk, approximately twenty-five miles southeast of Portsmouth, was the muster point that Muhlenberg and the 8th Virginia Regiment were assigned, and as spring approached, most of Muhlenberg's troops marched there by companies. Some passed through the capital, Williamsburg, where they collected pay and material to make hunting shirts and leggings.[1] Muhlenberg and his fellow field officers, Lieutenant-Colonel Abraham Bowman and Major Peter Helphinstine, appeared before the Committee of Safety on April 3 to subscribe to the Articles of War and receive their officer commissions.[2] Muhlenberg undoubtedly met with Major-General Charles Lee, who had arrived in Williamsburg just a few days before Muhlenberg to take command of all of the patriot forces in the South.

Lee, a former British officer with extensive military service in Europe, served with Washington in Massachusetts in 1775. Although he was a native of Britain and had only arrived in the colonies in 1773, Lee had earned the trust and admiration of many in Congress and held the third highest rank in the Continental army. He was the most militarily experienced and knowledgeable officer in the army and was highly esteemed throughout the colonies.

Concern in early 1776 that the British might strike the Southern colonies prompted Congress to send Lee south in March to oversee the region's defenses. He arrived in Williamsburg on March 29 and wrote to Washington about the situation he found: "The Regiments in general are very compleat in numbers, the Men (those that I have seen) fine—but a most horrid deficiency of Arms—no entrenching tools, no [effective cannon] (although the Province is pretty well stockd) . . . I have order'd . . . the Artificers to work night and day."[3]

Lee's attention soon settled on Lord Dunmore and the situation near Portsmouth and Suffolk. He received approval from the Virginia Committee of Safety on April 10 to forcibly evacuate a portion of the populace of Norfolk County and Princess Anne County in order to deny Lord Dunmore much-needed provisions from the local inhabitants.[4]

Lee ordered Colonel Muhlenberg, who for a brief time was the ranking officer in Suffolk during Howe and Woodford's absences, to prepare the town for a significant increase in troops and to detach two hundred men to Brickel's Ordinary, about halfway between Suffolk and Portsmouth.[5] Muhlenberg also had to address a case of insubordination from an officer in the 2nd Virginia Regiment who believed that riflemen were exempt from the daily parade and fatigue duties common in any army. Realizing the problems that would befall military discipline if the rifle officer was acquitted of disobeying orders, Muhlenberg referred the matter to Lee for a final determination. The explanation Muhlenberg gave for passing the buck was "[t]hat all his Regiment . . . consisted of Rifle Companies and that if [the accused lieutenant] was to be acquitted which [Muhlenberg was] apprehensive would be the case . . . that his officers would think as [the accused] does, that all Officers Commanding Rifle Companies, as they were raised as—Light Infantry, that no Commanding Officer has a right to make them do parade duty."[6]

When Lee learned of the case, he scoffed at the argument, proclaiming, "The idea hatched by some of the Rifle Companies that they are not subject to every duty of soldiers, is really a curious one, more especially when we consider that more than one half of the Virginian Troops are composed of Riflemen; at this rate, the Musqueteers would have a blessed time of it, to make the system consistent and complete, the latter ought to black the former's shoes, and wash their shirts."[7]

Lee complimented Muhlenberg's discretion in the matter, adding that he thought the colonel was very judicious in deciding to consult him before proceeding with a court martial.[8]

On April 23, Lee, accompanied by Colonel Woodford, arrived in Suffolk to take charge. Lee ordered Muhlenberg to march from Suffolk to Brickel's Ordinary that same evening and then proceed to

Portsmouth the next day with a number of wagons.[9] The forced evacuation of Portsmouth and the surrounding area was underway and Muhlenberg was ordered to inform the inhabitants still living in Portsmouth that they had five days to arrange their affairs before they were forcibly evacuated. Lee ordered that "Waggons shall be allowed for their Beds, Cloaths, and absolute necessary cooking utensils; their Tables, Chairs, and other Cooking Utensils cannot be carried off at the public Expense."[10] All black males of military age were also to be secured and sent to Suffolk as a precaution.[11]

While Muhlenberg carried out his orders, Lee received disturbing news from North Carolina. At least three thousand British troops had reportedly landed thirty miles south of the Cape Fear River.[12] Lee was concerned by the news but also determined to proceed with the evacuation of Portsmouth and the surrounding area. He replied to North Carolina officials who appealed for help that "I am occupied for a very few days in a very important busyness—when it is finished I shall set out for Halifax."[13] Lee explained that he could not at the moment spare any Virginian troops, but he expected reinforcements from Pennsylvania shortly, and once they arrived he would send a large detachment of Virginians southward.[14]

That detachment proved to be Peter Muhlenberg's 8th Virginians. They received orders to march to Halifax, North Carolina, sometime in the second week of May but did not get underway until May 16.[15] Lee noted that the 8th Virginia was selected to march south because it was the strongest regiment he had, meaning the troops were the best armed.[16] Two of Muhlenberg's companies had still not reached Suffolk, but one was on the way and Lee ordered Muhlenberg not to wait for it; the tardy company would follow Muhlenberg to Halifax.[17] The other company never joined the regiment and disbanded the following year.[18]

It took Muhlenberg and his troops five days to march the approximately seventy-five miles to Halifax, and when they arrived on May 21, they had lost about half a company of men to desertion.[19] General Robert Howe, who commanded North Carolina troops in Halifax, wrote to the Virginia Committee of Safety to express his concern: "A few days after our Arrival here, we were joined by Colo. Muhlenberg, with his Battalion. Many of his people seem'd discontented at March-ing farther, and about 20, or thirty have deserted. . . ."[20]

Howe's comment on marching farther referred to the determina-tion of Lee to move on past Halifax to New Bern, North Carolina, to be in better position to confront what he understood to be a large British operation near the Cape Fear River.

Lee also wrote to the Virginia Committee of Safety from Halifax regarding the 8th Virginia and blasted the Virginians for their unmil-itary conduct:

> The disorderly mutinous and dangerous disposition of the soldiers
> of the Eighth Regiment have detain'd me longer in this place than
> I cou'd have wish'd, more particularly as we hear (tho the ac-
> counts are not well authenticated) that the whole fleet of Trans-
> ports under Lord Cornwallis is arrived at Cape Fear. We have at
> length after infinite trouble got this Banditti out of the Town, and
> of course I set out myself immediately.[21]

Lee was not convinced that the British intended to stay in North Carolina; he suspected they were more likely to reboard their ships and sail to Virginia, so he did not want to proceed too far south until he was certain of their intentions.[22] Like Howe, Lee complained about the large number of desertions that had occurred in the 8th Virginia. "The spirit of desertion in these back Country troops is so alarmingly great, that I must submit it to the wisdom of the conven-tion, whether it is not of the utmost importance to devise some means to put a stop to it, before it spreads, by enjoining the Committees of the different Counties to seize every Soldier, who cannot produce an authenticated discharge or pass."[23]

Lee confessed that Virginia's civil authorities were better judges of what to do to stem the high desertion rate, but warned that

> I can only affirm that unless some effectual method is devised and
> adopted, it will be impossible for us to keep the Field. The old
> Countrymen, particularly the Irish, whom the Officers have inju-
> diciously inlisted in order to fill up their Companies, have much

contaminated the Troops; and if more care is not taken on this head, for the future, the whole Army will be one mass of disorder, vice and confusion.[24]

Lee was careful not to represent the officers of the regiment as the problem, writing that, "Altho I have so great reason to complain of the misconduct of this Regiment, I must do the Officers (particularly the Field Officers) the justice to say, that their conduct is in general very satisfactory."[25]

Within a week of Lee's letter to the Committee of Safety, he ordered the 8th Virginia Regiment to proceed even farther south, to Charleston, South Carolina, some 275 miles south of New Bern and over 400 miles from Virginia.[26] Reports that the British troops that had landed in North Carolina had reboarded ships and put to sea convinced Lee that Charleston was their true destination, so he ordered the 8th Virginia to march farther on and rode ahead to Charleston. Muhlenberg and his men trailed two weeks behind Lee, no doubt less than enthused to be marching even farther away from home.

By the time Lee reached Charleston on June 8, it was clear to everyone that the city was indeed the objective of the British.

The British force that sat off of Charleston in early June consisted of seven warships, over twenty troop transports, and multiple supply ships and smaller vessels, all under Commodore Peter Parker.[27] General Henry Clinton, aided by General Charles, Lord Cornwallis, commanded over 2,200 British troops aboard the transports.[28] They were originally meant to help loyalist forces in North Carolina regain control of the colony, but when many of these loyalists were routed by patriot troops at Moore's Creek Bridge in February, Tory strength evaporated and Clinton decided that Charleston was better suited for his efforts.

The British fleet arrived off Charleston in early June, and after a week of planning and preparation, Clinton and Commodore Parker took their first step toward breaching the patriot defenses outside of

Charleston by landing five hundred troops on a narrow island outside the mouth of Charleston Harbor called Long Island.[29] The key
patriot defensive position blocking the British approach by sea was
a palmetto log fort located on an adjacent island, Sullivan's Island,
four miles to the southwest of where the British troops landed. A
narrow cut of water separated the two islands and prevented the
British troops from marching straight at the fort.

Lee had arrived in Charleston on June 8, the day before the British
troops landed, and he had strong reservations about the usefulness of
the fort on Sullivan's Island. Although it sat within point-blank range
of the narrow channel that led to Charleston (the route British ships
had to navigate to avoid the many shoals of Charleston Harbor) and
it was large enough to hold a garrison of a thousand men, its sixteen-
foot thick walls were only ten feet high facing the water and even
lower on the other three sides.[30] In other words, the fort was vulnerable to both a land attack as well as enemy shots fired over the walls.
Lee was also very concerned that there was no reliable route of retreat
to the mainland should the fort be overrun by the enemy.

Nevertheless, the fort held thirty-one heavy cannon ranging from
twenty-six- to nine-pounders and a garrison of over 350 men commanded by a very determined officer, Colonel William Moultrie.[31]
Three miles up the shore of Sullivan's Island, an equally determined
Colonel William Thomson guarded the cut across from Long Island
and the British troops. Thompson had over 750 men and several cannon to repel the enemy should they attempt to cross onto Sullivan's
Island.[32]

On June 16, with Muhlenberg and the 8th Virginia still a week
away from Charleston, Clinton landed another 1,700 troops on Long
Island. Parker and Clinton had decided to attack, but moving several
of the large British warships across the sandbar that obstructed passage to Charleston Harbor proved a lengthy challenge. The wind,
tide, and weight of the ships had to be just right for the largest ships
to pass the sandbar. While the British struggled to accomplish this,
Muhlenberg and the 8th Virginia arrived on June 23.[33]

Despite his low opinion of the 8th Virginia soldiers at this point,
General Lee was relieved at their arrival and attached them to Gen-

eral John Armstrong's command at Haddrell's Point.[34] They, along with Armstrong's South Carolina troops, were to guard the mainland across from Sullivan's Island. In the enemy's camp on Long Island and aboard their ships, frustration mounted at their inability to overcome challenging weather to launch an attack.

An attack finally occurred on June 28, and at first it looked to be impressively coordinated between British land and sea forces. While Clinton's troops on Long Island gave every sign that they intended to fight their way across the cut to Sullivan's Island, Commodore Parker's warships sailed into position a few hundred yards from the American fort on the other end of the island to pummel Colonel Moultrie's garrison with cannon fire.

The British plan of attack quickly unraveled, however, because Clinton discovered he had no way to cross the cut between Sullivan's and Long Island without suffering unacceptably high losses. The narrow channel between the two islands was deeper than Clinton had been informed (seven feet at low tide) and thus unfordable, and the British commander believed any attempt to use boats to either cross the cut or land farther up the island would lead to enormous casualties among his troops.[35] So with Parker's warships fully engaged against the fort, the best Clinton could do was create a distraction by threatening to cross the cut, thereby keeping the hundreds of rebel infantry at the cut away from their fort.

The outcome of the battle thus turned on Parker's warships and Moultrie's garrison, and the barrage of shot and shell that each side expended was tremendous. Relatively safe behind their sixteen-foot-thick sand wall (lined with palmetto trees that absorbed British cannonballs rather than them splintering into sharp pieces) the American garrison punished the stationary British warships with twenty-six-pound, eighteen-pound, twelve-pound, and nine-pound ordnance.[36] Several of Parker's frigates attempted to sail past the fort but became grounded in low water and fell out of action. One of these was eventually abandoned and burned.

Lee, who was on the mainland when the attack began, crossed over to Sullivan's Island around 5 p.m. and was pleased to see that Moultrie had the situation well in hand.[37] Moultrie had lost over a score of men, but he was confident that the damage his men inflicted upon the enemy was far worse.[38] On that count Moultrie was correct, for the American fire did considerably more damage to the British navy than Commodore Parker's fire did to the fort.

Lee was surprised and impressed at the resolve of the garrison and described the intensity of the attack in a letter to the Virginia Convention the following day. "Yesterday about eleven o'clock the Enemy's Squadron, consisting of one fifty, one forty, and six frigates came to anchor before Fort Sullivan and began one of the most furious cannonades I ever heard or saw."[39] He went on to write that "The behavior of the Garrison, both men and officers, with Colonel Moultrie at their head, I confess astonished me; it was brave to the last degree. I had no idea so much coolness and intrepidity could be displayed by a collection of raw recruits, as I was witness of in this garrison."[40] Up to this point of the battle, Muhlenberg and his 8th Virginians had remained on the mainland in reserve. Late in the afternoon, Lee ordered Muhlenberg to reinforce Colonel Thomson's detachment at the northern end of the island.[41] Muhlenberg's men must have displayed some zeal to join the fight, for Lee paid them a direct compliment in his letter to the convention: "I know not which Corps I have the greatest reason to be pleased with, Muhlenberg's Virginians, or the North Carolina troops—they are both equally alert, zealous and spirited."[42]

Muhlenberg's Virginians may have been all of those things, but it appears they saw little of the action that occurred on Sullivan's Island. The honors of the day belonged to Moultrie's garrison, who withstood the British navy's intense bombardment and returned it with such deadly effect that Commodore Parker eventually disengaged and withdrew. The British threat to Charleston thus ended in defeat as Parker's ships suffered significant damage and heavy losses among their crew.

The damage was so great that the British did not make another attempt at Charleston. Nearly three weeks of repairs and preparation to sail passed before the British troops on Long Island reboarded their transport ships.[43] Clinton was eager to sail to New York to join William Howe's massive army on Staten Island, but Parker's warships had yet to cross the sandbar and it would take almost two more weeks to get all of Parker's ships across. Clinton refused to wait that long and ordered the transport ships to set sail on July 21.[44] The last of the British warships cleared the sandbar and set out to sea by early August.[45]

In the hours and days immediately following the battle of Sullivan's Island, Lee had kept his troops on alert, believing that the British would make another attempt at the fort. As the days passed, many of Muhlenberg's men fell ill, attracting the attention of Lee. He expressed his concern to General Armstrong and offered solutions to the problem.

> I am extremely concerned to hear that the Virginians and North Carolina Troops are falling down in sickness. I attribute it to three causes—being expos'd to the sun in the day time, lying on the damp ground at night, and bad water—I have prevail'd on the President [John Rutledge] to order 'em boards which will remedy the evil arising from their lying on the damp ground—a quantity of rum is ordered over as an antidote to the bad water, and the third evil that of being expos'd to the sun, I shou'd think you may remove by stationing 'em in the wood on your left instead of the old field where they at present are.[46]

When Lee finally realized that the British would not be returning for a second crack at Sullivan's Island or Charleston, he turned his attention to neighboring Georgia. Officials there had expressed concern about their defenseless state and appealed for assistance against British troops operating from St. Augustine and several smaller outposts in East Florida as well as attacks from Indians allied with the British.[47]

By the end of July, Lee had resolved to march to Georgia with a force that included the 8th Virginians. Muhlenberg's regiment was much reduced by the rigors of service in the field, and 150 of his men were unfit for duty due to illness.[48] Nevertheless, Muhlenberg and 375 of his men were capable of further service and they marched with Lee to Savannah in early August.[49] Before they marched, however, Muhlenberg expressed his concern to Lee about the status of his regiment in the army.

Although the troops of the 8th Virginia were considered regular, full-time soldiers (as opposed to militia) they had yet to be taken into Continental service by the Continental Congress. In the hierarchy of the army, this meant that Muhlenberg and his officers were viewed as provincial officers, equivalent to militia officers, and thus out-ranked by officers who held Continental commissions. Muhlenberg and his officers were frustrated by this arrangement and the colonel shared his concern with Lee.

> I am very anxious to have the affair I mentioned to your Excel-lency this morning, settled some way or other, before We leave this place, as it may otherwise perhaps, create confusion on the march—All the Continental Troops in this place have hitherto taken rank of my officers, because they have no commission to produce & suffer them to Rank only as Provincials. Since I men-tioned this affair to your Excellency, I have received another letter from Williamsburg, which mentions that the Convention had ap-ply'd to the General Congress to take the Seventh, 8th, and Ninth Regiments on the Continental Establishment—That the answer was, it could not be done immediately, but when those Regiments were completely mann'd & arm'd they might be taken.[50]

Muhlenberg and his fellow officers found the denial of Continen-tal establishment to the 8th Virginia because the unit was not "com-pletely manned and armed" particularly annoying because they had mustered at Suffolk in early April and were the only Virginia troops (outside of two independent rifle companies in 1775) to have marched out of Virginia (hundreds of miles, in fact) to help defend another colony. Muhlenberg worried that the delay of granting Con-tinental commissions to himself and his officers meant they would be outranked by less-deserving officers with far less service than they. He complained to Lee that "As this is the Case, I must beg leave to say, that I should use myself ill, were I to accept a Continental Com-mission after this date, when other Regiments, raised long after mine, would take rank before me; I should prefer being oldest Provincial Officer before the youngest Continental. I can assure your Excellency nothing should have prompted me to mention this, did I not conceive that my Regiment had been slighted in some respects."[51] Muhlenberg added that his service as commander of the 8th Virginia, especially during the period in the Carolinas, had come at great sacrifice to him.

> Perhaps of all the Virginia Colonels my Connexions, and Fortune are smallest, but according to my abilities I have sacrificed perhaps as much as they. I have cheerfully given up a salary of $350 pounds, & during my stay in this place my wages are scarce half sufficient to defray my necessary Expenses. I shall not trouble your Excellency any further, only request that the Rank of the Regiment may be settled before we go, if possible.[52]

Lee responded sympathetically to Muhlenberg the next day.

> What the Continental Congress can mean (if ever they so ex-press'd themselves) by not taking your Regiment and the others on their establishment until they are compleat, is above my con-ception—if they mean that it was to have its full complement to a man, or that it shou'd be compleat enough for service, I am at a loss—if they meant the former, it was almost impossible that these Regiments shou'd ever be on their establishment—if they meant the latter, your Regiment certainly must have the precedency over all the Regiments on the Continent. In all the services I am ac-quainted with, new levies are establish'd and take rank from the time two thirds of the Regiments is rais'd. They are then suppos'd on emergencies to be fit for service.[53]

Lee went on to compliment the 8th Virginia Regiment and assured Muhlenberg that Congress would correct its error and the colonel and his officers would receive their proper placement in the Continental army.

> On every principle your Regiment must be considered as Conti-nental, at least from the time you were ordered to march out of

the Province. You were ordered not because I was better acquainted with your Regiment than the rest—but because you were the most compleat, the best arm'd, and in all respects the best furnish'd for service—You may depend therefore when the Congress is inform'd of the Circumstances, your Rank will not be disputed—the fact is that the Congress having no military Men in their Body are continually confounding themselves and every body else in military matters—however to do 'em justice they will bear being corrected with candour & patience. . . . I shall write immediately on the subject if it is necessary for your satisfaction and that of your Officers, but think you need be in no pain about it.[54]

Lee wrote to the Board of War in Congress the next day and presented a very forceful argument in favor of Muhlenberg and the 8th Virginia Regiment. He also reiterated why he selected Muhlenberg's unit to march to the Carolinas with him.

Colonel Muhlenberg of the Eighth Battalion of Virginians has been made very uneasy by some letters He has lately receiv'd with respect to the rank of his Regiment—these Letters intimate that it was never the intention of the Congress to consider the seventh, eighth, and ninth Battalions of Virginians on the Continental Establishment until they were entirely compleat—that his Regiment never was intirely compleat, and that consequently after having so long thought himself on the Continental Establishment, and on this presumption having march'd five hundred miles from his own province under the Command of a Continental General, he now at last finds himself only a Provincial officer. I have ventur'd to assure him and his officers who are equally uneasy that there must be some mistake in this affair—in fact, the hardship wou'd be so great that I cannot believe their apprehensions are well founded— [The 8th Regiment] was (if I remember right) notify'd in April by the Committee of Safety in Virginia that they were then taken upon the Continental Establishment, and (tho in this I may be mistaken) without the proviso of their being compleat. It happen'd at this time tho not compleat to a man (for no Regiment ever is compleat to a man) that Muhlenberg's Regiment was not only the most compleat of the Province, but I believe of the whole Continent—it was not only the most compleat in Numbers, but the best arm'd, cloth'd and equip'd in all respects for immediate Service—I must repeat that I cannot conceive it was ever the intention of Congress that the establishment shou'd be fill'd to a man, but that they shou'd be competent to service in or out of their Province—in most services when new levies are rais'd one half of the propos'd complement entitles 'em to establishment; Muhlenberg's Regiment wanted only forty at most—it was the strength and good condition of the Regiment that induc'd me to order it out of its own Province in preference to any other—I certainly consider'd 'em at that time as Continental Troops otherwise I cou'd have no authority to order 'em out of the Province. I must now submit it to the consideration of the Congress if it wou'd not really be the greatest cruelty that their strength and good condition shou'd be turn'd against 'em—it was their strength and good condition which carried 'em out of their Province where had they remain'd and known that it was a necessary condition of their establishment to be compleat to a man, they certainly cou'd have accomplish'd it in three days—I do therefore most sincerely hope and confidently perswade myself that Muhlenberg's Regiment will at least date their Rank from the day I order'd 'em to march out of their Province, not only justice but policy requires it, for you will otherwise lose a most excellent Regiment.[55]

Congress acted quickly on Lee's letter and passed a resolution on August 13, placing the 8th Virginia Regiment on Continental establishment from the date they marched out of Virginia in late May.[56] Muhlenberg was undoubtedly relieved to learn the news; his rightful rank in the Virginia line had been restored.

In Lee's same letter to Congress, he outlined his plans against the British in East Florida. This largely wilderness region between Georgia and the British stronghold at St. Augustine held several British outposts from which incursions into Georgia had been launched. The losses suffered by Georgians from these British raids involved mostly slaves and cattle, but the potential for greater loss was high, so Lee resolved to break up the British posts in East Florida.[57]

Supply and transport problems delayed Lee's expedition to the point that much of August passed before his force reached Savannah.[58] Soon after he arrived, Muhlenberg was ordered to march approximately thirty miles past Savannah to the settlement of Sunbury.[59] Fortunately for Muhlenberg and his troops (many of whom became desperately ill), their stay at Sunbury was brief. Lee received instructions from Congress to march to Philadelphia in early September, which effectively ended his expedition to Florida.[60]

A portion of the 8th Virginia Regiment, including Colonel Muhlenberg and his fellow field officers, was sent back to Virginia, but a detachment remained behind. Lee had issued orders to General Armstrong in Charleston in mid-August to send the sick Virginians who had remained in Charleston (approximately 150 men) back to Virginia as soon as they recovered. Lee expected that these orders would have a miraculous effect on the health of many of the men and it is reasonable to assume that they made up a large part of the 8th Virginians who returned to Virginia in the fall.[61] Those that remained in South Carolina fell under Captain Richard Campbell's command.[62]

It is unclear when Muhlenberg set off from South Carolina for Virginia or how long the journey took, but we know he arrived home in mid-December.[63] A letter to his father on December 20 described the "arduous campaign" that he and his troops endured in the South.[64] Muhlenberg added that his "Regiment has suffered much from sickness, and that as soon as properly recruited, he had orders to march to Philadelphia."[65]

Another month passed before the remainder of the 8th Virginia Regiment in South Carolina was finally ordered to return to Virginia to rejoin the rest of the regiment.[66] Muhlenberg described their condition to Washington upon their arrival home in late February: "The detachment from the southward arrived here this week in a shattered condition, having only seventy men fit for duty; so that it will be almost impossible to march the men so soon as I could wish."[67]

Muhlenberg did not realize it at the time he wrote those words, but the 8th Virginia Regiment was no longer his concern. Two days before Muhlenberg wrote to Washington, Congress had promoted Muhlenberg to brigadier general.[68]

The thirty-one-year-old minister from Woodstock, Virginia, would now command a Continental brigade of thousands rather than a Virginia regiment of hundreds.

Four

North to the Brandywine

CONGRESS APPOINTED THREE NEW BRIGADIER GENERALS FROM Virginia on February 21, 1777: Peter Muhlenberg; George Weedon of the 3rd Virginia Regiment; and William Woodford, formerly of the 2nd Virginia but, at the time of his appointment, without a command. Woodford had resented the earlier congressional promotions of Hugh Mercer and Adam Stephens, two officers whose commissions came after Woodford's, so against the advice of Washington, Woodford resigned from the army in protest in the fall of 1776.

Woodford decided to accept his promotion (again at Washington's urging) the following February, but not without voicing strong complaints about his ranking last among the other new Virginia generals. The issue of rank lingered for years not only in terms of Virginia's officers but officers from every state, and the constant haggling over rank plagued Washington throughout the war.

For the time being though, the order of rank among Virginia's general officers in the Continental army in the spring of 1777 was Major General Adam Stephen, followed by Brigadier Generals An-

drew Lewis, Peter Muhlenberg, George Weedon, and William Woodford. When General Lewis resigned in April 1777 over the issue of
rank as well as health, Congress appointed Charles Scott as Virginia's
fourth brigadier general. More importantly for Muhlenberg, Lewis's
departure made Muhlenberg the highest-ranking Continental
brigadier among the Virginia officer corps.

So in mid-March, Muhlenberg's attention and efforts shifted from
restoring the 8th Virginia Regiment back to health to being tasked
to collect and organize "all the parts of the Virga Continental Battalions within your reach," so that they could be sent to Philadelphia
to join Washington's army as soon as possible.[1] Muhlenberg was ad-
ditionally ordered by Washington to "Let a sufficient number of
proper Officers from each Battalion be left behind for the purpose
of recruiting, with Orders to follow as soon as any of them has completed the quota allotted to him."[2] These instructions, dated March
9, 1777, reached Muhlenberg in a letter from George Johnson, an
aide-de-camp of Washington. The letter ended with the statement
that "His Excellency expects to see you here in a few days; there
being at present not a sufficient Number of Genl. Officers with the
Army."[3]

Muhlenberg likely set out for New Jersey as soon as he received
Johnson's letter. It appears that prior to his departure, or perhaps a
year earlier when he left Woodstock to command the 8th Virginia
Regiment, the Muhlenbergs purchased several slaves, probably for
the purpose of helping Mrs. Muhlenberg better manage affairs in
Woodstock during her husband's absence. In mid-May, General Muhlenberg's father wrote to Hanna to inform her that "Peter sent the
said money by a man from Virginia, named Hofmann, to her . . . in
order that she might pay what was still owing for her Negroes and
use the rest for an emergency."[4] This message is the only evidence we
have that Muhlenberg, or perhaps his wife, owned enslaved people
during the Revolutionary War.

It is difficult to determine the exact date on which Muhlenberg
reached Washington's army in the Watchung Mountains of New Jer-

sey. According to Muhlenberg's father's journal, he arrived in Trappe, Pennsylvania, on March 31 and stayed with his parents for nearly a week before proceeding to New Jersey to report to Washington.[5] The commander in chief's orders for April 11 gave Muhlenberg the responsibility of settling disputes over rank for multiple Virginia regiments, so he was obviously in camp by then.[6] Two days later, in a letter from one of Washington's aides, Muhlenberg was placed in command of a brigade of Virginians made up of the 1st, 5th, 9th and 13th Virginia Regiments.

> I am commanded by his Excelly to inform you, that he has arrang'd the 1, 5, 9, and 13, Va Battalions for your Brigade of wch You are hereby directed to take the charge, & diligently inquire into their present state; see that they are, without loss of time, completely equipped; in short that they be immediately put into a situation to take the Field without wantg any thing they ought to have. Their present dispers'd state will require your instant Attention; proper measures must be fallen upon to collect them into as compact [order] as possible. Of these You are the best Judge— However you had better consult with Genl. Stephen on this head.[7]

Similar instructions were given to Muhlenberg's fellow brigadiers as Washington prepared for the upcoming campaign.

The previous year had gone poorly for Washington and his troops with the loss of New York City and the near loss of New Jersey and Philadelphia, but Washington's bold actions at Trenton in late December and Princeton in early January provided a much-needed boost to American spirits. Washington's army had survived the winter in the Watchung Mountains of western New Jersey and the advent of spring brought new hope, along with reinforcements.

Although the American army grew significantly over the spring of 1777, Washington remained anxious about his troop strength and pressed his brigade commanders with orders to "enquire minutely into the State & Condition of your Brigade."[8] This included daily formations and roll calls to inspect the men and their gear (to ensure both were in good order) and also to prevent desertions. Muhlenberg and his fellow brigadier generals were also responsible for overseeing that fatigue duty (to supply the army and keep the camps in order) as well as guard duty (to maintain military order and security) were properly carried out in their brigades.

In late May, Washington rearranged the army, adding Colonel Baron de Arendt's German Regiment of Maryland and Pennsylvania Germans (also referred to as the 8th Maryland Regiment) with over 350 troops to Muhlenberg's brigade and placing Muhlenberg and General Weedon (who commanded the 2nd Virginia Brigade) under Major General Nathanael Greene's command.[9] Arendt's regiment made up for the missing 13th Virginia Regiment, which had still not arrived in camp from the frontier counties of Virginia. Muhlenberg's troop strength in May totaled approximately one thousand effective men, making it one of the stronger brigades but far smaller than its authorized troop strength.[10]

The regiments that comprised Muhlenberg's brigade varied considerably in military experience and composition. The 1st and 5th Virginia Regiments had seen action at Trenton and Princeton and had spent the whole winter in New Jersey; their effective troop strength of 120 and 127 men in May was testament to that. The 9th Regiment, which had been raised on the Eastern Shore of Virginia, did not arrive in camp until the spring and thus had three times the number of healthy men fit for duty, but they had little combat experience. The 13th Regiment, raised in and around Fort Pitt (which Virginia claimed) consisted of all riflemen with plenty of frontier experience, but they had yet to arrive. The most recent addition to Muhlenberg's brigade, the 8th Maryland (like the 8th Virginia, also known as the German Regiment) actually had as much experience, if not more, as the 1st and 5th Virginia Regiments, but the 8th Maryland had been plagued with poor officers and its latest commander, Baron de Arendt, was extremely unpopular with his men.[11]

While Washington's army steadily grew in strength over the spring in the Watchung Mountains, General Howe and the thousands of British and Hessian troops under his command remained just a few miles away in New Brunswick, baffling General Washington with their inactivity. Howe finally moved his troops westward toward

Washington on June 13. The British commander had no interest in attacking the fortified American positions in the mountains, however, and sought instead to draw Washington's army into the open. Washington refused to take the bait and sent only light parties forward to skirmish with the British. After nearly a week of inconclusive fighting, Howe disengaged and withdrew to New Brunswick. Then, inexplicably to Washington, Howe abandoned New Brunswick and marched to Perth Amboy, opposite of Staten Island.

Just as Howe had hoped, the British withdrawal emboldened Washington to send a portion of his army forward to harass Howe's retreat. On June 25, the British commander seized the opportunity to strike the pursuing American troops, who were now in the open. Fortunately for Washington, Howe's attempt to encircle the detached American advance troops with a march around their left flank was detected before the British could close their trap. Heavy fighting and speedy maneuvering by the Americans enabled them to escape and return to the relative safety of the Watchung Mountains. Disappointed, Howe abandoned further operations in New Jersey. He had a new plan in mind.

Muhlenberg and his brigade did not participate in the fighting that occurred in late June. He remained with Washington and the rest of the army on the main line in the mountains. It was there that Muhlenberg learned that his wife Hanna and their two-year-old son Henry had arrived at his father's residence in Trappe.[12] They stayed just a few days before moving on to Philadelphia to stay with Hanna's parents.[13] As pleased as Muhlenberg undoubtedly was that his wife and child were safely under the protection of her parents in Philadelphia, the likelihood of action against the British probably prevented him from leaving the army to see her.

Nearly two weeks of frustrating inactivity followed the British retreat from central New Jersey as Washington waited for Howe's next move. The British commander's movements thoroughly perplexed Washington, but by early July the American commander concluded—hesitantly—that Howe intended to cooperate with a second British army, with over seven thousand troops, moving through New York from Canada under General John Burgoyne.

Still unsure where Howe would strike, but aware that the bulk of his army was being loaded aboard transport ships, Washington shifted his army slightly north to Morristown, New Jersey. He wanted to be in a better position to march to New York to assist the American Northern army upon confirmation of Howe's movement to join Burgoyne. Such confirmation never arrived, however. What ensued instead were weeks of contradictory reports of British ship sightings along the coast of New Jersey, Delaware, and Maryland that perplexed Washington, keeping the American commander and his army on constant alert.

Washington's assumptions regarding Howe's intentions were mistaken, but it took weeks for Washington to discover this because bad weather had forced the British fleet carrying Howe's army far out to sea and out of sight of the coast. Howe, with approximately fifteen thousand British and German troops, had sailed from New York in July and had disappeared over the horizon. Washington believed this maneuver was a ruse and that they would soon reappear to sail up the Hudson River to cooperate with General Burgoyne marching through New York from Canada, so Washington ordered the American army to march northward, toward New York in mid-July.

As Washington was not certain that the New York Highlands was Howe's true destination, his march north was done with little urgency. During the twelve days the army moved north, seven were spent in camp, usually waiting for the weather to improve. The five days of extended marches (scattered over the twelve days) averaged approximately fifteen miles each day and took Muhlenberg's brigade from Morristown to the New York border.[14]

On July 24, Washington received startling intelligence that Howe was actually sailing southward, most likely to Philadelphia by way of the Delaware River or Chesapeake Bay. Alarmed that his army was well out of position to challenge Howe, Washington ordered his several divisions to march to Philadelphia by the most expeditious route they could.[15] What transpired was a difficult forced march across New Jersey for the American troops.

Averaging more than twenty miles a day in the hot July sun, Captain John Chilton of the 3rd Virginia Regiment described the ordeal Washington's troops endured. "As our March was a forced one & the Season extremely warm the victuals became putrid by sweat & heat—the Men badly off for Shoes, many being entirely barefoot and in our Regt. a minute [detailed] inspection was made into things relative to necessaries that the Men could not do without, which they were obliged to throw away."[16]

In just over a week, Washington's troops marched across New Jersey and crossed the Delaware River, camping on the outskirts of Philadelphia. Once again, however, Washington found himself uncertain how to proceed. Reports that Howe's fleet had once again disappeared over the horizon made it impossible for Washington to determine the British army's destination. Washington feared that Howe had doubled back and was actually heading to the Hudson River, so he prepared to move the American army back into New Jersey. They had only marched a short distance on August 10, however, when Washington received word from John Hancock, president of Congress, that a large fleet had been briefly spotted off the coast of Maryland before it disappeared over the horizon again. If the report was true and Howe was sailing south, he might be headed for the Chesapeake Bay to land his army below Philadelphia to strike the American capital from the south. Or perhaps Howe was heading to South Carolina. If so, there was little Washington could do to reach the Carolinas in time to help. Unsure what to do, Washington remained a few miles northeast of Philadelphia and waited for further word.

With ten days passing without further intelligence on the British fleet, Washington grew impatient. At a council of war attended by Muhlenberg and the other division and brigade commanders, it was agreed that since no new intelligence had arrived as to his whereabouts, Howe was likely sailing to Charleston. The council unanimously agreed that since there was little the army could do in time to assist Charleston, they should march to New York to reinforce the American Northern army against General Burgoyne's force of seven thousand British and Hessian troops.[17]

Upon this recommendation, Washington ordered the army to prepare to march, but within hours of these orders, news arrived that
the British fleet had finally been sighted passing the Virginia Capes.
It now appeared that the Chesapeake Bay was Howe's destination,
and Philadelphia his likely objective.

Washington immediately adjusted his orders: the army was to
march south to confront Howe. While Muhlenberg and the rest of
the army marched through Philadelphia and into Delaware, Howe's
troops sailed up the Chesapeake Bay and landed at Head of Elk near
the Maryland and Delaware border. Washington posted the bulk of
his troops just south of Wilmington, Delaware, in late August and
sent a 1,100-man detachment of light infantry (drafted from the several brigades including Muhlenberg's) farther south under General
William Maxwell to reconnoiter and challenge any British advance.

In early September, a sharp engagement at Cooches Bridge,
Delaware, occurred between Maxwell's light corps and Howe's advance guard, resulting in the Americans withdrawing toward Wilmington. Howe did not pursue the retreating Americans, however,
but marched his army north past Washington's right flank. Howe encamped at Kennett Square in Pennsylvania while Washington deployed his troops to Chads's Ford on Brandywine Creek, several
miles to the east of Howe, in order to block the British from advancing on Philadelphia.

The Brandywine was wide enough and deep enough to hinder an
army from easily crossing but not too wide or deep to completely
stop anyone determined enough to cross. Approximately fifteen
thousand American troops, including Muhlenberg and his brigade,
were posted on the eastern side of the creek and they intended to do
just that—stop the British army from crossing.

Washington centered the deployment of his army at Chads's Ford,
posting Nathanael Greene's 2,500-man division of Muhlenberg's and
Weedon's brigades on the heights overlooking Brandywine Ferry, a
few hundred yards south of the ford,[18] and Anthony Wayne's division
of 2,000 Pennsylvanians to guard the crossing at Chads's Ford and

the main road leading to Philadelphia. They were supported by General Francis Nash's Carolina Brigade of 1,500 soldiers.[19] Additional units, totaling approximately 8,000 men, were deployed for several miles up the creek.[20]

With a clash imminent, Washington sent Maxwell's thousand-man light corps across the creek to watch the enemy's movements and harass them if and when they moved against the Americans.[21] Back along the creek, Muhlenberg served as the field officer on picket duty and spent a sleepless night supervising Washington's pickets posted along the creek.[22]

A few miles to the west, Maxwell's men were also awake and in the predawn darkness braced themselves for battle. Howe ordered his advance guard forward at daybreak on September 11, and shortly afterward gunfire erupted in the countryside west of Brandywine Creek.

While Maxwell's light corps engaged the vanguard of Howe's army, more than half of the British forces, led by Howe himself, marched along a circuitous route to gain Washington's right flank and replicate Howe's rout of Washington at Long Island in 1776. This maneuver, which involved a nearly twenty-mile march around the American position, would consume a good part of the day before they were in position to strike the American flank. It was up to German general Wilhelm Knyphausen, therefore, to distract the Americans for most of the day with a direct, but measured, frontal assault toward Chads's Ford.

A running skirmish between Maxwell's light corps and Knyphausen's advance troops took up much of the morning. Maxwell's troops fought well, but they could not stop the far stronger enemy column and crossed Brandywine Creek to rejoin Washington's army before noon.

The ensuing lull in activity—for the enemy did not attempt to cross the creek—coupled with reports of enemy troop movements around his right flank, convinced Washington that Howe had split his army. Realizing the opportunity this provided, Washington made preparations to cross the creek and attack Knyphausen with what he assumed would be superior numbers. Just as his troops were about to cross, however, new reports on Howe's movements created uncertainty in Washington about the actual size of the enemy to his front. He opted to halt the attack until he could better determine the situation his army faced. By the time Washington ascertained that Howe had indeed divided his army and was moving against his right flank, the opportunity to exploit Howe's move had vanished and Washington scrambled to protect his flank.

With more than half of the British army bearing down on his right and rear, Washington ordered Generals Adam Stephen and Lord Stirling to abandon their position above Chads's Ford and rapidly march their divisions to high ground near Birmingham Meeting House in order to head off the British.[23] General John Sullivan was ordered to follow with his division and assume overall command of the redeployed right wing of Washington's army.

The march from Brandywine Creek to the heights near Birmingham Meeting House, with its narrow, winding roads over steep, wooded hills and deep ravines, tested the stamina of Washington's troops. They doggedly pushed on for three miles to the village of Dilworth, then swung north toward a hill overlooking Birmingham Meeting House and a road running north to Osborne Hill, where Howe and the British army had paused to rest after their long march around the American army.

Stephen deployed his troops upon a large, cleared hill just west of the Birmingham Road and Stirling's division formed to Stephen's left. When Sullivan arrived with his division, Stirling's and Stephen's divisions shifted right (Stephen crossing to the other side of a road) and Sullivan's division moved to form on Stirling's left flank. Sullivan assumed overall command of the American right wing and his troops were still getting into position when Howe's troops commenced their attack.

Despite the hastiness of the redeployment, the Americans had selected a strong position from which to fight. A British light infantry officer observed that "The position the enemy had taken was very strong indeed—very commanding ground, a wood on their rear and flanks, a ravine and strong paling [fence] in front."[24]

Unfortunately for the Americans, Sullivan's division on the left side of the line was still not set. While some of Sullivan's men fought well, many fell into disorder at the arrival of the British and withdrew to the rear. Sullivan, who had taken position near a battery of five cannon in the center of the entire American line to superintend the fight, sent his aides to reform his troops, but they had little success and most of Sullivan's troops retreated in disarray.[25]

With British troops to their front and now upon their exposed left flank, the pressure on Stirling's men in the center of the American line increased and they also began to give way. To their right though, Stephen's division of Woodford's and Scott's Virginians held firm.

The fight between Stephen's troops and the British light infantry to their front was severe, made more so upon the British by two American cannon that played very effectively upon the advancing enemy. A British officer who experienced the cannon fire recalled that there "was a most infernal Fire of Cannon & musketry— smoak—incessant shouting—incline to the right! Incline to the Left!—halt!—charge! . . . The trees [were] cracking over ones head. The branches riven by the artillery, the leaves falling as in autumn by the grapeshot."[26]

Stephen's division was well served by the cannon which, along with heavy musket and rifle fire, initially kept the British and German troops to their front at bay. The collapse of the American left flank and center, however, left Stephen's Virginians in an impossible situation. A British officer described the final assault on their position: "They stood the charge till we came to the last [fence]. Their line then began to break, and a general retreat took place soon after, except for their guns, many of which were defended to the last, indeed several officers were cut down at the guns."[27]

Aware that his right wing was in peril, Washington ordered Greene to rush his division northeastward to assist. It was impossible for Greene's troops to arrive in time to prevent the collapse of the right wing, but they did intervene in time to disrupt Howe's pursuit of Washington's broken right wing south of the village of Dilworth. This delay of the British, which lasted from twenty minutes to over an hour, depending on the observer, provided enough time for most of Washington's army to escape eastward before they were cut off by Howe's troops.

There has long been confusion about what role Muhlenberg's brigade played in covering the American retreat. As part of Greene's division, many historians assumed that Muhlenberg joined Weedon in stemming the British pursuit on the right. But several important sources give that honor solely to Weedon and his brigade.

Sullivan was one of these sources, writing a month after the battle that "Weedon's Brigade was the only part of Green's Division which was engaged. They sustained a heavy fire for near 20 minutes when they were posted (about sunset) to Cover the Retreat of our Army & had it not been for this the Retreat must have been attended with great loss."[28]

Greene himself, who led his troops toward Dilworth, recalled in a letter written nearly a year after the battle that,

> I marched one brigade of my division, being upon the left wing, between three and four miles in forty-five minutes. When I came upon the ground I found the whole of the troops routed and re-treating precipitately, and in the most broken and confused man-ner. I was ordered to cover the retreat, which I effected in such a manner as to save hundreds of our people from falling into the enemy's hands. Almost all of the park of artillery had an oppor-tunity to get off, which must have fallen into their hands; and the left wing posted at Chads ford, got off by the seasonable check I gave the enemy. We were engaged an hour and a quarter, and lost upwards of a hundred men killed and wounded. I maintained the ground until dark, and then drew off the troops in good order.[29]

Weedon offered a much less detailed account of the contributions of Greene's troops, humbly writing, "About 6 General Green's Divi-sion arrived to cover the Retreat, one of his brigades (Weedon's) gave the Enemy such a check as produced the desired effect."[30]

These three accounts, from perhaps the best sources possible, strongly suggest that Weedon's brigade alone saved the American army from more significant losses by holding back the British near Dilworth. And yet, although Weedon's brigade obviously distin-guished itself in this part of the battle, the whereabouts and involve-ment of Muhlenberg's brigade needs to be determined, if possible.

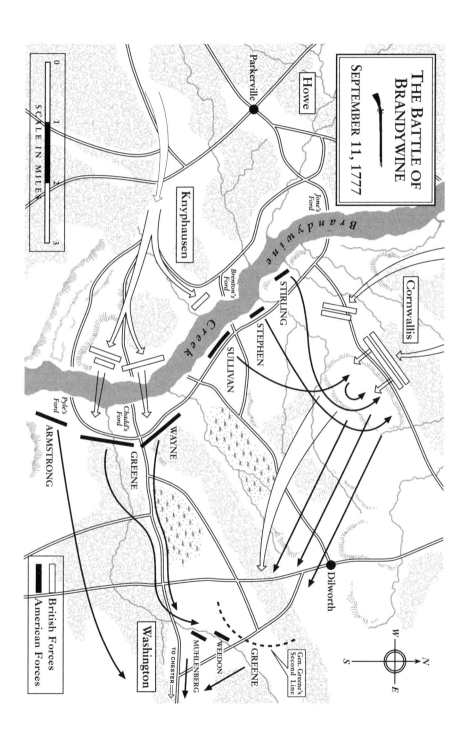

THE BATTLE OF
BRANDYWINE

SEPTEMBER 11, 1777

SCALE IN MILES

0   1   2   3

Parkerville

Howe

Knyphausen

Jone's
Ford

Brandywine

Brenton's
Ford

STIRLING

Cornwallis

STEPHEN

Creek

SULLIVAN

Pyle's
Ford

ARMSTRONG

Chadd's
Ford

GREENE

WAYNE

Dilworth

Washington

TO CHESTER

MUHLENBERG

WEEDON

GREENE

Gen. Greene's
Second Line

W

N

S

E

British Forces
American Forces

Although the accounts of Sullivan and Greene leave one to wonder if Muhlenberg was even present on the right flank, Weedon's brief account states that Greene's division arrived at 6 p.m. This suggests both his brigade and Muhlenberg's. This is supported by an account of an officer in the 3rd New Jersey, who also noted that Greene's division was sent to the assistance of the American right flank.[31]

Another consideration is that no account exists of Muhlenberg's brigade remaining near Chads's Ferry or Chads's Ford. If they had remained, surely in some account of the battle there would be a mention of this since a split of Greene's division would have been unique. Historian Michael Harris, who has extensively researched the Battle of Brandywine, offers the most plausible explanation of Muhlenberg's involvement in his book on the battle. He writes, "It is unlikely . . . that Muhlenberg remained on the southern part of the field [i.e. at Chads's Ferry], and indeed must have marched northeast behind Weedon's regiments. If he did so, it is equally likely that, with Weedon formed (or already fighting) east of the road [to Dilworth] as Greene's right wing, as the trailing organization Muhlenberg would have deployed his command west of the road with Sullivan's survivors gathered into line."[32]

If this is indeed what occurred, then Muhlenberg and his men would have participated in what Lieutenant James McMichael, a veteran soldier in Weedon's brigade described as "a severe and successive engagement [that] exceeded all I ever saw."[33] McMichael noted in his diary that "Our regiment fought at one stand about an hour under incessant fire, and yet the loss was less than at Long Island; neither were we so near each other as at Princeton, our common distance being about 50 yards."[34]

Several British combatants confirmed the intensity of the fighting around Dilworth, one officer noting that his troops "came upon a second and more extensive line of the Enemys best Troops drawn up and posted to great advantage, here they sustain'd a warm attack for some time & pour'd a heavy fire on the British Troops as they came up."[35] Another officer with the German Jagers recalled the "terrible firing" unleashed by the Americans that had a devastating effect on the advancing British.[36]

Such accounts support the view that the fight at the end of the day near the village of Dilworth was intense and deadly. Unfortunately, it remains uncertain as to who besides General Weedon's troops participated in the fight to stem the British advance. While it is very likely that Muhlenberg and his troops were present, the limited documentary evidence makes it difficult to determine with certainty what role they played in the heavy fighting around Dilworth. What occurred there in the fading light of day, however, was crucial because it spared Washington's army significantly more casualties by allowing the bulk of his troops to escape eastward.

Five

Germantown to Valley Forge

FOLLOWING THE BATTLE OF BRANDYWINE, WASHINGTON withdrew his battered army eastward to Chester and ordered his brigadier generals to send as many officers as they thought necessary back along the routes leading to the battlefield to gather stragglers and return them to the army. "In doing this," instructed Washington, "they will proceed as far, towards the enemy, as shall be consistent with their own safety, and examine every house."[1] The rest of the American army marched on to Darby and crossed the Schuylkill River on a pontoon bridge, then marched northwest past Philadelphia to the falls of the Schuylkill River near Germantown.

The following day Washington praised the army in his general orders, assuring the troops (incorrectly) that they had inflicted far more casualties on the enemy than they had suffered and that the next engagement would prove victorious.[2] Rum was liberally distributed (one gill per man per day while it lasted) and preparations to march the next morning were undertaken.[3]

Washington and his army recrossed the Schuylkill River the next day and marched southwestward, "intent on giving the Enemy Battle wherever I should meet them."[4] Howe remained in the vicinity of Dilworth for several days, but just as Washington expected, Howe proceeded to march in a northeasterly direction toward the upper fords of the Schuylkill River.

The two armies nearly clashed a few miles southwest of Valley Forge, but "a most violent Flood of Rain" damaged the bulk of the American army's musket cartridges and caused Washington to disengage and withdraw northward to Yellow Springs.[5] Concerned that General Howe was maneuvering to flank him as he had at Brandywine and Brooklyn, Washington marched farther north and west.[6] Reports that the enemy was actually marching toward Swedes Ford on the Schuylkill River, however, just a few miles from Valley Forge, prompted Washington to rush eastward to recross the river and head off Howe.

Washington's route took his troops through the village of Trappe and past Muhlenberg's childhood home. Muhlenberg's wife, Hanna, had returned to Trappe from Philadelphia with their son on September 10, fearful that the American capital would soon fall to the British.[7] It is unclear whether they were still in Trappe a few days later when the American army passed, for it appears that at some point before mid-October they moved in with Muhlenberg's brother, Friedrich, and his family a few miles away in New Hannover.[8]

Muhlenberg apparently did not get an opportunity to visit with his family at this time as there is no mention of him in his father's journal. He was likely far too busy managing his brigade as they rushed to get into position to intercept Howe. Washington's troops arrived at Fatland Ford, just north of Valley Forge, on September 20 and deployed for several miles up and down the Schuylkill River to guard against a British crossing.[9]

Washington was unsure of Howe's true objective; the British commander had placed his army about midway between the American capital at Philadelphia and a vital American supply depot at Reading. Having been defeated twice by General Howe's flanking movements, Washington was determined not to be outflanked again. When British troop movements on September 21 suggested that Reading was Howe's objective, Washington acted quickly and shifted his army toward that town.[10] Once again the American army passed through Trappe and halted near the village of Pottsgrove, closer to Reading than Philadelphia.

Unfortunately for the Americans, Washington had miscalculated. Howe was not interested in the supplies at Reading; Philadelphia was his true objective, and his army reversed direction and crossed the Schuylkill River at Fatland Ford unopposed.[11] Washington sheepishly informed Congress, which had removed to Lancaster days earlier, of this development.

> The Enemy, by a variety of perplexing Maneuvres thro' a County from which I could not derive the least intelligence being to a man disaffected, contrived to pass the Schuylkill last Night at the Flat land and other Fords in the Neighbourhood of it. They marched immediately towards Philada and I imagine their advanced parties will be near that City to Night. They had so far got the Start before I recd certain intelligence . . . that I found it in vain to think of overtaking their Rear with Troops harassed as ours had been with constant marching since the Battle of Brandywine.[12]

Washington felt obligated to offer an explanation of how he found himself out of position to challenge the British crossing of the Schuylkill.

> The day before yesterday they were again in motion and marched rapidly up the Road leading towards Reading. This induced me to believe that they had two objects in view, one to get round the right of the Army, the other perhaps to detach parties to Reading where we had considerable quantities of military Stores. To frustrate those intentions I moved the Army up on this side of the River to this place [Pottsgrove] determined to keep pace with them, but early this morning I recd intelligence that they had crossed at the Fords below.[13]

Addressing a question Washington was sure the entire Congress was thinking, he added, "Why I did not follow immediately I have mentioned in the former part of my letter. But the strongest Reason against being able to make a forced march is the want of Shoes; . . . at least one thousand Men are bare footed and have performed the marches in that condition."[14]

The commander in chief was not alone in his assessment that the American army was in no condition to undertake a forced march to catch and fight Howe's army. A war council of his general officers unanimously agreed that "from the present state of the Army, it would not be advisable to advance upon the Enemy . . . till the detachments and expected Reinforcements come up."[15]

Interestingly, Muhlenberg did not participate in this meeting. His absence might have been due to his duty as brigadier general of the day that day, or perhaps he was ill. Given the proximity of the American position to Trappe, he may have been granted leave to see his family. It is hard to imagine, however, with another engagement seemingly imminent, that Muhlenberg would choose to take, or be granted leave, even briefly, from his brigade.

Whatever the reason for his absence, Muhlenberg was at the next war council on September 28, where he agreed with a majority of officers that the army was not prepared to attack the enemy. Instead, Washington's commanders proposed that the army move closer to the British in Philadelphia and await either reinforcements or a more favorable opportunity to strike.[16]

Such an opportunity presented itself less than a week later and Washington seized upon it. Two developments occurred in the days following the war council. A brigade of Connecticut Continentals (about a thousand strong) that had been posted in the New York Highlands arrived in camp in late September while at nearly the same moment General Howe sent a thousand British soldiers from Philadelphia to Chester, Pennsylvania, to deal with several American river forts that prevented the British navy from sailing up the Delaware River to Philadelphia.[17] This left approximately eleven thousand British troops in the immediate vicinity of Philadelphia, three thousand in the city itself and the rest guarding the city five

miles away at Germantown.[18] It was this force at Germantown, estimated by Washington to be eight thousand strong, that the American
commander (with eight thousand Continentals and three thousand
militia) hoped to surprise and defeat with a dawn attack.[19]

Washington's plan was bold and complex. The army would march
throughout the night in four columns along four different routes and
converge on the enemy at sunrise in Germantown. The militia
brigades were instructed to strike the left and right flank and rear of
the enemy while the bulk of Washington's army, divided into a right
and left wing, would strike the enemy head on.[20]

General Sullivan commanded the right wing of Washington's
army. His force comprised his own division of Maryland troops
along with General Wayne's Pennsylvania division. General Greene
commanded the left wing of the army which included his division (of
Muhlenberg's and Weedon's brigades) and General Stephen's two
Virginia brigades. The recently arrived brigade of Connecticut Continentals under General Alexander McDougall also marched with
Greene's force, but they were to file off and attack the enemy's right
flank with the militia as soon as the fighting began.[21]

Washington attempted to inspire his army prior to the attack with
a challenge. Noting the recent success of the American Northern
army near Saratoga, New York, under Horatio Gates against John
Burgoyne's British army from Canada, Washington declared in his
orders that "Every circumstance promises success in that quarter. . .
."[22] Washington then challenged his troops:

> This army—the main American Army—will certainly not suffer
> itself to be out done by their northern Brethren—they will never
> endure such disgrace. . . . Covet! My Countrymen, and fellow sol-
> diers! Covet! A share of the glory due to heroic deeds! Let it never
> be said, that in a day of action, you turned your backs on the foe—
> let the enemy no longer triumph. . . . Will you suffer the wounds
> given to your Country to go unrevenged? Will you resign your par-
> ents—wives—children and friends to be the wretched vassals of a
> proud, insulting foe? And your own necks to the halter?. . . Every
> motive that can touch the human breast calls us to the most vigor-

ous exertions—Our dearest rights—our dearest friends—our own lives—honor—glory, and even shame, urge us to the fight—And my fellow soldiers! When an opportunity presents, be firm, be brave, shew yourselves men, and victory is yours.[23]

Muhlenberg's specific orders to his brigade, which were really just a reiteration of Washington's orders to the general officers, were far less inspirational: "Officers of Regts. Are to see that their men have three Days Provisions Cook'd (this day included). Their men are likewise to be furnish'd with 40 Rounds of Cartridges per Man . . . Flints, etc. in the best order."[24]

Washington's plan called for a multipronged attack on the enemy's outposts north of Germantown at 5 a.m. Greene's wing had one of the longest routes to march to get into position, so they commenced their march at 6 p.m. The troops left their packs and baggage in camp and were given white slips of paper to put in their hats to better distinguish themselves from the enemy in the dark (assuming it was still dark when they attacked). As there was no moon that evening, the men struggled over bad roads all night.[25]

By 5 a.m. three of Washington's four columns were in position to attack. Greene's column, however, had fallen behind and was late. That didn't stop Sullivan with the right wing of Washington's army from proceeding as planned. He approached Howe's light infantry outposts, which were situated about two miles north of the British main camp in Germantown, just after 5 a.m. A thick fog coupled with the dim light of dawn obscured visibility, but Sullivan had vastly superior numbers and he pressed on in the face of a scattering of enemy musket fire from the British picket line and cannon fire from two six-pound cannon.[26]

The British 2nd Light Battalion was now thoroughly alarmed, but they were also significantly outnumbered and had no chance of stopping Sullivan's men. The British gave ground and retreated to Benjamin Chew's large stone country house, called Cliveden, where the 40th Regiment of Foot (three hundred strong) was posted. Unable to stop the American advance, more than half of the 40th Regiment retreated with the light infantry back toward the main British camp.[27]

Importantly, however, over a hundred soldiers of the 40th, including their commander, Lieutenant Colonel Thomas Musgrave, barricaded themselves inside Cliveden and refused a call to surrender (actually mortally wounding the flag bearer who approached to seek their surrender).[28]

Washington, who had accompanied Sullivan's wing in the attack, came upon the scene and considered bypassing the obstinate enemy in the mansion, but General Henry Knox argued that it would be dangerous to leave them in the rear and convinced Washington to order an attack.[29]

Hundreds of Washington's troops now focused their attention and efforts on dislodging a hundred British troops from Cliveden, instead of joining the rest of Sullivan's wing in pushing on with the attack. Efforts to blast the British out with cannon, storm the mansion with infantry, and even burn the building to the ground all failed. The 40th Regiment refused to budge and in doing so, they helped undermine Washington's attack.[30]

It was during these efforts to capture Cliveden that some of Greene's troops arrived on the scene, forty minutes behind schedule. Woodford's brigade, on the far right of Greene's wing, was drawn to their right by the sound of the heavy fighting at Cliveden and when they reached the back of the mansion they joined the effort to take the house.[31] The rest of Stephen's division marched on past Cliveden. To their left marched the rest of Greene's wing, including Muhlenberg and his brigade, all deployed into a battle line.

Wayne, who had advanced several hundred yards past Cliveden with Sullivan's wing, heard the intense fighting to his rear and became worried that the enemy had somehow gotten behind him through the fog and smoke. He turned his brigade around and marched back toward Cliveden to investigate.[32] To his front appeared a long line of dark figures, mostly obscured by thick fog. Suddenly a volley erupted from this line, blasting the Pennsylvanians. Those of General Wayne's troops who didn't panic naturally returned fire, striking some of Greene's Virginians from Stephen's division.[33] A tragic case of friendly fire had occurred and the confusion of the moment caused many of the Pennsylvanians to assume they had been

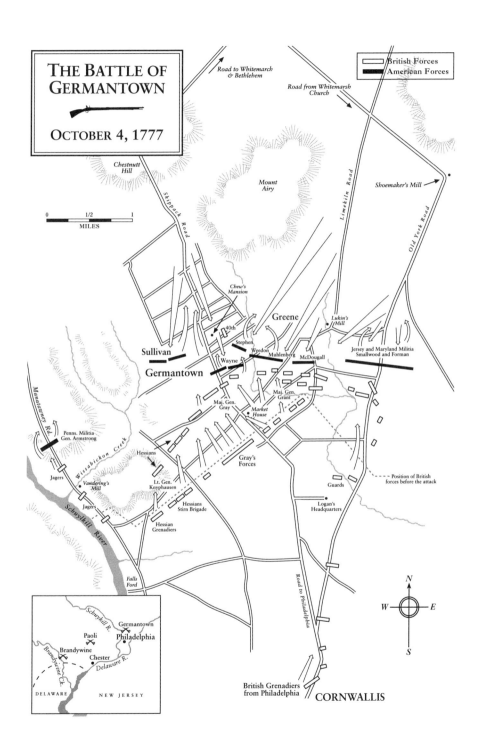

THE BATTLE OF
GERMANTOWN

OCTOBER 4, 1777

British Forces
American Forces

*Road to Whitemarsh
& Bethlehem*

*Road from Whitemarsh
Church*

*Chestnutt
Hill*

0   1/2   1
MILES

*Mount
Airy*

Shoemaker's Mill

*Chew's
Mansion*

Greene

*Lukin's
Mill*

40th

Stephen

Sullivan

Weedon   Muhlenberg

McDougall

Germantown

Wayne

*Jersey and Maryland Militia
Smallwood and Forman*

Maj. Gen.
Gray

Maj. Gen.
Grant

*Market
House*

*Penns. Militia
Gen. Armstrong*

Hessians

Gray's
Forces

*Vandering's
Mill*

*Lt. Gen.
Knyphausen*

Jagers

Guards

*Hessians
Stirn Brigade*

*Logan's
Headquarters*

Jagers

Hessian
Grenadiers

*Falls
Ford*

- - - *Position of British
forces before the attack*

Schuylkill R.

Germantown

Paoli

Philadelphia

Brandywine

Chester

Delaware R.

DELAWARE   NEW JERSEY

Road to Philadelphia

N

W   E

S

British Grenadiers
from Philadelphia   CORNWALLIS

flanked by the enemy. As a result, Wayne's brigade lost its order and began to retreat.[34]

Although the mishap between the Virginians and Pennsylvanians blunted the momentum of Washington's attack, the bulk of Greene's troops on the left, including Muhlenberg's Virginians, pressed forward and engaged the British 1st Battalion of Light Infantry (which up to this point had not been engaged). A British officer recalled, "The Rebels moving on, lined a Bank & Rail under cover of the Fog, & threw in a most severe fire upon the [Fourth] Regt . . . which knoc'd down almost the whole of their right wing."[35] Sixteen-year-old Joseph Plum Martin with the Connecticut troops who were alongside Greene's Virginians recalled that "the enemy were driven quite through their camp. They left their kettles, in which they were cooking their breakfast, on the fires, and some of their garments were lying on the ground, which the owners had not time to put on."[36]

Martin and his comrades in Greene's left wing briefly relished their apparent victory over Howe's advance troops. Muhlenberg's regiment of 9th Virginians (commanded by Colonel George Mathews) had pushed farther than any of Greene's troops, all the way to the Market House in the center of Germantown.[37] They soon discovered, however, that their accomplishment left them vulnerable. British reinforcements swarmed upon them, determined to push the Americans back, and with no support on their flanks, the 9th Virginia was quickly surrounded and their wounded commander forced to surrender his entire regiment.[38]

The situation was little better for the rest of Muhlenberg's brigade and Greene's wing. With most of Sullivan's right wing either halted or in retreat, Greene had little chance of victory on his own. To save his troops he grudgingly ordered a withdrawal.[39]

Washington was stunned at these developments. In a candid letter to his brother John Augustine two weeks after the battle, Washington admitted that he was still unable to identify the cause of their loss at Germantown:

After they [the British] had crossed [into Philadelphia] we took the first favourable opportunity of attacking them—This we attempted by a Nights March of fourteen Miles to surprise them (which we effectually did) so far as reaching their Guards before they had notice of our coming, and but for a thick Fog rendered so infinitely dark at times, as not to distinguish friend from Foe, at the distance of 30 Yards, we should, I believe, have made a decisive & glorious day of it. . . . But Providence—or some unaccountable something, designd it otherwise; for after we had driven the Enemy a Mile or two, after they were in the utmost confusion, and flying before us in most places, after we were upon the point (as it appeard to every body) of grasping a compleat Victory, our own Troops took fright & fled with precipitation and disorder. How to account for this I know not, unless, as I before observ'd, the Fog represented their own Friends to them for a Reinforcement of the Enemy as we attacked in different Quarters at the same time, & were about closing the Wings of our Army when this happened.[40]

Washington added that the fighting lasted nearly three hours during which many of his troops expended all of their ammunition.[41] With much of his army retreating on their own in a disorganized manner, Washington ordered them to return to their old encampment at Pennypacker Mills, about twenty miles from Philadelphia, where they could treat the wounded and reorganize themselves.

Unfortunately, like Brandywine, there are no direct eyewitness accounts of Muhlenberg's role at the Battle of Germantown. We know that he and his brigade were heavily engaged with the left wing of Washington's attack and that his 9th Virginia Regiment distinguished itself by advancing farther than any other American unit. That distinction came at a heavy cost, however, as nearly the entire regiment was captured.

Not everyone was pleased with Muhlenberg's troops. Accusations of cowardice were leveled against Muhlenberg's 13th Virginia Regiment at Germantown by Lieutenant James McMichael, who noted in his diary that "The cowardice of the Thirtheenth Virginia regiment gave the enemy an opportunity of coming around our left flank."[42] No formal charge was brought against the Virginians and we do not know the context of McMichael's complaint in his diary, suffice to say he was angry at the Virginians for retreating.

American losses at Germantown were significant and American morale suffered as a result. From Pennypacker Mills, Washington informed Congress that "My intention is, to encamp the Army at some suitable place, to rest and refresh the Men, and recover them from the still remaining effects of that disorder naturally attendant on a Retreat. We shall here wait for the Reinforcements coming on, and shall then act according to circumstances."[43]

Washington needed the reinforcements that were en route from Gates's army in New York because he estimated that he lost approximately a thousand troops at Germantown in killed, wounded, or missing. Washington speculated that not all of the missing were captured; some he felt had deserted under the fog of battle.[44]

Muhlenberg's brigade suffered the highest losses in the army at Germantown, losing nearly the entire 9th Virginia Regiment to captivity. To offset this loss, General Washington attached the 1st Virginia State Garrison Regiment, approximately 226 effectives, to Muhlenberg's brigade.[45] This regiment was raised the previous year as one of three state garrison regiments to offset the absence of the many Virginia Continental regiments that had left the state. Virginia's leaders wanted more than just militia available to defend the commonwealth, so three garrison regiments were formed in 1776. Soldiers in these regiments served full time for three years with the understanding that they would not be ordered out of the state.[46]

This was not an absolute restriction, however, and in the fall of 1777 Governor Patrick Henry and the Virginia Assembly responded to appeals for more assistance from Washington and Congress and ordered the 1st Virginia State Garrison northward to join Washington's army.[47] The regiment was commanded by Colonel George Gibson and arrived just prior to the Battle of Germantown.

In the weeks following Germantown, Washington's army struggled to address long-neglected issues such as supply shortages and military discipline. Muhlenberg and his fellow brigadiers were instructed to personally supervise the drafting of accurate troop returns as well as lists of missing clothing items that were needed to properly outfit each soldier in their brigade.[48] Four days after Washington requested these returns, with nine regiments not reporting as ordered, the totals from those units that did submit returns showed that Washington's army needed "3,084 coats, 4,051 waistcoats, 6,148 breeches, 8,033 stockings, 6,472 shoes, 6,330 shirts, 137 hunting shirts, 4,552 blankets, 2,399 hats, 341 stocks, 356 overalls, and 1,140 knapsacks.[49]

Along with struggling with the chronic supply shortage in the army, Washington used the weeks after Philadelphia's fall to address several disciplinary issues among his general officers. Accusations of misconduct in some form during the recent campaign were leveled against Generals Sullivan, Maxwell, Wayne, and Stephen.

Muhlenberg and many of his fellow general officers spent a sizable amount of time on boards of inquiry and courts martial to address the charges brought against their fellow officers. The only senior officer found guilty of significant wrongdoing was Adam Stephen; he was convicted of unofficerlike behavior during the retreat from Germantown and of also being too often intoxicated while in the service "to the prejudice of good order and military discipline."[50] Washington approved the sentence of the court (of which Muhlenberg was not a member) for Stephen—dismissal from the army—and it was so ordered. Stephen's departure left Muhlenberg as the ranking field officer among the Virginian brigadiers, but this status would prove to be short lived.

Washington and the rest of his army had welcomed the news about the decisive American victory over the British at Saratoga and the even better news that Burgoyne's entire force had surrendered, taking some of the sting out of the defeats at Brandywine and Germantown, not to mention the loss of Philadelphia. Returning his focus to that city, Washington authorized a long shot attempt to force the British army from Philadelphia by blocking their supply line on the Delaware River. Two forts on the banks of the river a few miles south of Philadelphia—Fort Mifflin in Pennsylvania and Fort Mercer in New Jersey—anchored American efforts to stop the British navy from reaching Philadelphia. The primary purpose of these two forts was to defend the water obstacles that blocked the channel in the Delaware River. As long as these forts were in American hands, gunfire from their cannon made it impossible for the British navy to dismantle and overcome the underwater obstacles in the river. Every day that the British navy was delayed created a greater logistical challenge for Howe and his army since they needed the supplies aboard the blocked British transport ships in the river.

Washington realized the significance of holding the forts and sent reinforcements to them after the Germantown debacle. Some of these troops helped the garrison at Fort Mercer repulse a Hessian effort to storm the fort on October 22. Hundreds of Hessians fell in the assault while American casualties were few.[51]

With winter approaching, Washington closely monitored the situation with the river forts. He pondered the idea of attacking Philadelphia to help relieve pressure on them and wrote a circular letter to his general officers asking for their opinion on that idea as well as on several other questions. Three days later, Muhlenberg and his fellow brigade and division commanders met with Washington in a council of war to provide the commander in chief their advice.

The war council opposed an attack on Philadelphia at that time and recommended instead that the army take position in the hills at Whitemarsh, about twenty miles north of Philadelphia, where they could gather forage for the coming winter.[52] The officers hoped that Howe would interpret such a movement as a threat, which might then dissuade him from sending additional troops against the river forts.

The war council also recommended that sufficient reinforcements be sent to the river forts to keep them at full strength. Washington had also asked the war council to consider plans for a winter encampment, but they deferred the matter of where the army should spend the winter for a later date.[53]

Washington accepted the council's recommendations and marched the army to Whitemarsh. A period of relative inactivity settled over the army as Washington waited for Howe to resume operations against him or go into winter quarters.

British efforts to subdue Fort Mifflin and Fort Mercer continued during this time, and some progress, at least against Fort Mifflin, was made by the British. For weeks, the garrison within Fort Mifflin endured heavy shelling from British cannon onshore and aboard ships, and by mid-November much of the fort had literally fallen down around the men. Despite a long and noble stand by the garrison, the destruction of Fort Mifflin left its commanding officer, Major Simeon Thayer of Rhode Island, little choice but to evacuate the garrison on November 16, 1777. A key link in the American defense of the Delaware River had fallen.[54]

Washington maintained hope that Fort Mercer, which was across the river from Fort Mifflin and still in American hands, might—by itself—be able to stop the British navy from neutralizing and passing the river obstacles. Unfortunately for the Americans, the commander of Fort Mercer, Colonel Christopher Greene of Rhode Island, informed Washington that British ships had found a passage up the river past Fort Mifflin and he feared his garrison at Fort Mercer was in danger of being besieged and captured.[55]

Washington was apparently not ready to give up Fort Mercer, however, and ordered several general officers in camp to proceed to the fort to evaluate whether an effort to keep it should be attempted.[56] They reported back on November 19 that they thought it was both feasible and important to keep possession of the fort.[57]

Washington acted immediately and ordered Nathanael Greene to cross the Delaware River with his division—Muhlenberg's and Weedon's brigades—and take command of all of the reinforcements sent to New Jersey to assist Fort Mercer.[58] "Very much will depend upon keeping possession of Fort Mercer," explained Washington, "as to reduce it, the Enemy will be obliged to put themselves in a very disagreeable position to them and advantageous to us, upon their Rear. Therefore desire Colo. Green to hold it if possible till the relief arrives."[59]

But it was too late to save the fort. On the night of November 19, Christopher Greene, who had valiantly defended Fort Mercer against a Hessian assault in October, feared that his garrison was about to be invested and trapped by the enemy and opted instead to save his troops by evacuating the fort.[60] Nathanael Greene, who had crossed the Delaware River above Philadelphia at Burlington, New Jersey, informed Washington of the news.[61]

There was still a chance for General Greene to inflict some loss on the large enemy force that had crossed into New Jersey to attack Fort Mercer. Greene had more than just his division of Muhlenberg and Weedon's brigades with him. General Varnum's Rhode Island brigade and General Jedediah Huntington's Connecticut brigade were in New Jersey, as were the remnants of Colonel Daniel Morgan's Rifle Corps (only 170 effectives) and Captain Henry Lee's troop of light horse. Greene also had over a thousand New Jersey militia in the field ready to follow his command and General John Glover's brigade of Massachusetts Continentals were expected to join him as well.[62]

With this sizable force Greene had hoped to attack Cornwallis in New Jersey, but Cornwallis had also been reinforced with British troops from New York and now outnumbered Greene's troops with approximately five thousand of his own.[63] The best Greene could do was harass the British rearguard when Cornwallis recrossed the Delaware River and returned to Philadelphia in late November.

Washington realized that with Howe's army concentrated in Philadelphia and his own army divided by the Delaware River, his troops at Whitemarsh were vulnerable to attack. He ordered Greene to return with his detachment as soon as possible.[64] Greene arrived along with Muhlenberg and the other general officers in his division in time to participate in another war council. The topic that the commander in chief put before his general officers was what to do with the army during the winter season. Washington requested that each officer put his advice in writing for his consideration.

Muhlenberg tended to agree with the more moderate—some might say cautious—recommendations of past war councils and continued that trend in his reply to Washington's inquiry.

> I would beg leave to premise that agreeable to my Sentiments, the Army should continue in a Position, where they can most effectu-

ally Annoy the Enemy, untill it shall be absolutely necessary on Account of the Severity of the Weather to Quit the Field—2dly That the Preservation of the Army by getting them into good Winter Quarters, will be of much greater Utility, than any small Advantages, which can be gain'd over the Enemy, by keeping the Army near their Lines.[65]

For winter quarters, Muhlenberg supported splitting the army between Lancaster and Reading instead of keeping it together at Wilmington, Delaware. He explained why in his reply:

With regard to the place, proper for the Army to take Winter Quarters, I must confess, I am more inclined to Join in Sentiment with those Gentlemen who propose Lancaster for the Right of the Cantonment & Reading for the Left, than with those who propose Wilmington—my reasons are these. Wilmington, &ca are so near the Enemy that there is the greatest probability of their frequent Alarming us, consequently the end intended, that is the Ease of the Army will not be Answered.

2dly Our Army will certainly diminish, at least for the Winter, by a Number of the Soldiers receiving permission to return to the different States they came from which would perhaps enable the Enemy to gain Material Advantages over us, especially if it should be found necessary, on account of Covering, to Quarter the Men some distance apart.

3dly The upper part of Pennsylvania would be left entirely to the Mercy of the Enemy, & the Communication with the Eastern States cut off.

4ly The Enemy will have it in their power to draw more Supplies from the Jersey, than it would be possible for them to draw from the lower Counties even if they were entirely given up to them, for if the Army lay at Wilmington, One Armed Vessell would be sufficient to prevent us from affording any relief to the Jerseys.[66]

Having explained in detail his opposition to Wilmington as a location for the winter encampment, Muhlenberg suggested that Washington might consider the area between Reading and Easton in Pennsylvania.

> Perhaps if your Excellency was to Order some Person to Reconnoitre the Country from Reading to Easton it would be found more eligible, to make Reading the right of the Cantonment, & Easton the left, than any other place proposed, especially if the Hint thrown out by a Gentleman in Council, was Adopted that is, to erect Huts for the more Robust & let the Feeble, be quartered in Houses &ct. In Reading the Refugees from Philadelphia, are less Numerous than in Lancaster, Lebanon, &ct. Reading, Allentown, Bethlehem & Easton lie in a direct line, very near the same distance from Philadelphia—a few Miles in front of this Line, in Matawny & Macungy, one, if not two Divisions may be Quartered with the greatest ease, & here the Troops would be ready, either to protect our Stores, or prevent any considerable Ravages in the Country.[67]

Before the general officers were able to assemble to discuss the question in person, Washington sent them another circular letter. Writing that "Particular reasons urge me to request your sentiments on this matter," Washington asked his officers for their opinions about conducting a winter campaign against the British that included an attack on Philadelphia, all contingent on the support of a large body of militia.[68]

General Muhlenberg's reply was reasonable, cautious, and convincing.

> I must confess that to me this Question seems so much interwoven, with the Question Your Excellency was pleasd to put a few days ago, [about a winter encampment] that I can hardly Separate them: The main point, I conceive, is still, whether A Winters Campaign is practicable. . . . A Winters Campaign to me, seems not only unadviseable, on account of our Situation, but impracticable, at least if I am to Judge of other Brigades by my own; One single Regt. of mine have turned out Ninety Men unfit for duty,

on Account of Shoes & other Necessarys. The Sick become Numerous, & the Men, notwithstanding the utmost Care of their Officers, will be Frostbitten, & Subject to many other disorders, if they are to keep the Field, untill the Militia can be Collected, which if we are to Judge From the past, cannot be done in less than two Months—In the meantime it cannot be expected that the Enemy will remain Idle, Their Works will be Continued, Their Vessels who are now before the Town, will not only furnish them with Cannon, but with Marines, Sailors &ct. so that in all probability, before the Militia can be Collected an Attack will be thought impracticable, upon the same Grounds & perhaps with more reason than at present.[69]

Muhlenberg admitted that when the idea to attack Philadelphia was first proposed in early November, he was open to it because he believed that, with the British focused on the river forts, there might be a chance for success. But the situation had changed considerably since then and Muhlenberg believed an attack on Philadelphia over the winter would be a disaster. "At the Time when this Hint was first thrown out in Council, I was pleasd with it, there seemd a probability of Success: but I had no Idea, that a Winters Campaign was so closely Connected with the plan, which in my Opinion would prove more fatal to the Army under Your Excellencys Command than an unfortunate Attack on the Town."[70]

Muhlenberg made clear, however, that he was not adamantly against attacking Philadelphia. He just believed such an attack would fail if launched in the near future or over the winter: "But I am far from thinking the plan ought to be dropped entirely, If the Army was to go into Winter Quarters where the Men could be refreshd & Clothd, & remain there, until the latter end of March; the Militia could be Collected in the mean time. Then a Vigorous Attack could be made with a probability of Success."[71]

Muhlenberg ended by acknowledging his relative youth, compared to most of the other general officers (he had recently turned thirty-one), and pledging to enthusiastically support what Washington decided to do.

Thus I have given Your Excellency my Sentiments on the Question proposd, as Clear as the shortness of the time I had for Consideration would permit me, which was only a few Minutes this Morning; The utility of hearing a Question be debated is great, at least to a young Soldier—should the Question be decided otherwise Your Excellency may be Assurd that any part entrusted to me shall be executed with the greatest Chearfullness.[72]

Muhlenberg was not alone in his opposition to a winter campaign against Howe in Philadelphia. The proposal was universally opposed by Washington's general officers, who believed the condition of the army would not allow for a winter campaign.

Ironically, even as replies to Washington's inquiry about a winter campaign were still arriving at headquarters, Howe made the issue a moot point by marching the bulk of his British army toward the American encampment at Whitemarsh. It seemed that perhaps the British commander had resolved to conduct a winter campaign against Washington.

It was not to be, however. Howe's brief foray into the Pennsylvania countryside alarmed the Americans and sparked some heated skirmishing, but little of significance resulted from Howe's movement and he retreated back to Philadelphia by the latter half of December.

With his general officers strongly opposed to a winter campaign and his army unable to serve in one, Washington realized it was time to go into winter quarters. Unlike the previous winter, in which Washington's troops were spread out among New Jersey's Watchung Mountains, the American commander wanted to keep the army intact and reasonably close to Philadelphia. Whitemarsh was rejected as too close to Philadelphia and, thus, too vulnerable to attack. Washington needed someplace farther away from Philadelphia—to allow for a proper warning if the British did try to attack over the winter—but also defensible and logistically sustainable. He settled on Valley Forge, about twenty-five miles northwest of Philadelphia, and marched the army there on December 19.

Six

Monmouth Courthouse and the Battles around New York

V ALLEY FORGE PROVIDED STRONG TERRAIN ON WHICH TO RESIST a possible British attack and yet was close enough to Philadel-phia for Washington to keep watch on Howe and harass his foraging parties. The Schuylkill River protected the American left flank and a steep hill, called Mount Joy, covered their rear. Although the front and right flank of the encampment possessed few natural barriers, the open terrain made an attack from those directions very haz-ardous, provided the Americans could build sufficient earthworks.

Washington ordered that log huts and earthworks be constructed immediately, but it took nearly a month before the entire army was adequately sheltered. Two lines of earthworks were built. The outer line extended along a ridge from the Schuylkill River to the foot of Mount Joy. Most of the army, including Muhlenberg's brigade, was stationed along this line in rows of huts behind the fortifications. Muhlenberg's troops were posted on the left flank of the outer line. An inner defense line was built along Mount Joy. It also ran to the river.

Muhlenberg did not oversee the hutting of his men or the con-struction of any earthworks at Valley Forge, his request for leave to transport his wife and young son back to Virginia was granted by Washington within a few days of their arrival at Valley Forge.[1] Muhlenberg arrived at his parents' house in Trappe on December 26 and continued on to his brother Friedrich's home in New Hannover by wagon to collect his wife and son.[2]

Seven weeks later, Muhlenberg's father recorded in his diary that his son Peter was back in Pennsylvania, so assuming the 230-mile journey took over two weeks by wagon and another ten days for Muhlenberg's return by horseback, he probably spent less than a month in Virginia.[3] It was long enough though to help Hanna get situated and to leave her expecting with their second child. (Of course, neither knew this when he departed in early February.) He also noted that Peter had been accompanied by a "Major Campbell" (probably Richard Campbell, one of Muhlenberg's former captains in the 8th Virginia Regiment) on his return. Muhlenberg apparently did not stop to visit his parents, but Major Campbell did, and he shared a harrowing account of their son's crossing of the Susquehanna River, which nearly ended in tragedy due to drift ice.[4]

Muhlenberg arrived back at Valley Forge in early March; he appears in the general orders for March 6 as the brigadier general of the day.[5] What he did in Pennsylvania in the nearly three weeks prior to his return is unclear. His father recorded in his journal of February 19 that Peter was in Tolpehaken, a German settlement fifty miles northwest of Trappe close to where his maternal grandfather, Conrad Weiser, had lived, so it is possible that he stayed there to recover his health after the long winter journey and mishap on the river.[6]

When Muhlenberg left Valley Forge in December his brigade numbered only 678 officers and men present and fit for duty.[7] His original four Virginia regiments—1st, 5th, 9th, and 13th—each had less than a full company of rank-and-file troops, and the 9th had so few soldiers left it was merged with the 5th Virginia. The other two regiments, the 1st Virginia State Garrison and the 8th Maryland, were similarly depleted. Many of these 678 officers and men remained at Valley Forge during Muhlenberg's absence in hastily built log huts. They suffered through difficult winter conditions and endured frequent shortages in both provisions and clothing. Hundreds became

ill and hundreds more were discharged in February when their enlistments ended.[8] Upon Muhlenberg's return, the total number of officers and men in his brigade who were present and fit for duty had
dropped below three hundred.[9] In fact, the five regiments of Peter
Muhlenberg's brigade combined could only field the equivalent of
two full companies of men.[10]

The situation remained bleak for the rest of March, but conditions
in camp improved with the arrival of spring, and by the end of April,
Muhlenberg's troop strength had grown considerably with new recruits and furloughed men arriving from Virginia as well as troops
who recovered from illness.[11]

Although the condition of his brigade undoubtedly accounted for
much of Muhlenberg's attention at Valley Forge, he was also greatly
concerned by recent developments concerning his ranking among his
fellow Virginia brigadier generals.

Scores of American officers were dissatisfied with their rank and
placement in the officer hierarchy and Muhlenberg's fellow brigadier,
William Woodford, was one such officer. Woodford had resigned
from the army in protest in 1776 because two officers of lower rank
at the time had been promoted to brigadier general ahead of him.
However, in early 1777 Woodford agreed to return to the army when
Congress offered him a brigadier general's commission. Unsatisfied
with his placement (third) among the four new Virginia brigadier
generals appointed in 1777 (Muhlenberg, Weedon, Woodford, and
Scott), all of whom had ranked beneath Woodford prior to his resignation in 1776, Woodford—and several of his allies in Congress—
let it be known for much of 1777 that he desired Congress to restore
him to his proper place (first) among the Virginia brigadier generals.

In addressing a similar dispute over rank among Pennsylvania officers in August 1777, Congress approved a Board of General Officers proposal (ironically of which Woodford and Weedon were
members) to establish the rank and precedence of the Pennsylvania
officers according to "that standing they held in the army immediately before their present commissions."[12]

Several months later, Congress wanted to apply this same measure to General Woodford. Henry Laurens, the president of Congress, instructed Washington on November 29 to regulate Woodford's rank based on the arrangement used for the Pennsylvania officers.

Washington rightly believed there would be strong opposition to elevating Woodford above the other Virginia brigadiers because Woodford had voluntarily left the army (against Washington's advice) in the fall of 1776. There was little sympathy among Woodford's fellow officers for his argument that he deserved a higher placement among them because he served as a colonel in the army well before the other officers had.

Recognizing the explosive nature of this issue, Washington sought further guidance from Congress. He also warned Congress of the importance of settling the question of rank once and for all and as quickly as possible:

> At the time Woodford was appointed he held no rank in the Army. His claim is to rank before such of the Gentlemen [Muhlenberg, Scott, Weedon] appointed when he was, as [they] were younger Colonels than himself. If this was intended by Congress . . . and I presume it was, or it can have no Operation as to him—An Explanatory and directory Resolve would answer every purpose, as from that a Commission might be filled up agreeable to their views respecting him. I wish this business to be determined on as early as possible . . . as no subject can be more disagreeable or injurious to the service than that of contested rank.[13]

Undoubtedly frustrated that Congress had failed to resolve the dispute itself and left him with the responsibility of resolving Woodford's rank, Washington included a brief lecture to Congress to be more careful in the future when addressing the issue of rank in the army. "I trust Congress will be more guarded in future. They may not be so intimately acquainted with them as I am; But they may be assured, there are none of a more fatal and injurious tendency, when rank is once given, no matter upon what principle, whether from mistake or other causes, the party in possession of it in most cases is unwilling to give it up."[14]

This was certainly the case regarding Woodford's attempt to rise above Muhlenberg and Weedon. Just as Washington expected, Weedon and Muhlenberg were adamantly opposed to any change in their status, especially one that placed Woodford above them. It was nothing personal, Weedon claimed; he held Woodford in the highest esteem and considered him an intimate acquaintance. It was the principle of honor that forced him to oppose the loss of his status through no fault of his own.[15]

Realizing the turmoil they had caused and the dilemma they were in, Congress formed a committee to go to Valley Forge to settle the dispute, but the committee members did not address the issue until mid-February and, after several deliberations, handed the problem off to yet another board of general officers. By this time, Muhlenberg and Weedon had both gone to Virginia on furlough.

The board of general officers met in early March to consider Woodford's case but refused to pass final judgment on the matter. They did, however, recommend to the Congressional Committee still at Valley Forge that Congress decide in Woodford's favor. Muhlenberg wrote to the committee shortly after his return to the army in March to explain his opposition to any rearrangement of rank.

> I beg leave to mention a few particulars on that Subject; & as General Woodford has already stated the case, I shall be as Concise as possible. At the time when General Woodford Resignd his Comission as Col. He Rankd as first Col. in the Virginia Line, myself as the fourth, but by the resignation of Col. Woodford & others, & by the disgrace of Col. Buckner I became first. Thus we stood on the 21 of Febry 1777, when Weedon, Woodford & myself were appointed Brigadiers.
>
> When Col. Woodford was promoted to the Rank of Brigadier, it was not on Account of his former standing in the Army as being a Senior Col. but merely as a favor for former Services done. This appears plainly by the Resolves of Congress at, & Subsequent to his promotion, & in this light I allways presumd, Genl. Woodford Viewed it himself, as He never Claimd precedency over Weedon & myself until almost twelve Months after his Promotion. The

Comission I recd, from the Honorable Congress as Oldest Brigadier in the Virginia Line was unsought for & unsolicited, This Comission mentions in a particular Manner, that I am to have precedency of Genl. Woodford, & this Comission is moreover supported by two Resolves of Congress, enough in Conscience to make it as the Laws of the Medes & Persians. Irrevocable— In short, Congress have been pleasd to Honor me with a Comission of importance; I have endeavourd to render myself worthy of it, by serving my Country to the utmost of my Abilities; nor am I conscious to myself of having any part of my Conduct while in the Army rendred myself unworthy of the Trust reposd in me, or of remaining in the Service of my Country, which in point of Honor I can only do, in that post, to which by my Comission I am entitled.[16]

Muhlenberg's letter, which hinted that he would resign if Woodford was advanced over him, and the recommendation of the committee were referred to Congress. On March 19, they ruled in Woodford's favor and ordered that "General Washington call in and cancel the commissions of Brigadiers Woodford, Muhlenberg, Scott, and Weedon; and that new commissions be granted them; and that they rank in future agreeable to the following arrangement, Woodford, Muhlenberg, Scott, Weedon."[17]

Muhlenberg and Weedon were understandably angry at the decision. Weedon resigned his commission in protest, refusing to return to the army. Muhlenberg acted a bit more cautiously and considered his response. Three weeks after the rearrangement, Muhlenberg, prompted by an inquiry from Washington asking if he had reached a decision on whether to resign or not, wrote to Washington. "Coll Mead was with me this Morning, desiring me to give Your Excellency a final Answer, in what manner I intended to Act, with regard to the dispute between Genl Woodford, Weedon & myself, Tho I have had time enough to consider of it, I have still put it off, as I expected nothing would be done in it, until Genl Weedons return."[18]

Muhlenberg acknowledged that the dispute had generated a lot of talk among his fellow officers, and the consensus of many was that Congress was biased from the beginning in favor of Woodford: "This Affair has been often Canvassed within my hearing, by the Officers in the Army, & I find the Generality of them are of Opinion that the Change would have taken place, if Genl Woodford had had no Claim, as Congress was determind to put him into a post, where He might have the first Chance of Promotion."[19]

Muhlenberg felt humiliated, and although he denied that honor played a large role in any of his thinking, it was precisely the issue he was most concerned about.

> I must Confess neither Honor or Ambition were the leading principles that Actuated me when I entred the Service; neither shall they be the cause of my quitting it at present; But Your Excellency will Acknowledge that much depends on Opinion & whenever an Officer degrades himself in the Opinion of his Brother Officers of inferior Rank his Influence & Authority become despicable. . . . As fond as I should be of continuing in the Service of my Country I do not think I could do it with propriety, unless some Reasons were given for the Change. This would Justify me to my Friends, & to the Army in Generall.[20]

Muhlenberg ended by offering a face-saving solution to continue his service in the army if ordered. "Your Excellency will I hope pardon me for writing my Sentiments freely, but should Your Excellency be of Opinion that I have not been injurd, & can serve, with propriety, I shall allways think myself happy in Obeying Your Excellencys Commands."[21]

Washington's reply was immediate and frank. He did not think Congress had shown any undo partiality, nor did he think that Muhlenberg's honor would be hurt if he accepted the decision and remained in the army. "You know my opinion, which has been given in a conversation between us. I cannot judge of the feelings of others, but my own should generally be regulated by the opinions of a set of Gentlemen, who I conceive have been actuated by the purest principles of impartiality and justice, and I do not think that any Officer will look upon a submission to their decision as dishonorable."[22]

Washington then pressed Muhlenberg for a decision, no doubt hoping that with the impending campaign season upon them, the affronted commander would choose to stay with the army. "I would not be thought to press you to a hasty decision upon this matter, but when you consider that we are upon the verge of the Campaign, you will think with me that no time is to be lost, because if a successor should be necessary, he will scarcely have time to be acquainted with the Brigade before they are called to action."[23]

A week later, however, Muhlenberg's situation was still unresolved. Washington informed Henry Laurens that Muhlenberg had "communicated his determination to resign, but has promised not to leave his Brigade, till Congress shall appoint another General in his room, provided it is done in any reasonable time."[24]

Muhlenberg was still waiting for his replacement more than a month later.[25] In the meantime, he carried out his duties in preparation for the upcoming campaign season. Congress apparently concluded that if they didn't name a successor for Muhlenberg he would just stay on with the army, and that is in essence what happened.

One of the duties executed by Muhlenberg at Valley Forge was to ensure that his troops properly performed the new manual of arms introduced by Baron Friedrich von Steuben, a Prussian volunteer who impressed Washington so much with his military knowledge that he named him inspector general of the army.[26] Another duty that fell to Muhlenberg and his fellow general officers was to administer an oath of allegiance to all of the officers in their brigades. Muhlenberg also attended to Weedon's brigade in Weedon's absence.[27] This was no simple task, as new troops and officers joined the army daily.

Muhlenberg's brigade saw a significant increase in its troop strength from April to June, rising from 673 officers and men fit for duty in April to 1,026 in June.[28] A large part of that increase came from the addition to Muhlenberg's brigade of the 2nd Virginia State Garrison Regiment, 229 strong, under Colonel Gregory Smith at the end of May.[29]

Muhlenberg's brigade was obviously not the only unit that had increased its troop strength as summer approached. Washington estimated that there were 12,500 troops fit for duty at Valley Forge in mid-June, although he acknowledged that the number capable of marching was closer to 11,000.[30]

In addition to the encouraging growth of the American army, fantastic news arrived in May of a French alliance with America. The promise of French military assistance boosted American morale and likely contributed to the decision of William Howe's successor, Henry Clinton, to abandon Philadelphia in June and return to New York.

It was Clinton's preparation to leave Philadelphia that prompted Washington to summon a war council of his general officers on June 17. Washington wished to know the opinion of his generals on how the American army should respond. He specifically sought advice on how aggressive the American army should be in response to what appeared to be the enemy's withdrawal from Philadelphia. Washington asked his generals to discuss the situation among themselves and then give him their individual opinions in writing.

Muhlenberg, like most of Washington's generals, advised caution:

> The Strength of the two Armies as Stated by your Excellency is so nearly equal, & the Situation of the Enemy in & near Philada so advantageous, that we can undertake nothing agt that Post, with the least prospect of Success—If Your Excellency wishes only to know, whether the Enemy really intend to evacuate or what Troops they have left in the City, this might be Ascertaind, by sending a Detachment of light Troops to drive in their Pickett on this side Skulkill, which they must either reinforce or give up, this may be performd without danger to the Army or the Detachment. The Army ought to remain in the present position until the Evacuation of Philada is ascertaind—because the Army can take no position on this side the Delaware where they can so effectually Cover the Country—Stores & Sick, as in their present position.
>
> No Detachments from the Army should be sent to Jersey, until we are better acquainted with the intentions of the Enemy—If the Enemy should Attempt to pass thr'o the Jersey to New York (which I confess is Contrary to my Opinion) They are so well prepar'd & the Obstructions the Militia will be able to throw in

their way so trifling that this Army will not be able to overtake them before they reach the place of their destination should this be the case it would be necessary to March immediately to secure the important post on the North River—But should the Enemy instead of Marching thr'o Jersey endeavor to establish themselves, and get a permanent footing in that State, it would then become necessary to risk even a General Action, if a favorable Opportunity offered, as the Destruction of that State would be productive of worse Consequences to the United States than a partial Defeat of their Army.[31]

As it turned out, circumstances abruptly forced Washington to act when he learned the next morning that the British had abandoned Philadelphia. He immediately issued orders for Charles Lee (who had returned to the American army in a prisoner exchange after an absence of a year and a half) to lead six brigades from Valley Forge toward the Delaware River to pursue the enemy, estimated by Washington to be around ten thousand strong, into New Jersey.[32]

Muhlenberg and the rest of Washington's army followed Lee early the next morning. They crossed the Delaware River two days later, where Washington reorganized the army for possible battle. Washington divided the army into three parts: a right wing, a left wing, and a second line. Lee commanded the right wing which consisted of the brigades of Woodford, Scott, Poor, Varnum, Huntington, and a brigade of North Carolina troops.[33] Stirling commanded the left wing, composed of the troops from Pennsylvania and Massachusetts, and the Marquis de Lafayette commanded the second or reserve line with Muhlenberg's and Weedon's Virginia brigades as well as troops from Maryland and New Jersey.[34] The marquis had come to America in 1777 as a volunteer enamored by America's cause, and, despite his youth, quickly won the confidence of Washington. Twenty-five select men from each brigade were also ordered to join Daniel Morgan's rifle corps to bring his force to six hundred men and allow him to better harass the enemy's flanks and rear.[35]

While Morgan's troops raced ahead of the army to catch up with the British and, in conjunction with a brigade of New Jersey troops under General William Maxwell and militia under General Philemon

Dickinson, annoy the retreating enemy column, Muhlenberg and the rest of Washington's main body followed as fast as they could, leaving their tents and heavy baggage to follow in the rear.

As the Americans drew closer to the British, Washington called another war council to once again seek the opinion of his generals on whether a general engagement was advisable and, if not, how they should proceed instead. Muhlenberg did not attend this council, but he would have likely supported their advice to Washington.

None of Washington's officers favored an outright general attack, but they did support sending another detachment of light troops ahead of the main army to assist the approximately 2,500 troops under Maxwell, Dickinson, and Morgan who were already engaging the enemy.[36] The size of this detachment was a point of contention among Washington's officers. Half of the officers in the war council, including Lee, favored an additional force of 1,500, but several others favored 2,500, while the rest argued for 2,000.[37] Washington was apparently unaware of the disagreement among his officers and ordered Scott to lead 1,500 picked men forward.[38] When several officers informed Washington of their support for a stronger force, however, he sent another thousand men forward under Lafayette and instructed the young Frenchman to take command of all of the advance detachments.[39]

With approximately five thousand troops in several detachments now engaged as an advanced guard, Lee, who had strongly argued against a general engagement, expressed his discomfort at not being in command of such a large part of the army. He was, after all, second in command of the army and thus, claimed Lee, entitled to lead such a force. Washington appeased Lee by sending him forward with yet another detachment—two brigades—with instructions to take overall command of the advance troops but not to interfere with any enterprise that Lafayette had already undertaken.[40] Washington hoped that this compromise would ease the egos of both officers.

By the evening of June 27, the American advance guard under Lee was within striking distance of the British column at Monmouth Courthouse. What occurred the next day was one of the fiercest battles of the war—a twelve-hour engagement in oppressive heat and humidity that tested the stamina and courage of everyone involved.

In spite of the caution of his war council, Washington was determined to strike a blow upon the enemy, so he ordered Lee to attack as soon as the opportunity presented itself. Lee sent a detachment ahead of his advance guard at dawn with orders to make contact with the enemy and ordered the rest of his troops to proceed forward to support the detachment. Lee needed accurate information about Clinton's movements, but unfortunately conflicting reports from the militia made it difficult to determine whether the British army was on the march or waiting for an attack at Monmouth Courthouse.

General Lee pressed forward and discovered that Clinton had resumed his march, leaving just a rear guard at Monmouth Courthouse. Lee was eager to envelope this force and maneuvered several detachments to do so, but Clinton undermined these efforts by sending a large portion of his army back to Monmouth to support his rear guard.

With his detachments spread out and difficult to coordinate, and the enemy pouring forward toward the Americans, Lee's officers acted on their own to adjust their positions. This, unfortunately, created confusion among the advance guard, as it appeared that detachments were retreating when they were really just redeploying to a better fighting position. The confusion undermined Lee's plan (which he had neglected to properly explain to his subordinates), and Lee was soon left with no choice but to abandon his attack and withdraw to a new defensive position to resist the unexpected British advance.

While all of this took place, Muhlenberg and his brigade were on the march, rushing forward with Washington and the main body of the army to support Lee's advance guard. Before they reached Tennent's Meeting House, which was only a few miles west of Monmouth Courthouse, Washington ordered Nathanael Greene to lead Woodford's brigade, along with four cannon, southeastward toward Monmouth Courthouse by way of a secondary road.[41] Washington, who was unaware of Lee's retreat at the time he issued the order, wanted Greene to screen the army's right flank while he marched with the rest of the army to support Lee's advance guard at Monmouth.[42]

While Greene and Woodford swept off to the right, Washington rode ahead of the main body and discovered that his advance guard, which he believed was pushing the enemy, was actually withdrawing in disarray. Washington encountered Lee on a small knoll on the road between Tennent Meeting House and Monmouth Courthouse and demanded to know why Lee's troops were retreating. Lee, taken aback by Washington's angry tone, stammered an answer, which Washington impatiently dismissed. Washington then ordered Lee to the rear of the main body and acted to slow the enemy advance by reforming some of the advance guard himself and posting them with orders to hold their position as long as possible. He then rode back to the main body to hurry them into position along a ridge overlooking the area.

Brief but fierce engagements erupted in the fields and orchards outside of Monmouth as pockets of Washington's advance guard challenged the British advance. They were too few, however, to stop the British alone, and by the afternoon the American advance guard had withdrawn across a creek and reformed behind the main American army, securely posted on Perrine Ridge. An intense artillery bombardment between the two sides ensued, but neither gave any ground.

Greene heard the gunfire on his left and adjusted his march, directing Woodford's brigade toward the fight to assist. Greene posted four cannon, covered by Woodford's brigade, upon a hill overlooking the left flank of the British line and commenced a deadly, enfilade fire that took a heavy toll on the British.

By the late afternoon, Washington was pleased with the situation. The American army was holding firm on Perrine Ridge, but Washington wished to force the enemy back, so he ordered attacks upon their flanks. Unfortunately, his orders came too late in the day to be carried out and the American army spent a tense night in the field expecting to renew the fight in the morning. To their surprise and likely their relief, Clinton retreated after midnight, resuming his march to Sandy Hook and the waiting British fleet that would take him to New York.

The American army was left to care for the wounded and bury the dead. Hundreds of troops on both sides perished in the battle, many succumbing to sunstroke under the blazing summer sun. Muhlenberg's brigade, as part of the reserve, never became significantly engaged in the battle, a battle that Washington and most of his troops proudly viewed as an American victory.[43]

Washington did not resume his pursuit of Clinton; he instead directed the army to march north. Washington wanted to cross the Hudson River above Manhattan Island and maintain pressure on the British, who he presumed were heading to New York City.

Washington and his army crossed the Hudson in mid-July and for the next two months remained in the vicinity of White Plains just fifteen miles north of Manhattan and the British army. Washington's deployment to New York allowed him to unite with the smaller American Northern army which was posted in the New York Highlands. This created issues over rank and command, as officers from the two armies, which had operated largely independent from each other for nearly two years, were now consolidated under Washington's direct command. Washington addressed these issues and also implemented changes to the composition of the Virginia brigades.

For Muhlenberg, Washington's new arrangement of the Virginia brigades meant that the 8th Maryland Regiment, which had been under Muhlenberg's command since the spring of 1777, was transferred to another brigade.[44] In its place came the 14th Virginia Regiment, some 250 strong, under Colonel William Davies.[45] The 13th Virginia Regiment had been detached from Muhlenberg's brigade in May to serve at Fort Pitt, and the other three original regiments to his brigade, the 1st, 5th, and 9th Virginia, had been consolidated into one regiment under Colonel Richard Parker in mid-June.[46] The two Virginia State Garrison regiments also remained with Muhlenberg's brigade.

The rearrangement of regiments resulted in a surplus of officers without commands (supernumerary officers) who were sent back to Virginia to recruit. It also led to the elimination of one of Virginia's four brigades, Weedon's. The remaining three, Woodford's, Muhlenberg's, and Scott's, were temporarily placed under the command of Major General Israel Putnam of Connecticut.[47]

In mid-September Washington redeployed most of the army approximately thirty miles north of White Plains to the vicinity of Fishkill and Fredericksburg, New York, and Danbury, Connecticut. Muhlenberg and his brigade, along with the two other Virginia brigades of Putnam's division, marched to the east bank of the Hudson River, just a mile and a half south of West Point (which lay on the other side of the river) to support this crucial post.[48]

Washington sought to form a defensive line stretching in an arc from Westchester northwestward to the main American army at Fredericksburg and Peekskill, across the Hudson River at West Point, then down to Clarkstown, New York, and ending at Elizabethtown, New Jersey.[49]

When Clinton launched a large foraging operation in late September involving approximately ten thousand troops on both sides of the Hudson River, Washington ordered Muhlenberg's and Scott's brigades to cross the river to protect West Point.[50] The British remained in the New Jersey and New York countryside for over two weeks collecting as much forage as possible against minimal American resistance.

Soon after their return to New York City in mid-October Washington received numerous intelligence reports that a large detachment of enemy troops (between ten to fifteen regiments) was preparing to sail out of New York City to the West Indies.[51] If true (and Washington believed it was true) the departure of so many troops signaled the end of British offensive operations in New York for the year. With this in mind, Washington solicited the opinion of Muhlenberg and several other general officers posted away from headquarters regarding preparations for winter quarters.[52] He then met with the general officers in camp two days later to hear their views on the same issue.[53]

Muhlenberg replied from West Point on the day the council met.

I have the Honor to transmit Your Excellency my Sentiments . . . relative to fixing upon a plan for the General disposition of the Army in Winter Quarters—I must confess it is with Dissidence I venture on the Subject, as I am too little acquainted with the

Country on the East of Hudsons River, to determine with propriety, what place will best answer the purpose, of covering our important Posts, as well as supplying the Army with Provisions & Forage. The Enemy with their Main Force at present Occupy New York, Long & Staten island; and as they have the Command of the Water, They will have it in their Power to make incursions into any State they think proper, but as it is impossible to Guard the whole Continent, We ought to keep particularly in View two Grand Objects, The Posts in the Highlands, & the French Fleet; To answer this purpose, and at the same time to cover as well as possible the Neighbouring States, The Army ought to be in such a position, that the whole might be able to Join in three or four days if it should be found necessary—The Main Body of the Army might lie near Fishkill, a very secure Post, which the Enemy cannot come at, but by marching thro' Mountains almost inaccessible, when in the least opposd—Three or four Brigades Advanced three days March on the Boston Road, to be in readiness to act in conjunction with General Sullivan and the Militia, to Counteract any designs the Enemy might have upon the French Fleet [in Boston], tho I hardly think it probable, the Enemy would undertake so dangerous an Operation in the Winter, especially when the Necessary preparations must apprise us of their design—Some Brigades in the Jersey who would serve as a Cover not only to the State but to the Highland Posts. A Strong Garrison at West point—The Spare Horses might be sent to the Jersey & Connecticut to be Wintred—In this Situation I presume We might be able to frustrate any designs the Enemy may have upon either the Fleet or the Highland Posts, and at the same time be in the best Situation possible to provide for the Army—but as it will be impossible to provide Houses for all the Troops at the different Posts, and it would be unadvisable to Canton them about in the Country, no time should be lost in providing Materials for raising temporary Barracks to cover the Soldiery during the Winter, & to keep them as Compact as the Situation of Affairs will permit—Your Excellency will please to remember that last Winter, many inconveniences might have been prevented, and our Winter Quarters rendered more Comfortable, if we could have begun upon them before the Severity of the Winter came on.[54]

Less than a week after sharing his views on a winter encampment for the army, Muhlenberg wrote to Washington to request permission to return to Virginia to "Settle my Affairs there." Muhlenberg shared some of the personal details with Washington.

As the present Campaign seems nearly at an end, I must request your Excellencys permission to go to Virginia, as soon as the Troops go into Winter Quarters, in order to Settle my Affairs there—I went to Virginia last Winter for that purpose but having receivd some intimation on my Way at York [Pennsylvania] how the dispute between Genl Woodford & myself was likely to be settled, I had no intention to continue in the Service on those terms, but thought to return to Virginia immediately, & should have done so, if Your Excellency had not Thought it necessary for me to stay at that time, as no other Genl Officer of the Virginia Line was present—I left my Household Furniture, Stock &ct. in the Glebe in Dunmore [County], which I rented for one Year from the 10th of January last under the care of an Overseer, who I am informd is gone on the Indian Expedition & The Vestry likewise inform me, They wish my Effects removd, to make room for a Minister. As the Enemy have nearly broke me up in Philadelphia I wish to Save the little I have left in Virginia, as I could not in Justice to my Family continue in the Service unless I knew them in some sort provided for. I do not mean to ask Permission to go, so long as Your Excellency shall Think my Services wanted.[55]

Interestingly, Muhlenberg did not mention the impending birth of his second child as a reason for returning home. His focus appeared to be on the financial security of his family. Muhlenberg had confided in Governor Patrick Henry about a similar concern nearly two months earlier. We do not have his letter, but Henry's reply survives and suggests that Muhlenberg placed much hope in western lands to compensate him for his financial sacrifice and loss during the war. Governor Henry wrote, "I received your favor last night . . . I am pleased at this instance of your confidence and friendship, on which I place a high value. The matter you represent reaches my feelings in the most affecting manner. You have served us on the most distressing terms hitherto, and it is not in the power of any country fully to compensate for the painful duty to which you have been exposed. But I trust the principles of common justice will so far prevail with our Assembly as to give preference to our officers and soldiers in the western lands."[56]

He pledged to do everything in his power to assist General Muhlenberg in his land claims in the west: "You may rest assured I shall exert myself to secure you some good land. I will represent the whole case to the next Assembly. . . . I shall endeavor to show the great hardship upon the gentlemen of the army, if any land is granted. . . [before] they have their choice, and if that avails not, I will secure some small share at least for you."[57]

Henry complimented General Muhlenberg and pledged, "If after all nothing can be done for you as an officer, I will secure some [land] for you as a private man. . . . In this I shall count myself happy if I can serve one for whose character both in private and public I have the most sincere esteem."[58] He added one more thought, a warning of sorts: "Let me take the liberty just to hint, that I think a resignation now might defeat a claim which otherwise I trust will be approved by everyone."[59]

It is impossible to determine what role Muhlenberg's desire or need for western land played in his decision to remain in the army. Six months had passed since Congress had promoted Woodford over Muhlenberg, and he had not carried out his stated intention to resign. One wants to believe that Muhlenberg's sense of duty convinced him to remain in the service of his country and there is evidence that this is so. But we should not overlook Muhlenberg's financial situation, which was admittedly comfortable before the war but had declined precipitously while he was away in the army. Perhaps Henry's warning reinforced a concern Muhlenberg already had that his resignation might jeopardize any compensation that he had rightfully earned in service to his country. Whatever the reason, Muhlenberg had served another campaign season in the army and was eager to return to Virginia to see his family and attend to his private affairs.

Washington replied to Muhlenberg's leave request within a week. "In answer to yours of the 22d I can only say that it is my wish to accommodate every Gentleman's situation in the Army to his private Affairs, as far as I can do it consistent with that duty which I owe to the public, and to the trust which is reposed in me. Genl Woodford is already gone to Virginia; by what I can learn Genl Scott will be obliged, from some late domestic Calamities either to go home for a time or resign, and if you go before a General Officer returns to superintend the Troops of the State, they will be left as they were last Winter without a Head and will dwindle to nothing."[60]

Washington needed Muhlenberg to remain with the army to superintend the Virginia troops, and the commander in chief saw in Muhlenberg's letter a willingness to do so if necessary. Washington noted this in closing: "From the tenor of your letter I am pleased to find that you are determined to wait until the service will admit of your absence with convenience and you may be assured that whenever that is the Case I shall give my consent to your visiting your family and Friends."[61]

It was well over a year before Muhlenberg returned home to Virginia. When he did so it was undoubtedly a joyous reunion; a young son born in November 1778 waited along with his wife and firstborn son in Woodstock to greet him.[62]

Washington followed some of Muhlenberg's advice about a winter encampment and ordered the army to their winter quarters on November 20, 1778. Muhlenberg and the Virginia troops were ordered to encamp at Middlebrook, New Jersey, with troops from Pennsylvania and Maryland. The New England troops spent the winter on the east side of the Hudson River in New York and Connecticut.[63]

In mid-December, Washington instructed Muhlenberg to offer extended furloughs to the Virginia troops whose enlistments were about to expire, provided that they agree to reenlist and return to the army in April.[64] One wonders if Muhlenberg felt the irony of granting the furloughs given his deep desire to return home to Virginia himself.

As one of the few general officers still in camp—responsible for over 2,500 Virginia troops at Middlebrook—Muhlenberg's winter was, to say the least, hectic.[65] Along with the typical guard and fatigue duty responsibilities of any encampment, there was the need to rearrange the Virginia officer corps due to yet another consolidation of Virginia's regiments.[66] Charles Scott's brigade was dissolved in May when he was ordered to lead recruits in Virginia to Charleston and his regiments were divided between Muhlenberg's and Woodford's brigades.[67]

The composition of Muhlenberg's brigade in 1779 had changed over the two years since he assumed command. He retained the 1st Virginia (which was bolstered by the remnants of the 15th Virginia—now designated the 10th Virginia), and the 1st and 2nd Virginia State Garrisons were still attached to his brigade, but the 5th Virginia had been merged with the 3rd Virginia in Woodford's Brigade, the 9th Virginia never recovered from Germantown, and the 13th was stationed at Fort Pitt.[68] Colonel Nathaniel Gist's Additional Continental Regiment, and the 6th Virginia Regiment (formerly the 10th Virginia) were added to Muhlenberg's Brigade in the spring of 1779, bringing Muhlenberg's troop strength of officers and men fit for duty in June to nearly 1,100 men.[69]

At the end of May, Washington asked Muhlenberg and his other general officers for their opinions on how to proceed with the upcoming campaign season. He had already decided to send Sullivan with several brigades into western Pennsylvania and New York to subdue the British-aligned Indians and Tories that had long plagued the region. The commander in chief desired to know what his generals thought he should do with the rest of the army: act offensively or defensively.[70]

Washington's inquiry became moot just days after he broached the subject when Clinton sent a large British force up the Hudson River to seize Stony Point and Verplanck's Point, eliminating Kings Ferry as a Continental crossing spot and threatening the American post at West Point, just fifteen miles upriver. Washington immediately ordered the army, which was still encamped in New Jersey, New York, and Connecticut, to move into better positions to defend West Point. Muhlenberg and his brigade marched north into New York and encamped just a few miles southwest of West Point.[71]

Over the ensuing weeks the British showed no sign of advancing any farther up the Hudson River and instead drew men away from

Stony Point and Verplanck's Point to support an expeditionary raid along the Connecticut coast under General William Tryon. The reduction of the British garrison at Stony Point, as well as desire to retaliate for Tryon's raid on Connecticut, likely prompted General Washington to proceed with his own bold attack.

On the night of July 16, General Anthony Wayne's recently formed light infantry corps staged a daring night attack upon Stony Point that resulted in the capture of over five hundred British troops. Muhlenberg, with three hundred troops from his brigade, supported the assault but did not directly participate in it. In his report of the attack, Wayne acknowledged Muhlenberg's support, writing, "General Muhlenberg . . . with three hundred men of his Brigade took post on the opposite side of the marsh so as to be in readiness either to support me, or to cover a retreat in case of accident, and I have no doubt of his faithfully, and effectually executing either had there been any occasion for him."[72]

As it turned out, Wayne's troops had everything in hand, and although they were unable to maintain possession of Stony Point, their successful raid significantly boosted American morale. Unsure whether the British would retaliate with a strike against West Point, Washington kept his army on alert. By the end of the month it was obvious that the British had no plans to respond, so Washington pondered a new strike on the British.

Paulus Hook sat on a peninsula that jutted into the Hudson River, within sight of New York City and the British fleet anchored in the harbor just a mile and a half away. The four-hundred-man British garrison at Paulus Hook was protected on three sides by the Hudson River and from the west by a large marsh that flooded at high tide.[73] The only land approach to the fort was over a long causeway through the marsh and over a drawbridge that spanned a tidal moat dug across the flat peninsula. A ring of abatis (piled-up brush designed to slow enemy attacks) encircled the post, which included two fortified redoubts bristling with cannon and two blockhouses.[74]

Although Washington was initially skeptical of a strike against Paulus Hook, Major Harry Lee of Virginia convinced both Washington and Lord Stirling (whose troops would participate in the attack) of its feasibility. Lee, just twenty-three years old, had developed a well-deserved reputation as a daring cavalry commander and had become a favorite of Washington, no doubt in part because Washington was well acquainted with Lee's father in Virginia (they had served together in the Virginia House of Burgesses).

On August 18, Lee led a detachment of 350 troops (that included men from Muhlenberg's brigade) from Stirling's headquarters in Hackensack, New Jersey, to Paulus Hook, some eighteen miles to the south. Lee hoped to time the long march so that his attack commenced at half past midnight, a few hours before high tide. Unfortunately, Lee's guide on the march went astray and several crucial hours were lost marching unnecessarily through difficult terrain.

When they finally arrived at the edge of the marsh they were three hours late and without a quarter of their force (who had straggled behind). Informed by a scout that all was quiet in the fort and the marsh and moat that defended it was still passable despite the rising tide, Lee decided to carry on with the attack. He explained his decision in a letter to General Washington: "I found my [original plan of attack] impracticable, both from the near approach of day, and the rising of the tide. Not a moment being to spare, I paid no attention to the punctilios of honor or rank, but ordered the troops to advance in their then disposition."[75]

Lee pushed his men forward, determined "to leave my corpse within the enemy's line," if the attack failed.[76] The main gate was open in expectation of the return of a large patrol so the Americans poured into the fort with relative ease. Enemy troops inside two redoubts and two fortified blockhouses were now alarmed, but Lee's troops acted so decisively that they quickly subdued all but one redoubt. It held the garrison's commander, Major Nicholas Sutherland, and he refused to surrender to Lee.[77]

Up to this point the Americans had not fired their muskets, relying instead on surprise and their bayonets. Most of Lee's troops were unable to fire their muskets anyway, as their gunpowder got wet fording the canals and moat. With alarm guns firing across the Hudson River and the British army and navy rousing themselves into action, it was imperative that Lee withdraw before his detachment became trapped. He therefore ended the assault and retreated from the fort with approximately 150 prisoners.[78]

After a harrowing march northward, Lee's exhausted detachment reached camp around 1:00 p.m. They had marched nearly twenty miles under difficult conditions to surprise the enemy at Paulus Hook. At the loss of just a handful of men, they captured over 150 enemy troops and killed or wounded another fifty.[79] They then marched another twenty miles past an alarmed enemy, burdened with enemy prisoners that they guarded with virtually empty muskets.

Praise for Lee and his expedition was extensive and included Washington, who expressed his gratitude to Lee and his men in the general orders: "The General has the pleasure to inform the army that on the night of the 18 instant, Major Lee at the head of a party composed of his own Corps, and detachments from the Virginia and Maryland lines, surprised the Garrison of Paulus Hook and brought off a considerable number of Prisoners with very little loss on our side. The Enterprise was [ex]ecuted with a distinguished degree of Address, Activity and Bravery and does great honor to Major Lee and to all the officers and men under his command, who are requested to accept the General's warmest thanks."[80]

Not everyone, however, was pleased with Lee's conduct. A group of Virginia officers in Muhlenberg's and Woodford's brigades accused Lee of misconduct in the attack. They charged Lee with lying about the date of his commission to deny Major John Clark—who actually outranked Lee—his rightful place of command of the detachment. They also accused Lee of leading a disorderly attack and an unnecessary and disorderly retreat from Paulus Hook. Muhlenberg and Woodford shared these accusations with Washington, who was more troubled by the fact that they had been brought forth than he was that they might be true. Washington tried to resolve the dispute quickly and quietly, but the accusers, who may have included Muhlenberg and Woodford themselves, insisted that Lee face a court martial, which he did in September. Lee was stung by the accusations, especially as they came from fellow Virginians. Lee shared his troubles with his friend, Joseph Reed, president of Pennsylvania's supreme executive council. "Generals and Colonels are now barking at me with open mouth. Colonel Gist, of Virginia, an Indian hunter, has formed a cabal. I mean to take the matter very serious, because a full explanation will recoil on my foes, and give new light to the enterprise."[81]

Lee confessed that he had actually been too generous in his praise for some of the troops in the attack. "I did not tell the world that near one half of my countrymen (fellow Virginians) left me—that it was reported to me by Major Clarke as I was entering the marsh,—that notwithstanding this and every other dumb sign, I pushed on to the attack."[82]

Lee asserted that he had been prepared to sacrifice his life in the attempt on Paulus Hook while the efforts of many of Clark's Virginians were "not the most vigorous." Lee ended the letter by assuring Reed that

> I am determined to push Colonel Gist and party. The brave and generous throughout the whole army support me warmly. . . . I have received the thanks of General Washington in the most flattering terms, and the congratulations of General Greene [and] Wayne. Do not let any whispers affect you, my dear sir. Be assured that the more full the scrutiny, the more honour your friend will receive and the more ignominy will be the fate of my foes.[83]

The charges against Lee at his court martial centered on his illegitimate command of the detachment—he was technically outranked by Clark—and his conduct of the attack and retreat, both of which were described as disorderly.[84]

Washington clearly wished the issue to be settled in Lee's favor and provided evidence in the form of a letter to discredit the charge that Lee's retreat was too hasty.[85] Even Clark helped Lee by testifying on his behalf.[86] After five days of testimony the court rendered its decision on September 11. Describing some of the charges against Lee as "unsupported" and "groundless," and some of his actions as necessary and fully justified, the tribunal acquitted Lee with honor on all charges.[87]

The extent of Muhlenberg's role in Lee's court martial is unclear. He very well could have been just a messenger for the disgruntled officers in his brigade who were worried that Lee's conduct might set a dangerous precedent concerning command in the field. Or perhaps Muhlenberg, who himself had been slighted by a dispute over rank, was sensitive to the issue. Evidence is lacking on what specific role Muhlenberg played in the affair.

Despite enduring two surprise American attacks on outposts considered safe and secure, attacks that cost the British army hundreds of soldiers, Henry Clinton had done nothing to retaliate. He seemed content to sit in New York City and wait for winter to arrive.

While Washington considered an attack on New York in coordination with the French (something the French never seriously contemplated), Muhlenberg and his Virginians remained encamped near West Point, guarding against a possible British surprise attack. He worked frequently with Woodford to manage the Virginia troops during this long lull in activity.

By late October, Washington grudgingly accepted that the French would not support an attack on New York and temporarily abandoned the idea. Frustrated by his inability to act and confused by the inactivity of the enemy, Washington confessed in a letter to his friend and fellow Virginian, Benjamin Harrison, that he was thoroughly perplexed on how to proceed against the British. "The enemy have wasted another Campaign. . . . There is something so truely unaccountable in all this that I do not know how to reconcile it with their own views, or to any principle of common sense."[88]

Washington did not understand why Clinton had taken the trouble to establish two strong outposts at Stony Point and Verplanck's Point in June, only to abandon them a few months later at the loss of hundreds of troops. Clinton had also done nothing to assist his Indian allies against a summer expedition that Washington had launched in western Pennsylvania and New York. Clinton's brief naval raid on Virginia in May under Commodore George Collier, although destructive and disruptive to those in southeastern Virginia, seemed rather arbitrary and without a purpose. Washington observed to Harrison that "We are now, in appearance, launching into a wide and boundless field—puzzled with mazes and o'erspread with difficulties."[89]

Some clarity began to appear to Washington in November when he learned of British preparations to embark a large force aboard ships in New York.[90] He did not know it at the time, but Clinton had decided to send eight thousand troops south to capture Charleston, South Carolina.

Two weeks after Washington discovered that Clinton might have a new operation planned, he received instructions from Congress to send the Continental troops from North Carolina, as well as whatever other troops he could spare, to Charleston to reinforce Benjamin Lincoln's Southern army.[91]

Washington, convinced that the active campaign season for 1779 had ended in the north, was well into planning for his winter encampment in New Jersey, New York, and Connecticut when he received these instructions. He initially ordered just the North Carolinians and some dragoons to march south.[92] Upon further consideration (and urging from Congress) Washington grudgingly agreed that the Virginian troops should proceed as well and ordered them southward on December 8.[93] Woodford, as the ranking Continental officer from Virginia, received orders from Washington to lead all of Virginia's Continentals to South Carolina: "I have this minute been honoured with a Letter from Congress . . . directing the Troops of the Virginia line to be put in motion immediately. You will put everything in train and march the whole, with their Tents & baggage as soon as possible to Philadelphia, where you will receive farther Orders from Congress."[94]

Seven

Benedict Arnold's Invasion of Virginia

W ASHINGTON'S DECISION TO SEND THE ENTIRE VIRGINIA
Continental line south to reinforce Benjamin Lincoln
brought Muhlenberg's long dispute with Woodford over their rank
to a head. Muhlenberg wrote to Washington on December 10 to address the matter, and although this letter has not been found, Washington's reply four days later suggests that Muhlenberg had informed
Washington that he was leaving the army.[1] Months earlier Muhlenberg had hinted in a letter to Virginia's congressional delegates in
Philadelphia of a possible solution to the rank dispute, asserting, "I
cannot in Justice to myself accept an inferior [rank] unless it can be
done in a manner that will Give no reason to think I was superseded
for Misconduct."[2]

Congress failed to respond to Muhlenberg's hint at the time, but
his impending departure in December prompted the legislature to
act, and they offered a face-saving resolution on December 29. Acknowledging that "uneasiness has arisen" among the Virginia
brigadier generals regarding the reordering of rank among them, and
most particularly at assumptions made about the reordering of rank

that are "prejudicial to the characters of those gentlemen who are placed inferior in command," Congress passed the following resolution:[3]

> Resolved, That Congress entertain the most favourable opinion of the merit and characters of the gentlemen mentioned [Muhlenberg, Scott, Weedon] in the resolution before recited.
>
> Resolved, That the arrangement made therein was founded upon principles not affecting the personal characters or comparative merits of these officers.[4]

Samuel Huntington, the president of the Congress, followed this resolution with a letter directly to Muhlenberg in early January to ensure that Muhlenberg was aware of Congress's action.[5]

While not the ringing endorsement Muhlenberg likely sought, the sentiment expressed by Congress was apparently enough to persuade the aggrieved general to keep his commission and remain in the Continental army. His brigade had marched south in mid-December with Woodford, so with no troops to command Muhlenberg found himself with little to do. In late February, however, the Board of War instructed Muhlenberg, who had remained in Philadelphia, to return to Virginia to oversee Continental recruitment efforts there. Muhlenberg was to "superintend the collection of troops, provisions, and munitions of war for the southern armies, in such a manner as to keep them constantly effective, and if any hostile attempt should be made on Virginia, to assume the command of all forces necessary for its defence."[6]

Delayed by bad weather, he did not set out until March 10, arriving in Richmond, the new capital of Virginia, in early April.[7] With the bulk of the Virginia Continental line in Charleston, South Carolina, under Woodford and no funds available to recruit or authority to draft new troops, Muhlenberg could not carry out his assignment. He informed Congress of the bleak situation in mid-April. "The numbers collected are small, and the officer appointed by the government of the state to collect them will, I am apt to believe, meet with little success."[8] Muhlenberg expressed hope though that the Virginia legislature would soon pass a new draft law to address the shortage of troops.

Stunning news from Charleston in late May added urgency to such action. On May 12, the American southern army under Lincoln, which included the bulk of the Virginia Continental line, surrendered to the British. It was the biggest defeat of the war for the Americans and it left the Carolinas, Georgia, and even Virginia in a perilous situation.

While the Virginia General Assembly hammered out the details of a new draft law for the state, Washington instructed Muhlenberg and Horatio Gates, who was tapped in July to rebuild the shattered American southern army, on how he wanted the remnants of the Virginia Continental line organized. Washington used the Virginia officers not captured at Charleston (most of whom, for various reasons, were still in Virginia when Charleston fell) as the basis of a new Virginia line. Field officers from the 2nd, 6th, 7th, 8th, 9th, 10th, and 11th Virginia Regiments commanded the seven severely under-strength regiments from which Washington hoped to rebuild Virginia's Continental line. They were joined by an assortment of company officers from the old Virginia line who had also avoided the disaster, mostly because they had remained in Virginia to recruit or to deal with personal matters.[9]

Although there was an adequate number of field- and company-level officers for the remaining Virginia regiments, each was extremely deficient of troops. Fortunately, Virginia's new draft law in early August gave Muhlenberg and his officers, along with the civilian officials of Virginia, authority to raise three thousand new Continental troops.[10] The troops were to serve until the end of 1781, making them eighteen-month men, and although Washington would have preferred that they serve for the duration of the war, eighteen months was far better than a month or two, which was the typical service of militia.

Muhlenberg and his officers found that raising the troops was not as difficult as supplying them with clothing and equipment.[11] He shared his frustration with Washington in late August. "The whole of the old soldiers at Chesterfield . . . are at present formed into five companies of sixty men each. They would have gone on before this time, but there is a total want of everything necessary to fit them for the field. There are neither teams, tents, nor blankets, and it is but a few days since we have been able to procure arms fit for service."[12]

With Virginia's treasury empty and the state unable to adequately supply the needs of these troops, Muhlenberg sent Colonel Christian Febiger of the 2nd Virginia Regiment to Philadelphia to personally solicit the help of Congress.[13]

While he waited for Congress to act, Muhlenberg and his officers worked tirelessly to organize the remnants of Virginia's old Continental line troops at Chesterfield Courthouse and send them to Gates in South Carolina before the eighteen-month levies arrived. But Gates and the rebuilt American southern army had suffered another significant defeat on August 16, outside Camden, South Carolina, and fell back to Hillsborough, North Carolina. By the end of August, however, Muhlenberg had better news for General Washington. "To-morrow morning [August 27] Colonel [Abraham] Buford will march from this place with 350 men for Hillsborough, well armed, and I hope I shall have it in my power to send in a party every week. Thirty-five hundred stand of arms, and one hundred and eighty boxes of musket cartridges have arrived at Fredericksburg, with other military stores, and I have ordered all the wagons in that neighborhood to be pressed, in order to bring them on."[14]

Several smaller detachments totaling 150 men marched south a week later to join their comrades in Hillsborough.[15] Overcoming several significant obstacles, including the lack of clothing, gear, tents, transport, and arms, Muhlenberg had managed to send to Gates over five hundred desperately needed Virginia Continentals and he hoped to send many more soon. Unfortunately, properly supplying the new recruits that arrived daily at Chesterfield Courthouse remained a challenge. Some of the new troops, unarmed and ill equipped, did not report to Chesterfield; they travelled straight to Gates's army in Hillsborough, instead. General Gates pleaded with General Muhlenberg to take measures to stop this. "More of the eighteen months men from the adjacent counties in Virginia keep pouring upon me with neither clothes, blankets, arms, or accoutrements. Such a naked rabble only increase distress, and can be of no service; I have nothing to supply them with here."[16]

Muhlenberg actually had close to a thousand troops at Chesterfield Courthouse in the fall of 1780, but not being able to "procure such articles as are essentially necessary for the troops in the field," he refused to send them southward.[17] Muhlenberg offered Gates hope of further reinforcement in mid-October, however, reporting that although providing the troops with blankets for the colder weather was "totally out of the question," he did have material on site to make approximately a hudnred tents and was hopeful that in a few days he could send troops southward adequately supplied with tents.[18]

While Gates and the remnants of his army anxiously awaited reinforcements at Hillsborough, Charles Cornwallis moved to expand British control of North Carolina. Cornwallis's commander, Henry Clinton, sent a 2,200-man expedition from New York under the command of General Alexander Leslie to Virginia to assist Cornwallis in his efforts. Leslie's force was to distract the attention of Virginia away from Cornwallis and, if possible, interdict or delay whatever military assistance (in the form of both troops and supplies) intended for Gates in North Carolina.

Escorted by six warships, Leslie's expedition sailed into Hampton Roads on October 20, 1780, and landed troops at Portsmouth the next day.[19] Additional troops landed at Newport News and marched to Hampton where Leslie learned through the local gazette of the stunning defeat of British major Patrick Ferguson at Kings Mountain in South Carolina. Approximately a thousand frontiersmen from the Carolinas and Virginia had crushed an equal number of provincial troops (Americans fighting for Britain) under Ferguson and, in doing so, they undermined Cornwallis's plans to subdue North Carolina. Unsure how to proceed, Leslie remained in Portsmouth to await instructions from Cornwallis. While he waited, Governor Jefferson summoned the militia of Virginia to defend the state.

At this stage of the war, the vast majority of troops available to defend Virginia were county militia, many poorly armed. Jefferson initially sought ten thousand troops but reduced that number by more than half when he realized the size of Leslie's force.[20] Muhlenberg commanded eight hundred newly raised Continentals at Chesterfield Courthouse, and he marched them south toward Portsmouth as soon as he learned the British had landed. Muhlenberg apprised Gates of his actions in early November from his camp in Isle of Wight County: "On the enemy's landing in this state, I marched with all the regulars we had embodied, consisting of eight hundred men, to oppose them, and prevent their ravaging the lower counties with impunity. It was near six days before I got near them, when they immediately retreated to Portsmouth, where they commenced entrenching themselves."[21]

Muhlenberg added that he expected to soon have a "respectable force" to oppose the enemy.

> The post I at present occupy is fifteen miles distant from the enemy's outpost; and I only wait a reinforcement to move lower down. I have, since my stay at this place, been reinforced with six hundred militia. Eight hundred more will join me in a few days, and General Weedon is on his march to join me with a thousand men, besides a corps of volunteers commanded by Colonel Lawson, consisting of eight hundred infantry and one hundred horse; so that in a few days we shall have a respectable force.[22]

To Governor Jefferson and Virginia's credit, a respectable force was indeed assembled to confront Leslie. Unfortunately, this force was neither as organized nor as armed as Jefferson wished. In a letter to General Edward Stevens, who commanded Virginia militia in North Carolina under Gates, Jefferson confided, "The force called on to oppose the Enemy is as yet in a most Chaotic State, consisting of fragments of 3 Months Militia, 8 Months Men, 18 Months men, Volunteers and new Militia. Were it possible to arm men we would send on Substantial reinforcements to you notwithstanding the presence of the Enemy with us, but the prospect of Arms with us is very bad indeed."[23]

Despite the "chaotic state" of the forces assembled against the British in Portsmouth, Leslie's relative inactivity gave the appearance that Virginia's forces had indeed confined the British to Portsmouth. And when they reboarded their transport ships and sailed away, a good number of Virginians may have even believed they had driven the enemy away. The reality, of course, was that Cornwallis had directed Leslie to proceed to the Cape Fear River in North Carolina to cooperate with his movements in the Carolinas.

With the crisis abated, Muhlenberg returned with his Continentals to Chesterfield Courthouse. In late November, Major General Friedrich von Steuben arrived in Virginia and took charge of organizing the Virginia Continentals. He was eager to send as many men as he could to the new commander of the American southern army, Nathanael Greene, and made arrangements for 450 troops to march south in December. Steuben was shocked to learn, however, of their refusal to march. He informed General Greene,

> Yesterday a paper was handed me signed by the Officers complaining of ill usage from the state, and of the distressing situation of the officers and men concluding that till some thing was done for them they could not think of Marching. You may suppose I was exceedingly shocked at such a proceeding. However as it was not addressed to me I thought it most prudent to take no other notice of it than to speak to Genl Muhlenberg on the Subject. I represented fully to him and to Cols Harrison and Green the fatal consequences of such a proceeding and they promised to speak to the Officers.[24]

There is no record of what Muhlenberg and the other officers said or did to convince the disgruntled officers and men to march, but on December 14, 1780, 450 Continental troops under Colonel John Green marched south to reinforce Greene's southern army.[25]

Soon after these reinforcements headed south, Muhlenberg rode in the opposite direction, eager to see his family. In Richmond, Muhlenberg penned a letter to Congress requesting reimbursement for his many expenses of the past year.

> The command I have been honoured with during the summer and fall, has from unavoidable circumstances proved much too expen-

sive for a man of my fortune. At the time when I was ordered on this command, I expected to be at more than the ordinary camp expenses, but had no idea that they would be so heavy as to compel me to distress my family to make them good. . . .

In February I was ordered from Philadelphia to Virginia. I was compelled to take my baggage with me, and the severity of the weather with the badness of the roads occasioned me to be about a month on the journey. When I arrived in Virginia, three places of rendezvous were appointed, Winchester, Fredericksburg, and Chesterfield. The first and last were one hundred and eighty miles apart, but still it was necessary I should visit them by turns, which I did once a month; besides this, my attendance at Richmond was necessary, so that I was almost entirely on the roads.[26]

As a result of the great expense involved with all this travelling, Muhlenberg requested that Congress reimburse him $6,000 in Virginia currency.[27] He confessed that his expenses far exceeded that figure, but he only had vouchers (receipts) for that amount. "If this sum is made good to me, I shall be content to relinquish the remainder of my expenses though far exceeding $6,000."[28]

While Muhlenberg was on the road to Woodstock, Virginia, Governor Jefferson learned that a large fleet of nearly thirty ships had sailed into Hampton Roads.[29] The dispatch Jefferson received on December 31 failed to identify the ships, so there was no way to determine their intent, but Jefferson thought it best to apprise Steuben of the news and both believed further information would be forthcoming. Unfortunately, two days passed before Jefferson and Steuben learned that the mysterious fleet was the enemy and that they were making their way quickly up the James River.[30]

Clinton had sent the notorious American traitor Benedict Arnold, now a brigadier general in the British army, to Virginia with 1,800 troops to accomplish what General Leslie had failed to do, namely disrupt Virginia's support of the American southern army and establish a strong British post at Portsmouth.[31]

Alarmed by Arnold's rapid advance up the James River, Jefferson once again summoned the militia for duty.[32] Some of these troops, along with a battalion of Continentals at Chesterfield Courthouse that Steuben had hoped to send southward to General Greene as soon as they were properly equipped, fell under Steuben's command.

Unfortunately, it took several days to assemble the militia, during which Arnold swept up the James River to Westover Plantation and then marched rapidly to Richmond where his troops dispersed a small militia force, burned several public buildings, and seized tobacco and other valuables. Arnold was also able to destroy an important arms manufactory and foundry a few miles upriver from Richmond. His force returned to their ships at Westover relatively unscathed and by January 10 were headed back downriver by boat. Muhlenberg only learned of the invasion through an errant dispatch from Steuben that finally reached him in Woodstock on the same day Arnold departed.[33]

When Steuben wrote to Muhlenberg on January 2, he was unaware of Arnold's rapid move up the James River and was concerned that Arnold might try to strike the important arms manufactory and foundry at Fredericksburg. Steuben thus instructed Muhlenberg to "take proper precautionary measures for the safety of northern Virginia."[34] Muhlenberg, who had only been home for three days, responded to Steuben's dispatch immediately and reached Fredericksburg, approximately ninety miles from his home, the next evening. Too exhausted to write, he informed Steuben of his arrival the next day, January 12.

> On the 10th in the morning, I was honoured with your favour of the 2nd, and in consequence of your order set out immediately, and arrived at this place [Fredericksburg] last evening. This morning I saw a letter from General Weedon, wherein he mentions that the enemy had embarked, and that it was thought they were destined for Potomac. As this is the case, I shall continue at this place, collect the militia, and endeavor to make head against the enemy should they attempt to land.[35]

Alas, Muhlenberg was mistaken about Arnold's destination. Pleased with the destruction and disruption he had caused thus far, Arnold also realized he had alarmed the Virginia countryside. It was time to establish a fortified post and hold his ground, so Arnold sailed downriver to Isle of Wight County and then marched from there to Portsmouth, arriving on January 19.

When Steuben realized that Arnold's foray into the Virginia interior had concluded and that he intended to remain in Portsmouth, he ordered Muhlenberg to proceed to Cabin Point, on the south side of the James River about sixty miles upriver from Portsmouth.[36] Muhlenberg arrived on January 25 and met with Steuben, who returned to Richmond the next day to update Governor Jefferson, leaving Muhlenberg in command of Virginia's forces south of the James River.[37]

Those forces included eight hundred militia under Muhlenberg's immediate command at Cabin Point, over eight hundred militia under General Robert Lawson at Mackie's Mill (several miles south of Smithfield), and five hundred militia under Colonel Josiah Parker just outside of Suffolk on the road to Portsmouth.[38] Across the James River, General Thomas Nelson commanded another thousand militia.

Although the combined strength of the assorted militia detachments likely discouraged Arnold from venturing too far outside his fortified position in Portsmouth, the Virginians faced a multitude of supply problems and initially kept their distance from Portsmouth. The lack of tents or tools to build huts or shelters of any kind left many of the militia exposed to the elements and they suffered greatly in the field. Muhlenberg informed Steuben at the end of January that "General Lawson complains heavily of the wretched situation of the sick in his camp, who are without medicine, physicians, and necessaries. We are here in the same situation and no other alternative is left us then to disperse the sick in the neighbouring houses. General Lawson would have erected huts to shelter his men, but finds it impossible, for want of as."[39]

Three days before Muhlenberg's letter, General Lawson described an even more dire situation at Mackie's Mill to Governor Jefferson.

We have no Tents; and are posted where we cannot have the benefit of Houses. The severity of the Season coming on daily, The Baron order'd us to build Hutts; but this cannot be done without proper Tools, and those we have not as yet been able to procure. ... Indeed it is a lamentable fact that we have not as many As are essentially necessary for the purpose of cutting Wood to make fires for the Men, who are decreasing my strength daily by sickness, occasion'd I am confident from their expos'd state to the severity of the excessive bad weather we have had in this quarter. We want exceedingly ammunition Waggons, with proper military Chests, Cartridges, and almost every article of Camp Equipage.[40]

Muhlenberg informed Steuben in his report on January 31 that Lawson's effective force was down to 654 out of 830 men and it was likely that both Muhlenberg and Parker also had large numbers of sick given their similar camp situations.[41]

While Muhlenberg and his officers struggled to provide for their troops and constrain Arnold to Portsmouth, an additional audacious mission was proposed to Muhlenberg by Jefferson: capture Benedict Arnold. "Acquainted as you are with the treasons of Arnold, I need say nothing for your information, or to give you a proper sentiment of them. You will readily suppose that it is above all things desireable to drag him from those under whose wing he is now sheltered."[42]

Jefferson left the details of how to capture Arnold up to Muhlenberg, but he suggested men from Muhlenberg's region of Virginia to be the most dependable ones for such a task.

Having peculiar confidence in the men from the Western side of the mountains, I meant as soon as they should come down to get the enterprize proposed to a chosen number of them, such whose courage and whose fidelity would be above all doubt. Your perfect knowledge of those men personally, and my confidence in your discretion, induce me to ask you to pick from among them proper characters, in such number as you think best, to reveal to them our desire, and engage them to undertake to seize and bring off this greatest of all traitors. Whether this may be best effected by their going in as friends and awaiting their opportunity, or other-

wise is left to themselves. The smaller the number the better; so
that they be sufficient to manage him.[43]

Acknowledging the great danger those involved with this enterprise faced if they were discovered, Jefferson offered five thousand
guineas, and glory, if they succeeded in capturing Arnold alive.
"Every necessary caution must be used on their part to prevent discovery of their design by the enemy, as should they be taken, the laws
of war will justify against them the most rigorous sentence. I will undertake if they are successful in bringing him off alive, that they shall
receive five thousand guineas reward among them, and to men
formed for such an enterprize it must be a great incitement to know
that their names will be recorded with glory in history."[44]

If, however, Arnold was somehow killed in the attempt, their reward would be reduced to two thousand guineas, "as our satisfaction
would be reduced."[45]

Jefferson justified his authorization to use deadly force against
Arnold because he was "a deserter from the American army, who
has incurred the pain of death by his desertion, which we have a right
to inflict on him and against which he cannot be protected by any
act of our enemies."[46]

It is unclear what, if anything, Muhlenberg did to fulfill Jefferson's
wish to capture Arnold. If an attempt was made, it obviously failed,
for Arnold remained in command in Portsmouth into the spring of
1781.

Upon his arrival in Portsmouth on January 19, Arnold ordered his
1,800 troops to construct earthworks, redoubts, and abatis along the
land approaches to Portsmouth (mostly on the western edge of
town). The fleet of warships and transports that had reunited with
Arnold on his return from Richmond defended the water approach
to Portsmouth, and two outposts were established well outside of
Portsmouth to help secure the surrounding countryside.

One of these outposts, the Great Bridge over the southern branch
of the Elizabeth River, about nine miles south of Norfolk, remained
the key access point into Norfolk and Princess Anne County from

the south. Control of this crossing point secured much of the area around Portsmouth and Norfolk from attack or encroachment. Within days of his occupation of Portsmouth, Arnold sent a strong detachment to Great Bridge to secure the bridge and erect a redoubt to be garrisoned by a hundred men and two cannon. Captain Ewald, who accompanied the detachment to Great Bridge, described the location in his diary: "Great Bridge is an important position in Virginia if Portsmouth is to be designated and maintained as a fortified post. It consists of a village of twenty-five fine buildings and is inhabited by tradespeople, who had . . . all flown [away]."[47]

Ewald noted that several small creeks flowed into the southern branch of the Elizabeth River at Great Bridge and created "an impenetrable marsh of fifteen or sixteen hundred paces."[48] The marsh was overcome by "a single causeway [which] passes over this swampland, and there is a wooden bridge in the middle which rests on trestles and piers."[49] The wooden bridge was over two hundred paces in length and was the primary crossing point for nearly all travelers to and from northeastern North Carolina and southeastern Virginia. Thus, control of the Great Bridge was essential for the security of General Arnold and his men in Portsmouth.

The other important outpost that Arnold fortified outside of Portsmouth was a few miles to the northeast of Great Bridge. Three roads converged on the village of Kemp's Landing, which was located at the headwater of the eastern branch of the Elizabeth River. From Kemp's Landing, one could travel straight to Norfolk, just seven miles to the west. The village of Kemp's Landing was three times the size of Great Bridge, yet the British garrison left to defend this important intersection in Princess Anne County numbered only sixty men, just over half of the force guarding the Great Bridge.[50]

Arnold undoubtedly would have preferred to leave more troops at these outposts, but with so many men needed to build and defend the lines of the western edge of Portsmouth, he had few to spare, especially since he sent regular patrols into the countryside to reconnoiter and forage. One such foraging party was ambushed in late January on the road to Great Bridge by a party of Princess Anne County militia led by Major Amos Weeks.

In fact, in the first weeks of Arnold's occupation of Portsmouth, Major Weeks and his militia staged a series of daring ambushes and raids throughout Princess Anne County upon both Arnold's troops and the loyalists who looked to Arnold for protection. Their aggressive actions prompted General Arnold to send two strong detachments to subdue Weeks, an effort that nearly cost Arnold possession of Portsmouth and ultimately his life.

With Steuben in Richmond, Muhlenberg was the ranking officer of the American troops outside of Portsmouth. Although his men were still poorly equipped and provided for, their numbers had grown to the point that Muhlenberg believed it was safe to march closer to the enemy. In mid-February, he led his troops southward from Mackee's Mill in Smithfield to a new camp site at Scott's Old Field, just a few miles northwest of Suffolk. He also posted detachments at several points along the road between Suffolk and Portsmouth to serve as both a deterrent to enemy patrols that might venture that far out from Portsmouth and also an early warning measure if Arnold tried to surprise Muhlenberg with a significant attack on his militia.

The arrival of several French warships soon after his move toward Suffolk prompted Muhlenberg to become more aggressive and tighten the noose around Arnold in Portsmouth. He explained his increased aggressiveness to General Steuben: "As I knew the British army in Portsmouth was already in want of forage as well as provisions, it was the opinion of the officers with me, as well as my own, to increase their wants, by drawing our own forage from places in the vicinity of their camp."[51]

To accomplish this, Muhlenberg led over a thousand troops from Scott's Old Field through the ruins of Suffolk (which had been burned by the British in a raid in 1779).[52] They marched on past Muhlenberg's outposts on the road to Portsmouth and halted at a crossroads approximately eight miles south of Portsmouth. Muhlenberg described what occurred next to General Steuben.

At one o'clock this morning, Colonel Matthews was ordered to march towards Portsmouth, with his regiment [of riflemen],

Colonel Dick's corps of light infantry, and Colonel Armand's and Major Nelson's cavalry. Colonel Matthews formed an ambuscade near the town, and sent the cavalry to surprise the picket, which was within sight of the works. The picket, consisting of a sergeant, corporal, and twelve men, were taken, without firing a shot. . . . A wagon and eight horses were likewise brought off. We have waited for Mr. Arnold, within one mile and a half of the town, for three hours, but as he shows no inclination to turn out, we shall this evening return to Colonel Matthew's camp.[53]

A Virginia soldier who participated in Muhlenberg's attempt to draw Arnold out of Portsmouth (and into an ambush) described the plan in detail.

A detachment of horse was sent forward to skirmish with the pickets of the enemy. . . . They were ordered to retreat in haste and draw the enemy on to Hall's Mill dam, they were then to wheel and attack in front while the Militia took them in flank and rear. It was hoped that they might easily be taken. The Militia passed the night under arms. It was a dreadful night, thundering and lightening, though in the depths of winter and clearing off so piercingly cold that the ponds were covered with ice before morning. The enemy did not follow.[54]

Alas, Arnold would not take the bait and leave the safety of his works, and for good reason. His troop strength in Portsmouth at the time was approximately three hundred men fit for duty due to the large detachments Arnold had sent out to pursue Major Weeks, as well as rampant illness within his ranks. Fortunately for Arnold, Muhlenberg was unaware of this. Had he known, he may have risked a direct assault on Arnold's lines.[55] Unfortunately for the Americans, the opportunity passed, and the departure of the French ships on February 19 (surprisingly after a successful engagement with Arnold's fleet in which they captured the forty-four-gun *Romulus* and two privateers), coupled with the return of Arnold's detachments (approximately five hundred men) secured Portsmouth for the time being.

The remainder of February saw little activity between the two sides. Muhlenberg explained the main reason for his restrained actions in a letter to Greene on February 24:

> I must acknowledge it is derogatory to the honour of the state to suffer such a handful of men [under Arnold] to retain possession [of Portsmouth for] so long; but what . . . is to be done? They are strongly fortified; I have near two thousand men, but among the whole about three hundred bayonets and two brass six pound [cannon]. With such a military apparatus, we cannot think of attacking the works by regular approaches, and all my hopes at present are, that I shall be able to coop up Arnold so close that he will be obliged to make an attempt to dislodge us.[56]

Of course, the problem with Muhlenberg's plan to keep Arnold cooped up was that Arnold was content to remain behind his fortifications.

Steuben, who was informed by Washington that Lafayette would soon arrive in Virginia with 1,200 Continental light infantry and a French fleet, moved quickly in late February to ensure Arnold did not escape Portsmouth. He ordered Muhlenberg to send eight hundred troops from his camp near Suffolk to reinforce General Isaac Gregory's force of seven hundred North Carolinians who were already posted below Great Bridge to block a movement in that direction by Arnold.[57]

Muhlenberg received Steuben's orders after three days of prodding and probing Arnold's pickets at Portsmouth. Replying to the orders on March 4, Muhlenberg wrote that

> Last evening I returned from the enemy's lines at Portsmouth without being able to effect anything material. On the 28th, I marched from this place [near Suffolk] with 1,200 men; when we got to the forks of the road below Hall's . . . I detached Colonel Parker with 300 chosen men to make an attempt on the enemy's post at that place [Great Bridge] as I had certain intelligence that the garrison consisted only of 120 men; and with the main body I marched towards Portsmouth, drove in the pickets, and kept them

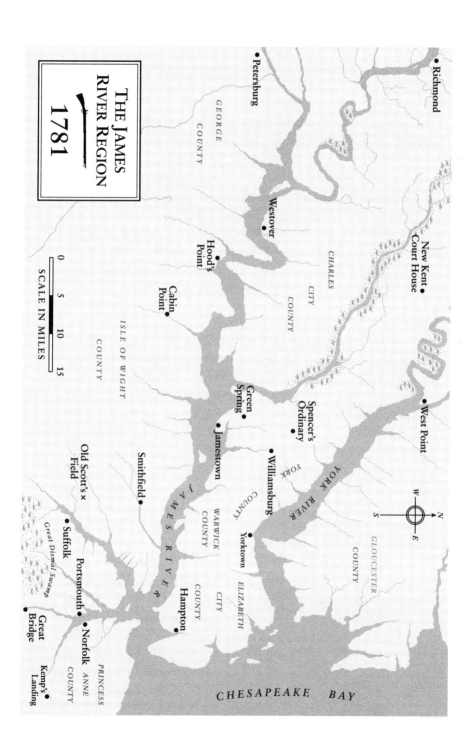

THE JAMES RIVER REGION

1781

SCALE IN MILES

0   5   10   15

• Richmond

• Petersburg

GEORGE COUNTY

• Westover

CHARLES CITY COUNTY

New Kent Court House •

Hood's Point •

Cabin Point •

ISLE OF WIGHT COUNTY

Green Spring •

• Jamestown

Spencer's Ordinary •

• West Point

YORK

• Williamsburg

YORK RIVER

GLOUCESTER COUNTY

Old Scott's × Field

Smithfield •

JAMES RIVER

WARWICK COUNTY

Yorktown •

ELIZABETH CITY COUNTY

• Suffolk

Great Dismal Swamp

Portsmouth •

• Norfolk

Hampton •

PRINCESS ANNE COUNTY

Great Bridge

Kemp's Landing •

CHESAPEAKE BAY

N   E   S   W

alarmed, to prevent their sending any reinforcement to the Bridge.
I left the lines at Portsmouth yesterday morning [March 3] at 9 o'
clock.[58]

On his way back to Suffolk, Steuben's orders to reinforce Gregory
reached Muhlenberg and he immediately carried them out.

In doing so, a curious incident occurred at Great Bridge that
greatly troubled Muhlenberg and his fellow officers. A party of
Colonel Josiah Parker's men attacked and sank a British gunboat
heading back to Portsmouth from Great Bridge. Among the items
captured were the papers of Captain Stevenson of the Queen's
Rangers, and among these papers were two letters curiously addressed to General Isaac Gregory. The letters suggested the existence
of a plot by Gregory to surrender his troops to Arnold:

> G.G.
> Your well-formed plan of delivering those people now under
> your command into the hands of the British General at
> Portsmouth gives me much pleasure. Your next [letter] I hope will
> mention the place of ambuscade, and the manner you wish to fall
> into my hands.[59]

Parker was stunned. Writing to Muhlenberg the same day the letters were discovered, Parker declared that the "contents embarrassed
me amazingly [largely because] General Gregory had furnished the
guards for the night.[60] [The General] was present when I examined
the papers," continued Parker, "and declares himself innocent of any
correspondence."[61] Although Gregory was regarded as a devoted patriot, so was Arnold before his treason at West Point. With his trust
in Gregory shaken, Parker quietly ordered his own guard detachments out to ensure the safety of the camp.

Muhlenberg was equally troubled by the letters and wrote to General Steuben to inform him that he had relieved Gregory of his command. "From [Colonel Parker's] report, as well as from other
circumstances, I am fully convinced that some treasonable practices
have been carried on by General Gregory. I am sorry these circum-

stances compel me to make some little alteration in your plan, but am convinced, were you present, you would approve the alteration."[62]

A week later, after further investigation, Muhlenberg admitted to Steuben that he was unsure of Gregory's guilt. "I confess myself at a loss to judge," wrote Muhlenberg. "He may be innocent, and I hope he may prove himself so."[63]

Although Gregory remained under suspicion for weeks, it appears he was indeed innocent of any plot to surrender his troops, for according to Lieutenant Colonel Simcoe, Captain Stevenson's letters were fictitious, "written by way of amusement, and of passing the time."[64] Simcoe noted that his officers at Great Bridge were at first amused at the trouble the letters had caused Gregory, but when they learned that he had been placed under arrest, "Capt. Stevenson's humanity was alarmed," and he wrote to Parker to explain the origin of the letters and clear Gregory of any wrongdoing.[65] The damage to Gregory's reputation had already been done, however, and suspicion lingered.

The distraction caused by the incident with General Gregory did not interfere with Muhlenberg's preparation for a strike against Arnold. He sent reinforcements to Great Bridge and continued to harass Arnold's lines. "On the 8th, [of March] I marched to the fork in the road below Hall's where we encamped. On the 9th, at break of day, Colonels Parker and Meade marched with their detachment for the Great Bridge, while a party from my corps marched towards Portsmouth in order to amuse the enemy."[66]

When Parker's and Meade's detachment safely reached Great Bridge, Muhlenberg returned to Suffolk, expecting to meet significant militia reinforcements that had been called into the field in anticipation of the attack on Portsmouth. He was disappointed at what he found and also concerned about the lack of arms, and most notably ammunition, available for the few troops that had turned up. "I returned to camp in hopes of finding the promised reinforcement, but am sorry to inform you that only between four and five hundred men are yet arrived, and those are totally without arms. . . . We are likewise in the utmost want of cartridges, as I have not a single one on hand to supply the troops coming in, and even the detachment under

Colonel Parker was obliged to march with less than ten rounds per man."[67]

Despite these problems, Steuben and Muhlenberg pressed on with their preparations. Within the works of Portsmouth, Benedict Arnold grew increasingly anxious as reports of the impending arrival of a large French fleet reached him. Captain Johann Ewald recalled that, in response to this news, "General Arnold, who had constantly beaten the French and Americans at table, lost his head and wanted to make up all at once for what had been neglected up to now. We now worked hastily to make this post impregnable, although the entire place consisted of miserable works of only six to eight feet on the average."[68] The Hessian officer continued, "General Arnold, the former American Hannibal, now stayed on horseback day and night, galloped constantly from the fortified windmill up to the blockhouse on the left and back, and had a dam constructed across Mill Point Creek to create a flood in front of the right."[69]

The English warships that were still with Arnold, namely the forty-four-gun *Charon*, twenty-eight-gun *Guadaloupe*, twenty-gun *Fowey*, several privateers, and a fire ship, were brought closer to Portsmouth, both for their own protection and that of the town. They anchored off of Mill Point and waited. Ewald, who was posted on the picket line at Scott's Creek guarding the road to Suffolk, remembered that "No one wanted to venture out of his hole to reconnoiter the enemy, and so we lived in anxiety for twenty-four hours."[70]

Arnold and his men were right to be anxious, for the force that the Americans and French were sending to reinforce the Virginia militia (and ultimately attack Portsmouth) was substantial. It included a powerful French fleet to wrest control of Hampton Roads from the British and 1,200 of Washington's best troops, light infantry from New England and the mid-Atlantic states, under the Marquis de Lafayette. In February, Washington ordered Lafayette and his corps southward to Virginia. They reached Annapolis, Maryland, on March 10 but proceeded no further. The presence of British warships in the Chesapeake made it too dangerous to transport Lafayette's corps by ship to Virginia; the light infantry corps waited in Annapolis while Lafayette, with a small escort, eluded the British and sailed to

Virginia in a small, swift, ship. He reached Yorktown on March 14 and, after a stop in Williamsburg, crossed the James River and arrived at General Muhlenberg's camp at Sleepy Hole, on the Nansemond River, on March 19.

Lafayette was disappointed to learn that the French navy had yet to arrive (not aware that it had been turned back by a powerful British fleet off the Virginia capes). He was even more disappointed to discover the severe shortage of ammunition among the Virginians that Muhlenberg had complained about earlier. Unwilling to move all of Muhlenberg's poorly supplied force closer to Portsmouth, Lafayette settled for accompanying a detachment of riflemen and militia forward to reconnoiter Arnold's works. A sharp skirmish ensued on the outskirts of Portsmouth along Scott's Creek that cost each side a handful of men and prevented Lafayette from getting a thorough look at Arnold's works.

On the same day of the skirmish at Scott's Creek, General George Weedon, who had marched to Williamsburg a week earlier with militia troops from northern Virginia, wrote to Governor Jefferson with news that an unidentified naval squadron had arrived in Chesapeake Bay.[71] Weedon speculated that the ships were part of the long-expected French fleet, but the following day, Commodore James Barron in Hampton informed the governor that the fleet was British.[72] British Vice Admiral Marriott Arbuthnot, with twelve powerful warships, including the ninety-eight-gun HMS *London*, had prevailed in an engagement off the Virginia capes on March 16, against an equally powerful French naval squadron under the command of the Chevalier Destouches.

The two fleets had blasted each other with broadsides for nearly two hours, inflicting extensive damage and a number of injuries but disabling no ships. It was actually the British who broke off the engagement, but in doing so, they sailed back into Chesapeake Bay while the French fleet headed back to Newport, Rhode Island, to refit.

The news grew worse for the Virginians on March 26 when the British naval presence in Lynnhaven Bay more than doubled with the arrival of numerous transport ships. Captain Richard Barron (James

Barron's brother) counted over thirty vessels and, upon word of this, Steuben concluded what Virginia's authorities feared, that the transports were loaded with British reinforcements for Portsmouth.[73] These new troops, nearly 2,500 strong, were commanded by General William Phillips, an experienced British commander who had been captured at Saratoga in 1777 and held for a few months in Virginia until his exchange in 1780. The arrival of Phillips and his men altered Lafayette's plans. He explained to Washington that

> The Return of the British fleet with vessels that Must Be transports from New York is a Circumstance which destroys Every Prospect of an operation Against Arnold. The Number of men is Not what I am afraid of [as] the French and Continental troops joined with the Militia must be Equal to a pretty Serious Siege, But Since the British fleet Have Returned and think themselves Safe in this Bay, I entertain very little Hopes of Seeing the French flag in Hampton Road.[74]

In other words, the opportunity to capture Benedict Arnold had eluded the marquis.

Eight

Defending the Old Dominion

THE ARRIVAL OF 2,500 BRITISH REINFORCEMENTS TO PORTSMOUTH under General William Phillips forced Lafayette, Steuben, and Muhlenberg to adjust their plans. The long-hoped-for assault on Portsmouth, to be led by Lafayette and his yet-to-arrive light corps, was scrapped. In fact, the young Frenchman disappointingly returned to Annapolis, Maryland, and turned his troops around, marching north to rejoin Washington's army in New Jersey.

Muhlenberg, with Steuben's concurrence, acted to contain the British in Portsmouth as best he could, but as he was significantly outnumbered, the best he could do was pull his troops farther back from Portsmouth and watch and wait. He informed Steuben of his actions, explaining, "I did not think my position [between Suffolk and Portsmouth] secure, and therefore removed the main body to my old camp near Scott's, leaving Col. Matthews' and Col. Wills' regiments with Nelson's horse at my old camp at Cowpers Mills, and sent Col. Dick's battalion to reinforce the troops stationed at Chuckatuck."[1]

With these defensive posts, Muhlenberg guarded the main land routes to the west from Portsmouth. Whether he could hold them if attacked was doubtful, especially as his militia force decreased daily in numbers. Most of his men had been in the field since January and they wanted to return to their families. More importantly, they believed their three-month commitments were up and they increasingly took it upon themselves to leave on their own. Muhlenberg described his dilemma to General Steuben.

> The militia, who have served their term of three months, have partly discharged themselves, and compelled me to discharge the remainder. I tried every method in my power to prevail on them to continue until I could be reinforced from some other quarter, but in vain. About one hundred deserted within two nights out of my camp; and this morning one hundred out of Colonel Downman's regiment, stationed at Chuckatuck, stacked their arms and marched off. The remainder marched into camp with their arms and accoutrements, and now claim their discharge, which I shall be compelled to give them, as their stay will ruin the few troops I have left. Colonels Bowyer and Matthews with the riflemen will march off on Tuesday. Fleming's regiment have likewise served their term, so that I shall be left with about seven hundred. . . . I can see nothing to prevent the enemy from breaking me up, if I continue in their reach.[2]

With reports arriving daily of intensifying preparations for a British movement by water (probably up the James River), Muhlenberg moved his main camp northwestward, to the Broadwater River, about thirteen miles from Scott's Field.[3]

Detachments of approximately a hundred men were maintained on the road connecting Suffolk to Portsmouth and near the old encampment at Scott's Field, but the bulk of Muhlenberg's force, reduced to just five hundred troops, encamped on the Broadwater.[4]

On April 18, British general Phillips confirmed the speculation about his plans by sailing up the James River with approximately 2,500 troops. Benedict Arnold accompanied Phillips and reported to Clinton in New York that the British force consisted of two battalions of light infantry, parts of the 76th and 80th Regiments of Foot, all of the Queen's Rangers, and jaegers, as well as Arnold's small American Legion corps.[5]

Muhlenberg remained at Broadwater and readied his troops in case Phillips landed at Pagan Creek, near Smithfield, but it became evident by the afternoon of April 19 that Phillips had another destination farther up the river in mind. Muhlenberg broke camp at Broadwater and marched northwest to Wall's Bridge, where he encamped. However, before night passed Muhlenberg broke camp again and marched to Cabin Point, well upriver from Phillips, who had halted his movement up the James River near Williamsburg. On April 20, Phillips sent troops ashore at Burwell's Ferry, just four miles from Williamsburg. He also sent part of his force farther upriver past Jamestown Island to the Chickahominy River to destroy a shipyard there.

Colonel James Innes, who commanded the outnumbered and overwhelmed militia around Williamsburg in place of the severely ill General Thomas Nelson, observed the danger his troops were in with two strong enemy forces on each flank and wisely retreated northwestward out of reach of the British.[6]

While Phillips settled into Williamsburg unopposed on April 20, Lieutenant Colonel Simcoe led forty cavalrymen on a dash to Yorktown to surprise a small garrison of rebel artillerists posted along the York River. They routed the rebel garrison, spiked the abandoned cannon, and rode back to Williamsburg to rejoin Phillips.[7] A few miles west of Williamsburg, Lieutenant Colonel Robert Abercrombie, against no opposition, destroyed a Virginia State Navy shipyard along with naval stores and vessels under construction on the Chickahominy River.

As these events unfolded in and around Williamsburg, Muhlenberg remained at Cabin Point, waiting to see if Phillips intended to go farther upriver than the Chickahominy. Governor Jefferson, perhaps still sensitive to the criticism he received for Virginia's slow response to Arnold's invasion in January, was more decisive and called out the entire militia of several nearby counties with orders to assemble in Richmond, Manchester, and Petersburg.[8]

For several days it appeared that the British meant to stay in Williamsburg, but on April 23 they sailed up to Hood's Point (which was undefended). Muhlenberg had moved to Prince George Courthouse, about midway between Cabin Point and Petersburg in part as a precaution and in part to meet new militia that were coming into the field.[9]

The following day Steuben reconnoitered the British force, which had sailed past Hood's Point and had anchored opposite Westover. What he saw—thirteen ships, twenty-three flat-bottomed boats, and 2,500 men—concerned Steuben and although he was still unsure of their destination, he sent orders to Muhlenberg to march to Blandford, a village immediately east of Petersburg along the Appomattox River, as a precaution.[10]

That same evening, the British moved a bit farther upriver and landed their entire force at City Point at the mouth of the Appomattox River. Steuben recalled that this "fully envinced that their first object was Petersburg," and as a result, "I made a choice of Blandford for the place of Defence & the Bridge of Pocohuntas for our retreat. The troops were disposed accordingly and passed the Night under Arms."[11]

The town of Petersburg lay about twelve miles up the Appomattox River from City Point and served as an important supply depot for the Virginians. The British landing at City Point signaled their intention to march to Petersburg and prompted Steuben to challenge them there with Muhlenberg's force of approximately a thousand troops, almost all militia. Steuben explained his decision to oppose the vastly superior enemy at Petersburg to Nathanael Greene:

> I had not more than One thousand men left to oppose the Enemies advance. In this Critical situation there were many reasons against risking a Total Defeat. The Loss of Arms was a principal one, & on the other hand to retire without some shew of Resistance would have intimidated the Inhabitants and have encouraged the Enemy to further incursions. This last consideration determined

me to defend the place as far as our inferiority of numbers would permit.[12]

Outnumbered more than two to one, Steuben and Muhlenberg organized a defense in depth, similar to what Daniel Morgan and Greene had used at Cowpens and Guilford Courthouse earlier in the year. A detachment of infantry was posted at the sole bridge across the Appomattox River at Petersburg. They were supported by two six-pound brass cannon on the heights overlooking the bridge. Should the rest of Muhlenberg's troops fail to stop the enemy advance into Petersburg, this bridge would be their only way across the river.[13]

Two militia battalions (over five hundred men) under Lieutenant Colonel Ralph Faulkner of Chesterfield County and Lieutenant Colonel John Slaughter of Culpeper County, were posted on the south side of the river about half a mile to the east of the bridge on the edge of Petersburg.[14] They were deployed behind a shallow but wide marshy creek (Lieutenant Run), their left flank anchored on the tobacco warehouses along the Appomattox River and their right flank positioned about six hundred yards to the south on high ground upon the estate of Mrs. Mary Bolling.[15]

To their front, a half mile farther east on the edge of the village of Blandford, were two additional battalions under Lieutenant Colonel Alexander Dick and Major Thomas Merriweather. Both were experienced officers and the three hundred men under their command were probably Muhlenberg's best troops.[16] Dick's battalion comprised light infantry specifically selected for such duty from among the several militia units under Muhlenberg.[17] Merriweather's battalion, the remnants of the 1st and 2nd Virginia State Regiments, were more similar to Continental troops than militia; many were enlisted for the duration of the war and had valuable experience in the field already.[18] Muhlenberg placed these troops on rising ground, partially behind Poor's Creek; their left flank under Dick anchored on the Appomattox River and their right flank under Merriweather fixed on high ground to the south. Together these troops formed a thin line extending southward approximately six hundred yards from the river.

Small parties of militia patrolled in advance of the first line to warn of the enemy's approach. Muhlenberg apparently moved between the two lines of troops during the battle, displaying "great Gallantry" in the execution of the battle plan, according to Steuben.[19]

Phillips and his troops (with four six-pound cannon) began their march from City Point to Petersburg around mid-morning on April 25. Eleven flat-bottomed boats armed with swivel guns and loaded with men and supplies advanced up the Appomattox River alongside the British column. Small militia parties posted in the neck of land between the James and Appomattox Rivers first noticed the enemy boats and fired ineffectively at them.[20] The British continued their advance and halted outside of Blandford around 2:00 p.m. to rest and refresh themselves.[21]

Phillips was aware that his force significantly outnumbered the rebel troops before him, so he formed his men into a line of battle that extended past the Virginians' right flank and ordered a frontal assault. Lieutenant Colonel Abercrombie led a battalion of light infantry and the jaegers straight at the rebel troops deployed behind Poor's Creek while Lieutenant Colonel Dundas marched around their right flank with the 76th and 80th Regiments in an attempt to force the Virginians toward the river.[22]

Although they were indeed greatly outnumbered, Muhlenberg's first line resisted fiercely. One of Petersburg's most prominent residents, John Bannister, described the fight:

> [The enemy] proceeded at about 2 o'clock to advance in two columns, one by the old road leading to the Church, the other along the lane and across the ravine at Miller's old mill. Here they received a fire from Captain House, of Brunswick county, at the head of forty militia, which was supposed to do execution but only a Jaeger was known by us to have been killed. Captain House continued to retreat and fire until he came to Taylor's mill, where he joined Col. Dick at the head of 300 picked militia, who kept up a constant fire, and prevented their taking the heights, for upwards of half an hour.[23]

The Virginians at the first line used hedges, fences, and buildings for cover and kept up a hot fire on the British.[24] When British boats threatened the left flank of Colonel Dick's battalion, Colonel Faulkner at the second line rushed a company of militia to the river to confront the boats. Daniel Trabue was part of this company and recalled that

> Colonel [Faulkner] called out for volunteers to go with him to take a britesh vesil that was 1/2 mile below and aground. . . . The company was made up and started in 5 Menuts. We went in a run, and before we got to them they fired on us. We went on the bank oppersit the vessil within 60 or 70 yards and fired on them as fast as we could load and shoot. They fired several times at us. When Capt. Epperson saw them putting their Mach to their cannon he would cry out, "Shot!" All of us would fall Down and the cannon ball generally went over our heads. We would Jump up and fire again at the men we could see on Deck and Did actually kill the most of them. . . . [Suddenly] Col. [Faulkner] came riding as fast as he could, hollowing, "Retreat! Retreat! Retreat!" We started and when he Met us he told us their was several hundred of the enemy a surrounding us. We run a long [way] up the river . . . to our redgement.[25]

The sheer size of the British assault, combined with the eventual use of their artillery, overwhelmed Muhlenberg's first line of troops and they withdrew toward Petersburg before the British fully enveloped them.

The larger second line of militia, partially reinforced by some of the more resolute troops from the first line, made an equally determined stand on the edge of Petersburg. They had the advantage of a wide swath of marshy land to their front that ran along the creek they were posted behind. This would surely slow any direct frontal advance of the enemy and over the span of an hour, two British charges were repelled.[26] Private George Connolly claimed that once the fighting started at the second line, he fired twenty-three rounds (virtually an entire cartridge box) before wounds forced him to retire.[27]

Connolly was soon joined in retreat by the rest of the second line, which withdrew in the face of deadly enfilade artillery fire as well as overwhelming infantry pressure on their front and right flank. Muhlenberg and his Virginians then withdrew through Petersburg toward the lone bridge across the Appomattox River. They were pressed hard by the British, but Muhlenberg's rear guard used the town's warehouses and buildings for cover and maintained a hot fire that slowed the British pursuit.[28] As the militia crossed the river, they fanned out on the other side to provide support for the beleaguered rear guard. Daniel Trabue remembered:

> As soon as we Got over the bridge we went above and below the bridge on the edge of the water to save the Retreat over the bridge. . . . When the enemy Discovered our men crossing the bridge they rushed after them. . . . The bridge was not wide enough for the men to get over fast enough. The enemy came Rushing Down to cut off our rear . . . charging with their bayonets. And our men resisted and Defended themselves some little, but at last they [captured] about 40 or 50 of our men before our faces within 60 or 70 yards of us but they paid dear for these men. Our regiment at the bridge fired 10 or 12 times each. I fired 13 very fair shoots. . . . And when I fired I looked where I shot at and I could see them tilt over. And when they [the British] Retreated up the hill from the bridge they run, as our men would keep on fireing at their flanks so as not to hurt our men who was Just made prisoners.[29]

Muhlenberg also provided details of the battle, particularly of the action at the bridge, to his brother Frederick the day after the battle. "Every inch of ground to the bridge was warmly disputed. The dispute was very hot at the bridge, for some time; but at length they cannonaded us so severely, that we broke up the bridge and retreated in the greatest regularity after maintaining the fight for nearly two hours."[30]

Heavy cannon and small arms fire from the opposite riverbank, along with the removal of the bridge planks by the retreating militia, prevented the British from charging across the bridge.[31] Phillips'

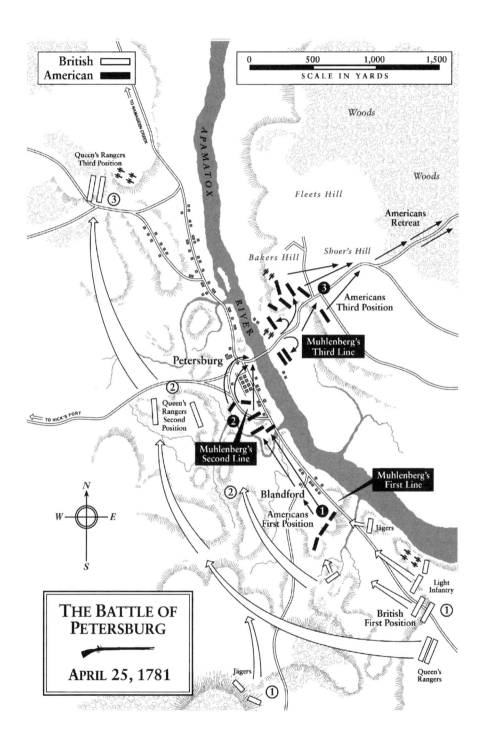

THE BATTLE OF
PETERSBURG

APRIL 25, 1781

troops contented themselves with a few parting artillery shots at the Virginians to conclude the affair.

The Battle of Petersburg ended, as expected, in a British victory. Casualty reports, as is often the case, varied significantly. Lafayette (presumably reporting losses received from Steuben) informed Greene three days after the battle that "our loss it is said is about 20 killed and wounded."[32] Muhlenberg estimated that casualties "will not exceed sixty."[33] Governor Jefferson reported a similar number to Washington, noting that "Our Loss was between sixty and seventy killed, wounded and taken." Jefferson added that the enemy's losses were probably equivalent, "As they broke twice and run like Sheep till supported by fresh Troops."[34]

Not surprisingly, British estimates of American casualties were much higher, with Arnold and Simcoe both claiming a hundred militia killed and wounded. Arnold, writing to Clinton on behalf of a gravely ill Phillips in early May, reported British losses at Petersburg as only one man killed and ten men wounded.[35] It is hard to believe given the stubborn resistance of the Virginians at Petersburg that the British suffered so few casualties, but all the British accounts of their losses at Petersburg describe them as trifling.

Although victory belonged to the British, Steuben and Muhlenberg were pleased that their outnumbered troops fought as well as they did.[36] Muhlenberg proudly reported to his brother that "the militia behaved with a spirit and resolution which would have done honour to veterans."[37] Steuben was equally complimentary of Muhlenberg, reporting to Greene that "General Muhlenberg merits my particular acknowledgements for the good disposition he made & the great Gallantry with which he executed it."[38]

As night fell on Petersburg, Muhlenberg, accompanied by Steuben, led his troops northwest toward Chesterfield Courthouse, ten miles above Petersburg. They continued on another seven miles past the courthouse and old encampment where Muhlenberg had spent much of the previous year and halted near Falling Creek Church west of Richmond.[39] Phillips did not pursue and spent the night at Petersburg, satisfied that his army had driven the Virginians from an important rebel supply depot. The British lingered in Petersburg another day, burning some tobacco warehouses along the river (along with four thousand hogsheads of tobacco) and a few small boats but sparing the town from destruction.[40]

On April 27, Phillips marched his army across the Appomattox River, dividing his force. Arnold led the 76th and 80th Regiments, the Queen's Rangers, his own American Legion, and part of the jaegers toward Osborne's Landing, ten miles northeast of Petersburg on the James River, to destroy or capture the remnants of the Virginia State Navy (which he easily accomplished). Phillips led the remainder of his force, which included two battalions of light infantry, the cavalry of the Queen's Rangers, and the rest of the jaegers, to Chesterfield Courthouse.[41] With no rebels there to confront, General Phillips contented himself with burning 150 empty huts and destroying three hundred barrels of flour.[42]

Phillips joined Arnold at Osborne's Landing (seven miles east of Chesterfield Courthouse) in the afternoon of April 27, and the reunited army spent the next two days repairing some of the captured rebel vessels. On April 30, Phillips marched the whole army north toward Richmond, halting in Manchester (a village directly across the James River from Richmond) where his troops destroyed 1,200 hogsheads of tobacco. Lafayette, who had reached Richmond the day before with nine hundred Continental soldiers, observed the destruction from across the river.[43] With Steuben and Muhlenberg's militia a day's march from the capital and Lafayette's cannon and baggage yet to arrive in Richmond, there was little Lafayette could do to oppose Phillips except post troops on the heights of Richmond, summon Steuben to join him with Muhlenberg's militia, and hurry along his artillery and baggage train.

Upon observing Lafayette's troops deployed on the heights overlooking the capital and river, Phillips, unaware of Lafayette's lack of cannon, canceled his planned attack on Richmond. Lafayette bemusedly reported to Washington that an observer with Phillips claimed the British general "flew into a Violent passion and Swore Vengeance against [Lafayette]" for spoiling his plan to attack Richmond.[44] Phillips instead ordered his army to march southward from Manchester to reunite with his naval force still at City Point.

Phillips and his army boarded transport ships on May 2 and proceeded down the James River. Lafayette feared that Phillips was headed for Fredericksburg to attack Hunter's Forge, "the Great Resource of the Southern department."[45] This important foundry and forge was one of the few sources of muskets and other war material in Virginia, and given the severe shortage of weapons in the state, it was vital that the forge remain in operation. Lafayette therefore marched eastward out of Richmond to Bottoms Bridge in order to be in a better position to cross the Chickahominy River and march to Fredericksburg if Phillips did indeed intend to sail up the Rappahannock River to attack the town.

Steuben along with Muhlenberg, who still commanded a brigade of Virginia militia, were ordered to join Lafayette at Bottoms Bridge. They did so on May 4.[46] Steuben almost immediately returned to Richmond to confer with Governor Jefferson about renewing efforts to support Greene in South Carolina; Muhlenberg and his militia now fell under General Lafayette's command.[47]

Their stay at Bottoms Bridge was brief, for Lafayette discovered by May 7 that Phillips had reversed course below Jamestown and sailed back up the James River. Phillips landed the bulk of his army at Brandon, a large plantation on the south bank of the James River, twenty-five miles southeast of Petersburg, and commenced to march from Brandon with six days' rations.[48]

Lafayette presumed that Phillips was marching south toward Halifax, North Carolina, to unite with General Cornwallis and his 1,500 tired but battle-hardened troops, who were marching north toward Halifax from Wilmington.[49] The young French commander therefore led the American army across the James River at Richmond to pursue Phillips.

To Lafayette's surprise, however, Phillips marched not southwestward toward North Carolina but northwestward to Petersburg, occupying the town again on May 9. Upon this news, Lafayette halted at Osborne's Landing where he described his dilemma to a friend, the Chevalier de La Luzerne:

> My situation, Monsieur le Chevalier, cannot help being a bit confining. When I look to the left, there is General Phillips with his

army and absolute command of the James River. When I turn to the right, Lord Cornwallis's army is advancing as fast as it can go to devour me, and the worst of the affair is that on looking behind me I see just 900 Continental troops and some militia, sometimes more and sometimes less but never enough not to be completely thrashed by the smallest of the two armies that do me the honor of visiting.[50]

Realizing that his force was not strong enough to confront either Cornwallis or Phillips, much less both combined, Lafayette ordered most of his troops back across the James River on May 10. Muhlenberg, with approximately five hundred militia, remained on the south side of the James to escort a supply of ammunition past Petersburg. The gunpowder was desperately needed by a detachment of North Carolina militia posted on the Roanoke River that Lafayette hoped, once adequately supplied, might slow Cornwallis's march.[51]

To distract British attention away from the transport of ammunition (which moved southwestwardly around Petersburg) Lafayette sent four cannon to the heights overlooking the Appomattox River and Petersburg to cannonade the town for several hours while the ammunition wagons passed around Petersburg. The artillery was supported by a battalion of Lafayette's Continental light infantry.[52] Both this detachment and Muhlenberg and his militia withdrew across the James River the next day to join Lafayette at Wilton, a large plantation along the north bank of the James owned by the Randolph family.[53]

While the news of Cornwallis's march toward Petersburg was worrisome for Lafayette, he likely became even more concerned when he learned that yet another large enemy reinforcement from New York had just arrived in Virginia by ship.[54] All told, over seven thousand British troops were converging on the Old Dominion, far more than double what Lafayette had in his command.

Lafayette expressed his growing anxiety to General George Weedon in Fredericksburg on May 15, bemoaning the situation he found himself in: "The Arrival of the Enemy at Petersburg, their Command of the James and Appomattox Rivers, the approach of Lord Cornwallis . . . Such are the Reasons which Render our Situation precarious and with the Handful of Men I have, there is No chance of Resisting the Combined Armies unless I Am Speedily and powerfully Reinforced."[55]

Just such a reinforcement of Pennsylvania Continentals under Anthony Wayne had been ordered to Virginia weeks earlier by Washington, but morale and transport problems delayed their march and it would be another month before they joined Lafayette. In the meantime, the young French commander of the American forces in Virginia had to demonstrate some sort of resistance to the vastly superior enemy in order to maintain patriot morale in the state. The trick was to do so without risking his army, which, Lafayette reported on May 18, amounted to approximately 900 Continentals, 1,200 militia (half commanded by Muhlenberg and the other half commanded by General Thomas Nelson), six artillery pieces, and a handful of cavalry.[56]

Across the James and Appomattox Rivers, Phillips and his men seemed content to remain in Petersburg. What Lafayette did not know was that Phillips had become gravely ill and died on May 13, leaving Benedict Arnold in command. Arnold opted to sit tight and await the arrival of Cornwallis, who reached Petersburg with approximately 1,500 men on May 20.[57]

Lafayette reacted to the arrival of Cornwallis by moving his army upriver from Wilton to Richmond. On May 22, he candidly described the challenge before him to the Chevalier de La Luzerne:

> We are still alive, Monsieur le Chevalier, and so far our little corps has not received the terrible visit. . . . The proportion of [the enemy's] regular infantry to ours is between four and five to one and their cavalry ten to one; there are a few Tories, with whom I hardly bother. Our militia is not very numerous on paper, and it is even less so in the field. We lack arms, we haven't a hundred riflemen, and if we are beaten, that is to say if we are caught, we shall all be routed. The militia is used to advantage in the North, but in this country there are so many roads that one's flanks are constantly exposed wherever one turns. We must maneuver, we

must reconnoiter, and all that (especially without cavalry) is very difficult for us.[58]

On May 24, Cornwallis led the British army out of Petersburg and across the James River to Westover, twenty-five miles southeast of Richmond. Two thousand reinforcements from New York met Cornwallis there. The British commander sent a portion of them back downriver to Portsmouth and absorbed the rest into his powerful army, now over five thousand strong. Arnold, whose "present disposition renders him unequal to the fatigues of service," returned to Portsmouth with the detached reinforcements and continued on to New York, concluding his time in Virginia.[59]

The British took their time crossing the James, spending three days at the task. While Cornwallis patiently waited for his army, he penned a letter to General Clinton in New York, explaining his intentions: "I shall now proceed to dislodge La Fayette from Richmond, and with my light troops destroy any magazines or stores in the neighbourhood which may have been collected either for his use or for General Greene's army."[60]

Dislodging Lafayette from Richmond proved a simple task. The American commander had no interest in a general engagement with Cornwallis, so when the British army broke camp from Westover on May 26 and marched northwestward to Turkey Island Creek (about twelve miles from Richmond) Lafayette and his outnumbered army abandoned the capital and marched north, away from Cornwallis.

When the British army changed direction and swung directly north toward Bottoms Bridge, Lafayette concluded that Hunter's Foundry in Fredericksburg was Cornwallis's target. He informed Governor Jefferson on May 28 that "The Enemy's intention has been to destroy this army and I conjecture would have been afterwards to destroy the stores which it covers. They have now undertaken another movement and it appears they are going through the country to Fredericksburg. Their Dragoons were this morning near Hanover Court House and (unless this is a feint) I expect the Army will be there this evening."[61] Recognizing that he was powerless to stop

Cornwallis, Lafayette added, "We shall be upon a parallel line with the Enemy keeping the upper part of the Country."[62]

Lafayette's goal was to hover on the British left flank to deter any westward movement of the enemy while, at the same time, closing the gap between his army and the 1,200 Pennsylvania Continentals Anthony Wayne was leading southward from Pennsylvania. Lafayette hoped that the addition of Wayne's troops would give his outnumbered American army a better chance of success, slim as it might be, against Cornwallis when the time came to fight.

Until Wayne and his troops arrived, however, Lafayette was determined to avoid a general engagement with Cornwallis. The challenge was to do this without appearing weak and ineffectual against the enemy, hence Lafayette's measured movements on a parallel track with Cornwallis. When Cornwallis marched north, as he did on May 29 and 30 to Newcastle and Hanover Courthouse, Lafayette followed suit, marching to Scotchtown and Anderson Bridge on the North Anna River. With him marched Muhlenberg, still in command of a brigade of militia that had grown to over 1,100 men.[63]

In early June, Cornwallis changed his strategy and ended his movement north, turning his attention and army instead to the west. He explained his decision to do so in a letter to Clinton:

By pushing my light troops over the North Anna, I [threatened both] Fredericksburgh, and . . . [Lafayette's] junction with General Wayne, who was then marching through Maryland. From what I could learn of the present state of Hunter's iron manufactory, it did not appear of so much importance as the stores on the other side of the country, and it was impossible to prevent the junction between the Marquis and Wayne: I therefore took advantage of the Marquis's passing the Rappahannock, and detached Lieutenant-Colonel Simcoe and Tarleton to disturb the assembly then sitting in Charlottesville, and to destroy the stores there, at Old Albemarle court house, and the Point of Fork.[64]

Cornwallis sent Simcoe and Banastre Tarleton with strong detachments westward ahead of the army on June 2 and trailed behind them with the rest of his troops.

It took a couple of days for Lafayette to realize Cornwallis's sudden shift in strategy. He had continued to march north, across the Rapidan River into Culpeper County, hoping to unite with Wayne's reinforcements at any moment. The Pennsylvanians were still a week away, however, and when Lafayette realized that Cornwallis had redirected his army westward to threaten Virginia's political leaders in Charlottesville and the important military stores stockpiled at Point of Fork, he adjusted his own march route southwestward, sending word to Wayne to catch up to him as quickly as possible.

Lafayette still recognized that his army was too weak to directly challenge Cornwallis, but he wanted to position it so that, when he was finally reinforced by Wayne, he might be able to defend some of the military stores in central Virginia. Unfortunately, it was too late to protect the General Assembly in Charlottesville or the military stores at Point of Fork; Tarleton and Simcoe had already struck those places.

Although neither raid resulted in significant loss of life for the Virginians—a handful of legislators were captured at Charlottesville and military stores at Point of Fork were destroyed, but few troops were lost—the raids demonstrated how vulnerable and weak Virginia still was.

Cornwallis trailed behind Tarleton and Simcoe with the main army, leaving a swath of destruction in parts of Hanover and Goochland Counties. On June 7, he halted at Elk Hill, a plantation owned by Thomas Jefferson situated on the James River, and remained there for several days, using Jefferson's house as his headquarters. The British commander did nothing to stop his troops from plundering the estate as well as neighboring properties. Elk Hill was soon, according to Governor Jefferson, reduced to "an absolute waste."[65]

While Cornwallis and his five-thousand-man army enjoyed the offerings of Jefferson's property and conducted several other raids in the surrounding area to destroy tobacco and military stores, Lafayette marched southwestward from the Rapidan River. Wayne had still not joined Lafayette, but the Pennsylvania Continentals (reduced to only seven hundred effectives due to fatigue, illness, and desertion) were only a few days behind and finally caught up with the marquis in Orange County on June 10.[66]

The arrival of these Continental reinforcements prompted Lafayette to restructure his army. Wayne remained in command of his Pennsylvanians and took on the Continental light infantry that had marched to Virginia with Lafayette. General Thomas Nelson—who was elected governor of Virginia in June—commanded most of the militia troops, while Muhlenberg was given command of a light corps of newly arrived riflemen (some mounted) and light troops (picked men from the militia) that served as the advance guard of the army.[67]

Cornwallis remained at Elk Hill until June 13 and then led his army eastward to Richmond. Muhlenberg's riflemen harassed the rear of the British army on their march, earning praise from Lafayette: "We make it seem we are pursuing him, and my riflemen, their faces smeared with charcoal, make the woods resound with their yells; I have made them an army of devils and have given them plenary absolution."[68]

Cornwallis halted in Richmond for several days, during which he sent Tarleton with his legion westward to surprise Muhlenberg's light corps. Tarleton claimed that Muhlenberg evaded the attack with a timely retreat, but Lafayette viewed the affair differently.

> I Received Information that the Ennemy about 700 in Numbers were Within 12 miles of us. General Muhlenberg with the Light Corps was Sent to Cut them off and to Make Sure work of it. The Continental Line Moved down with Unloaded arms. The party proved to be Tarleton's who I am told Intended to Surprise Muhlenberg. But some Rascals Having given them Information of our movement they precipitately Retreated to Richmond.[69]

Lafayette's "pursuit" of Cornwallis, led by Muhlenberg and the light corps, continued on June 20 when the British army resumed its march eastward from Richmond. Lafayette explained his actions to Nathanael Greene.

> I Hear the Ennemy Have Evacuated Richmond and Gone the Road to Bottom's Bridge. I have ordered the Light Corps to pursue

and By all means to try to Strike at them. What Lord Cornwallis Means I do not know But this Retreat will not Read well in [the] Newspaper. I follow and one Would think I pursue Him. But as the fate of the Southern States depends on the preservation of this Army, If Mylord chooses to Retreat I Had Rather Loose Some Share of glory than to Risk a defeat By which Virginia would Be Lost.[70]

Lafayette directed that all of the mounted riflemen "should lose no time in joining General Muhlenberg."[71] Lafayette also suggested to Wayne, who trailed a few miles behind Muhlenberg, that he send a detachment forward to reinforce Muhlenberg. "I think we might derive advantage by a well chosen detachment of about 200 from your line, under Col. Butler, who should gain Muhlenberg with all practicable expedition. Besides the addition to his force, we shall be profited by Butler's services. If the enemy are to be injured, they must first be impeded by the troops with Muhlenberg, which I wish to strike their rear."[72]

It appears that before Muhlenberg and his light corps had an opportunity to strike the enemy's rear guard, Lafayette had a command dilemma. The arrival on June 19 of 420 new Virginia Continentals and militia was soon followed by General Steuben himself.[73] Steuben outranked Wayne and Muhlenberg, yet he was extremely unpopular in Virginia because of his failure to defend the military stores at the Point of Fork two weeks earlier.

Despite these sentiments, Steuben was entitled to and likely expected a command in Lafayette's army, so to accommodate him Lafayette divided his force into two wings. Wayne commanded the left wing of the army, which included his Pennsylvania Continentals as well as most of the riflemen, part of the cavalry, and the advance guard under Colonel Richard Butler. Steuben commanded the right wing of the army, which included the original nine hundred Continental light infantry Lafayette had led to Virginia as well as some riflemen and cavalry. Muhlenberg was given command of the Continental light infantry in Steuben's wing while Nelson and the militia were held in reserve.[74] Muhlenberg's new command was with the main body of Lafayette's force, several miles behind the advance corps, so Muhlenberg passed command of the advance corps to Wayne and rode west to take command of the light infantry.

Wayne, who was near New Kent Courthouse with the advance corps as well as his Pennsylvanian Continentals, ordered Butler to advance farther ahead with some cavalry and infantry in an effort to strike at the rear of the British before they reached Williamsburg. On the morning of June 26, the horsemen of Butler's detachment, riding two men to a horse, surprised John Simcoe's Queen's Rangers and Johann Ewald's jaegers a few miles northwest of Williamsburg at Spencer's Ordinary. The skirmish that erupted was hot yet inconclusive, and both sides disengaged after heavy fighting, each side suffering roughly thirty casualties.

Muhlenberg did not participate in this battle—he and the bulk of Lafayette's force were still miles to the northwest. Lafayette was pleased with Butler's efforts, expressing to Greene in a letter that "I am under great Obligation to Colo. Butler and the Officers and Men of the Detachment for their Ardor in the pursuit and their Conduct in the Action."[75]

Despite his satisfaction with the skirmish at Spencer's Ordinary, Lafayette worried that his advance troops were now too close to the enemy's main body in Williamsburg so he ordered Wayne to withdraw to Byrd's Ordinary. Lafayette moved the rest of his army, including Muhlenberg's light infantry, to Tyree's Plantation on the west side of Diascund Creek, about twenty miles from Williamsburg.

Both armies remained largely stationary for a week, Cornwallis seemingly unsure of his next move and Lafayette waiting to respond. In truth, the day after he arrived in Williamsburg, Cornwallis received a request from his commanding officer, Henry Clinton, to send a portion of his army to New York.[76] Resigned to comply, Cornwallis made arrangements with the British navy to transport his army across the James River. He departed Williamsburg on July 4 and planned to cross at the ferry at Jamestown en route to Portsmouth. Lafayette responded to the news of Cornwallis's departure by marching toward Jamestown. He hoped to take a swipe at Cornwallis. Cornwallis expected this and planned accordingly.

Cornwallis surmised there was a good chance the youthful Lafayette might be lured into a trap at Jamestown so he sent the army's baggage, escorted by Simcoe and the Queen's Rangers, across the James River on July 6 and hid the rest of his troops along the northern shore of the river. Pickets were placed on the road to Green Spring, a plantation two miles northeast of the river crossing. Cornwallis wanted to convince Lafayette that only his rear guard remained on the north side of the river in hopes that the young French general would rashly attack. He instructed his pickets to draw the Americans toward Jamestown and a trap.

Lafayette's advance guard, which numbered around five hundred troops under Wayne and included a regiment of Pennsylvania Continentals, a company of light infantry, and detachments of riflemen and cavalry, halted at Green Spring at 2 p.m.[77] Conflicting reports on the number of enemy troops that had actually crossed the James River concerned Lafayette. He had no desire to risk his army in a general engagement against Cornwallis. Instead, he hoped only to strike the British rear guard as it covered Cornwallis's retreat across the river. Ever cautious, Lafayette ordered the rest of his Continental troops (who had halted at Norrell's Mills and Chickahominy Church, eight miles to the rear) forward to Green Spring. Muhlenberg and his three light infantry battalions, along with Wayne's two other regiments, hurried to Green Spring in the early afternoon. The Virginia Continentals and militia remained farther back at Byrd's Ordinary, twelve miles away.

Lafayette ordered Wayne forward with his advance guard prior to Muhlenberg's arrival at Green Spring. Led by small parties of volunteer horsemen and riflemen (who fanned out in skirmish order and slowly advanced along both sides of the road to Jamestown), General Wayne's force cautiously crossed a causeway over marshy ground and continued on through the open fields of Green Spring Plantation.

About half a mile into the march the road entered a long stretch of woods. Waiting in the woods were small parties of British skirmishers with orders to strongly resist the rebel advance. Cornwallis believed that such a show of resistance would convince the Americans that they were indeed confronting the British rear guard and, thus, the rebels would push on into the trap that Cornwallis had set. He explained his thinking to General Clinton after the battle: "Concluding that the enemy would not bring a considerable force within our reach, unless they supposed that nothing was left but a rear guard, I took every means to convince them of my weakness, and suffered my pickets to be insulted and driven back."[78]

Cornwallis's rear guard waged a spirited two-hour skirmish in the woods against the American riflemen, grudgingly yielding ground under the "galling" and steady fire of the rebel riflemen.[79] The British troops (whose determined resistance and lack of reinforcement suggested to Wayne that his riflemen were indeed engaged with the rear-guard of Cornwallis's army) eventually withdrew from the woods. They hurried across an open field and redeployed among some farm buildings and fences.

Lieutenant Colonel James Mercer was with a detachment of riflemen on the right flank of the American line that dislodged the British rear guard and discovered a shocking sight upon his advance. "The horse of Tarleton were form'd, at the respectable distance of four or five hundred yards; their left flank was protected by a skirt of woods, in front of which was form'd a Pickett of 100 or 150 men, beyond this on the right of Tarleton, & across the main road & in front of the church appeared, indistinctly, the main body of the British army."[80]

Thousands of British troops stood on the opposite side of a large farm field across the road to Jamestown, waiting to join the battle. Lafayette had indeed fallen into a trap, and the potential consequences increased significantly when Wayne's two other regiments and a battalion of Muhlenberg's light infantry arrived to join the fight against what everyone believed was only the enemy rear guard. Now these troops were also at risk. Lafayette, who was still at Green Spring but now aware of the danger to his army, ordered Muhlenberg to prepare his remaining light infantry at Green Spring to cover the inevitable American retreat and rushed forward to try to salvage the situation.

Wayne reacted quickly to the unexpected appearance of the enemy army, deploying his reinforcements alongside the advance guard and

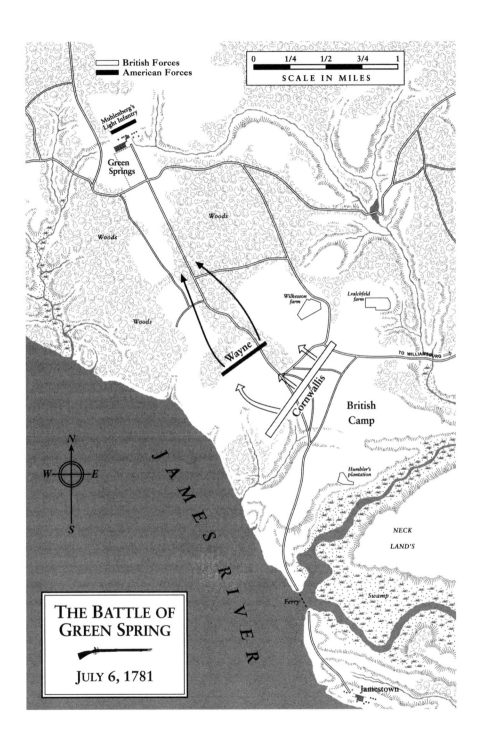

British Forces
American Forces

0   1/4   1/2   3/4   1
SCALE IN MILES

Muhlenberg's
Light Infantry

Green
Springs

Woods

Woods

Woods

Wilkesson
farm

Lralchfeld
farm

TO WILLIAMSBURG

Wayne

Cornwallis

British
Camp

Humbler's
plantation

N
W   E
S

J A M E S   R I V E R

NECK

LAND'S

Swamp

Ferry

Jamestown

THE BATTLE OF
GREEN SPRING

JULY 6, 1781

taking bold, many would even say rash, action. With his flanks and front pressed hard by the enemy, Wayne ordered his vastly outnumbered troops to advance. He explained his decision to attack in this desperate situation to Washington after the engagement: "It was determined among a choice of difficulties, to advance and charge them. This was done with such vivacity as to produce the desired effect, that is, checking them in their advance, and diverting them from their [attempted encirclement]."[81]

Lieutenant William Feltman of the First Pennsylvania Regiment described the advance: "We . . . displayed to the right and left, the Third battalion on our right, and the Second on our left, being then formed, [we] brought on a general engagement, our advance [was] regular at a charge till we got within eighty yards of their whole army, they being regularly formed, standing one yard distance from each other. . . . We advanced under a heavy fire of grape-shot at which distance we opened our musketry."[82]

Ensign Ebenezer Denny, who was also in the center of Wayne's line with the 1st Pennsylvania Regiment, was thrust in charge of his company after his captain was wounded and candidly described the experience in his journal. "We could not have been engaged longer than about three or four minutes, but at a distance of sixty yards only." [83]

All who participated or witnessed the engagement noted the intensity of those few minutes when Wayne advanced. Tarleton actually complimented the American Continentals for their gallantry: "The conflict in this quarter was severe and well contested. The artillery and infantry of each army . . . were for some minutes warmly engaged not fifty yards asunder . . . on the left of the British, the action was for some time gallantly maintained by the Continental infantry."[84]

Major William Galvan with the American light infantry recalled that the American line advanced about thirty yards, which prompted the British to halt their advance and pour "an immense fire upon us."[85] Wayne's bold advance had momentarily frozen Cornwallis's troops, but the Pennsylvanians soon halted too. Galvan noted, "Our stop encouraged the British and, tho' our fire was as brisk as could be expected from so small a line, they began to move rapidly upon us and the right of the Pennsylvanians to give way, the left followed, and the enemy making a devil of a noise of firing and huzzaing (tho' by the by they did not push on very fast) all on our side became a scene of confusion."[86]

Wayne, realizing that his unexpected advance had achieved all that it could achieve, ordered a retreat. He explained to Washington that "being employed by numbers, [vastly greater than his and with] many brave and worthy officers and soldiers killed or wounded, we found it expedient to fall back half a mile to Green Spring Farm."[87]

Luckily for the Americans, the lateness of the day prevented an aggressive pursuit from Cornwallis, and Wayne's battered force, which had lost approximately 150 men to only half that amount for the British, withdrew, screened by Muhlenberg's light infantry.[88]

Nine

The French and American Alliance

ENERAL CORNWALLIS COMPLETED HIS MOVEMENT ACROSS THE James River the day after the battle of Green Spring and marched the bulk of his army to Portsmouth. Tarleton and his cavalry were sent in the opposite direction to raid the Virginia countryside before joining Cornwallis at Portsmouth.[1]

Across the James River, Lafayette misinterpreted reports of Tarleton's movements westward to mean that Cornwallis and his army were heading back to the Carolinas.[2] Lafayette marched his army to Richmond to cross the James River and follow Cornwallis, but before they arrived Lafayette learned that Cornwallis had actually split his army. He still believed (incorrectly) that a portion of Cornwallis's force was marching for the Carolinas, but he was also informed that the rest were marching back to Portsmouth.[3]

Not wanting to leave Virginia defenseless against the British returning to Portsmouth, Lafayette divided his own army and sent Wayne with eight hundred troops (his five hundred Pennsylvanians and a battalion of three hundred Virginia Continentals) across the James River.[4] Wayne was to march to Goode's Bridge (which spanned the Appomattox River) in Amelia County where Daniel Morgan would meet him with five hundred Virginia riflemen.[5] Lafayette remained in Richmond for several days and then marched to Malvern Hill with the rest of his army—the backbone of which was the Continental light infantry under Muhlenberg.

Malvern Hill was located about seventeen miles downriver from Richmond and just a few miles from Four Mile Creek, where a number of boats were kept to allow Lafayette to cross the James River if necessary.[6] Just as important, however, was the healthy climate of Malvern Hill. Lafayette described it as "the Most Airy and Healthy place this Side of the Mountains."[7] If the army had to remain stationary in the Virginia tidewater in July, Malvern Hill was probably the best place to be.

Tarleton's return to Portsmouth after a two-week, four-hundred-mile circuit through south-central Virginia, surprised Lafayette, for it meant that no part of Cornwallis's army was marching to the Carolinas. This realization caused Lafayette to hold Wayne at Goode's Bridge until he better understood what Cornwallis was up to. Activity in Portsmouth pointed to the transfer, by ship, of at least a portion of Cornwallis's force, but how many troops were leaving and where they were going remained unanswered, so Lafayette held all of his troops in place until Cornwallis's intentions became clearer.

As the end of July approached, the continued uncertainty nagged at Lafayette so he sent General Muhlenberg with a battalion of light infantry and some riflemen and cavalry across the James River to Bland's Mill in Prince George's County.[8] It was a place Muhlenberg knew well from his time in the area the previous spring. Muhlenberg proceeded to march toward Portsmouth, but news that Cornwallis had abandoned the town and had sailed to the York River spurred Lafayette to recall Muhlenberg and order Wayne to march to Bottoms Bridge to be within supporting distance of the main army, which Lafayette moved to New Castle on the Pamunkey River.[9]

Cornwallis's commander, Henry Clinton, desired a secure, deep water port in Virginia for the British navy to winter in (Portsmouth was considered unhealthy), so Cornwallis selected Yorktown in early August. The process of transferring the British army from Portsmouth had actually begun in mid-July, before Cornwallis had even settled on Yorktown, and it took nearly a month to complete.

Lafayette initially worried that the movement to Yorktown was just a feint; he still believed Cornwallis intended to send at least part of his force to the Carolinas.[10] By the second week of August, however, Lafayette realized that Yorktown was to be the new base of operation for the British in Virginia.

Lafayette was challenged by more than a powerful enemy with the ability to sail wherever it desired in Virginia; his own troops (specifically the Pennsylvanians and Virginians under Wayne) were near the point of attacking each other. The situation was so tense that Lafayette wrote to Washington on August 11 about his concern: "The Pennsylvanians and Virginians Have Never Agreed but at the Present time, it is worse than Ever. I Receive Every day Complaints. Some from the [Governor]. . . . Gal. Waine thinks He and His people Have not Been well used. In a Word, I perceive the Seeds of a future Dispute Between States—and Every Day the troops Remain Here adds to the Danger."[11]

Lafayette informed Washington that, due to the mounting tension between these troops, he had decided to send Wayne's Pennsylvanians to Greene in South Carolina as soon as six hundred Continentals from Maryland arrived.[12] Until then, Lafayette depended on Wayne to keep order in his brigade, which he kept near Bottoms Bridge, about twelve miles north of the James River.

Muhlenberg's light infantry (who were not part of the problem) and the Virginia militia moved closer to the enemy in Yorktown, encamping on the north bank of the Pamunkey River a few miles upriver from West Point.

Once again, Lafayette found himself in a situation in which he had to wait for Cornwallis to act. Hundreds of miles to the north, however, Washington was working on a plan that would not only swing the initiative toward the Americans but determine the outcome of the war.

———————

Washington had come to the disappointing realization in mid-August that his long-desired joint operation with the French to recapture New York City from the British was not going to occur in 1781. The failure of the northern states to meet their recruitment quotas, combined with the decision of French admiral de Grasse to sail his powerful West Indies fleet to the Chesapeake Bay instead of New York, forced Washington to once again accept that New York was out of reach.

The developments in Virginia, however, offered Washington an alternative and he seized upon it, writing in his diary on August 14 that "I was obliged . . . to give up all idea of attacking New York; & instead thereof to remove the French Troops & a detachment from the American Army to the Head of Elk to be transported to Virginia for the purpose of cooperating with [de Grasse] against the Troops in that State."[13]

Washington wrote to Lafayette the next day to inform him of de Grasse's intentions to sail to the Chesapeake. Washington instructed Lafayette to position his army "as will best enable you to prevent [the enemy's] sudden retreat thro North Carolina" and told Lafayette to expect reinforcements from New York.[14]

Lafayette received Washington's instructions on August 21 and immediately wrote to Nelson, in his capacity as governor, to request that six hundred militia be called out for service on the south side of the James River. Wayne was ordered to march toward Westover and be ready to cross the river, but Muhlenberg and the rest of Lafayette's army remained near West Point, twenty-five miles up the York River from Yorktown.

Lafayette informed Washington that the troops presently in Virginia fit for service consisted of 400 Virginia Continentals, 600 Pennsylvania Continentals, 850 Continental light infantry, 120 dragoons, and 3,000 militia.[15] Lafayette also expected six hundred Maryland Continentals to arrive at any moment. As for supplies and provisions, Lafayette lamented that "There is Such a Confusion in affairs in this part of the World that Immense Difficulties are found for a proper formation of Magazines. . . . We Have No Cloathing of any Sort— no Heavy Artillery in order. Some Arms will Be wanting—Some Horse Accoutrements—and Great deal of Ammunition."[16]

Lafayette urged Washington to come to Virginia himself, unaware that the American commander in chief had already begun the march south with French general Jean-Baptiste comte de Rochambeau and the French army.

Washington faced a daunting challenge in moving a portion of the American army and all of the French from New York to Virginia, a journey of over four hundred miles. The logistical challenges of moving thousands of troops hundreds of miles as quickly as possible were compounded by difficulties in communication that saw Washington and Lafayette receive messages from each other that were usually a week old and often older. This meant that Washington usually had to make decisions based on outdated information.

Unsure whether Cornwallis would still be in Virginia when he and Rochambeau arrived, Washington pushed forward, asking de Grasse in a letter on August 17 to send all of his frigates and transport ships to the Elk River at the head of Chesapeake Bay in order to meet the allied troops and hasten their movement southward.[17] Washington proceeded on faith that de Grasse would first secure control of the bay and then send the requested transport ships up the bay to the Elk River.

Leaving troops in New York under General William Heath to defend West Point and the New York Highlands, Washington led a detachment of approximately 2,500 Continentals across the Hudson River and southward through New Jersey. Three thousand French troops marched south as well.[18] Fortunately for the allies, the heavy French siege guns and ordnance were transported by a French naval squadron out of Rhode Island.

While Washington and Rochambeau's troops made their way south, Lafayette pressed forward with his vital mission to prevent Cornwallis from escaping to North Carolina. Part of this effort involved distracting Cornwallis with a probe into Gloucester County. Lafayette sent a battalion of Muhlenberg's light infantry, along with a detachment of cavalry, across the Mattaponi River into Gloucester County to alarm the British detachment at Gloucester Point. Little fighting came of it and it is unclear whether Muhlenberg led the detachment in Gloucester, but Lafayette thought it might "throw the Enemy" a bit.[19]

The excursion into Gloucester County was brief, and by August 25, Muhlenberg's light infantry corps was back together with the main army on the Pamunkey River.[20] Several tense days passed for Lafayette, made worse by the lack of provisions, particularly liquor, for the troops. He appealed to Governor Nelson for assistance. "Eleven days have passed since they had one drop of spirits; consequently the Continentals are falling sick, and their diminution is the more to be lamented, as in the manner the militia are going off and no relief coming in these poor Continentals will soon become our sole dependence. Another cause of disgust is the absolute want of flour; not a grain of which has been seen in camp for a long while."[21]

General Lafayette wrote frequently to Governor Nelson in August, and one of his most critical letters to the governor came upon his discovery that the six hundred militia that Lafayette believed had been called out to serve on the south side of the James River (to help prevent Cornwallis from escaping if the British commander decided to make a run for North Carolina) had been sent home when the last British troops left Portsmouth. Lafayette was livid when he discovered what had happened and wrote a stinging letter to Nelson. "The loss of ten Days During Which I thought the Measure Would Be Adopted May Have a Very Bad Consequence. . . . I Beg Your Pardon Sir, to Be So particular on this Point—But Upon My Honor I do Assure You that the Unhappy Alteration that Has taken place May Have fatal Consequences."[22] Lafayette declared that had he known sooner that the militia had been sent home he would have ordered General Wayne to cross the James. He continued, "My Anxiety on this Head was So Great that Yesterday I sent Genl. Muhlenberg with orders to Arrange Matters in that Quarter. May I Request that the County lieutenants be directed to Answer His Calls, and that a thousand Armed Militia with What Ammunition May Be Collected Immediately to Rendezvous at Long Bridge Upon Black Water."[23]

Muhlenberg crossed the James River and ordered the local militia to muster in Surry County.[24] Wayne and his troops also crossed the river at Westover and marched to Surry County as well.[25] Both only stayed a few days; the arrival of the French fleet and French troops (which significantly reduced Cornwallis's ability to retreat through

North Carolina, prompted Lafayette to order their return to his army (which was accomplished with the assistance of the French navy).

As French troops landed at Jamestown, Lafayette led his reunited army into Williamsburg on September 4 and deployed Muhlenberg and his light infantry two miles outside of town on the road to York-town to guard the approaches to Williamsburg.[26] They were relieved from picket duty the next day and marched back through Williams-burg to encamp about a half mile west of the college.[27]

No one in camp realized that, just off the Virginia coast, a naval battle was fought that same day that helped determine the fate of the British at Yorktown and perhaps the American Revolution itself. The Battle of the Capes, between the British and French navies, was in-conclusive in terms of a tactical victor, but it did result in a crucial strategic outcome—French control of the Chesapeake Bay; the French navy remained on station to blockade Cornwallis at Yorktown while the British navy sailed back to New York to refit and regroup.

Back in Williamsburg, with Wayne temporarily unavailable for duty due to a shooting incident with a sentry a week earlier (in which Wayne was wounded by buckshot in his thigh), it appears Muhlen-berg may have remained on the picket line when Wayne's troops re-lieved his light infantry. In a letter to Washington dated September 8, Lafayette noted, "I have upon the lines General Muhlenburg with one thousand Men four hundred of whom are Virginia Regulars and one Hundred Dragoons."[28] Those Virginia regulars were likely Colonel Thomas Gaskin's Virginia Continentals who were attached to Wayne's brigade. If Muhlenberg remained on duty with the picket he would have likely been present when British dragoons drove a de-tachment of American cavalry back to the advance picket line near Colonel Nathan Burwell's mill on King's Creek.[29]

Lieutenant Colonel St. George Tucker, an aide-de-camp to Thomas Nelson (who was both governor and commanding general of all of Virginia's militia), acknowledged Muhlenberg's role in guarding Williamsburg while the Americans and French awaited the arrival of General Washington and Count Rochambeau. "Genl. Muhlenberg with Gaskin's Regiment of Virginians, a Regt. of Rifle Men and Detachmts. Drawn from [General Edward] Steven's &

[General Robert] Lawson's [militia] Brigades form'd an advanced Corps which guarded the several Roads & passed from York to Williamsburg, with the assistance of the Horse under Col. Benjamin Temple."[30]

In Tucker's account, Muhlenberg commanded a detachment of Gaskin's Virginia Continentals, Virginia militia, and cavalry on the picket line facing Yorktown. This should not be surprising, as Lafayette rotated the pickets daily and likely did not need to assign entire brigades for such duty. Such duty likely required only a portion of a brigade and was, thus, probably rotated among the battalions within the brigades.

While Lafayette eagerly awaited the arrival of Washington and Rochambeau and their reinforcements, he struggled to obtain adequate provisions for the thousands of troops at Williamsburg. Lafayette's burden was lifted, however, when Washington arrived in Williamsburg on September 14.[31] The American commander in chief would now have the responsibility of coordinating the logistics of the combined American and French forces in Virginia.

The American and French troops from the north were still over a week behind their commanders; they and most of their gear and supplies were aboard transport ships sailing down Chesapeake Bay from Head of Elk, Maryland. Washington refused to draw closer to Yorktown until the rest of his troops could join him. Williamsburg therefore played host to thousands of American and French troops who waited for their comrades to arrive. Ensign Ebenezer Denny, a Pennsylvania Continental in General Wayne's brigade, described the effect the arrival of General Washington and his staff had on Williamsburg. "The presence of so many general officers, and the arrival of new corps, seem to give additional life to everything. Discipline the order of the day. In all directions troops seen exercising and maneuvering."[32]

Not all of the American military activity, however, was drill. St. George Tucker recalled in his diary that "Genl. Mulenburg in the mean time had made frequent excursions to the Lines of the British near York, but nothing material happened as he could not draw the Enemy out on any Occasion."[33]

On September 23, Muhlenberg updated General Washington on his attempts to reconnoiter the enemy lines at Yorktown.

> Since the Evening before last I have not been able to procure the least intelligence from York neither have we had a Deserter from the Enemy since that time. I have had parties continually in the Hampton—Warwick & halfway roads, who have been within sight of their Pickets, but some of the Enemy have been out. It is certain that their number of Shipping is much diminished at York, But whether they attempted to get out the Night before last, or whether the Enemy have sunk them in the Channel I cannot yet find out; a large Smoke was seen Yesterday Morning below York, which has confirm'd a report the Enemy have burnt some of their shipping.[34]

The smoke Muhlenberg reported was from a failed British attempt to launch a fire ship against the French fleet at the mouth of the York River, and the diminished presence of British ships off of Yorktown was indeed the result of several ships being scuttled in the channel to prevent the French navy from creeping closer.[35]

The American and French troops from the north arrived at Burwell's Landing, just outside of Williamsburg, on the same day as Muhlenberg's reconnaissance report. This prompted Washington to reorganize his Continental troops. Muhlenberg maintained command of the light infantry troops from New England—the same troops he had commanded since June (and the ones who marched to Virginia in the spring with Lafayette). Washington formed five other brigades of Continentals, comprised of troops from Virginia and all of the states north of Virginia.[36]

With preparations for the march to Yorktown nearly complete, Washington ordered Muhlenberg's brigade (with nearly a thousand officers and men fit for duty) along with Wayne's brigade and the 3rd Maryland Regiment, to march to the advance encampment outside of Williamsburg on the Yorktown road.[37] They spent September 27 posted there while the last details for the march and siege of Yorktown were finalized. Washington announced the order of battle for the army on the eve of the march.

Till circumstances shall render a change of disposition Necessary, the following will be the order of Battle for the Army, the American Troops composing the Right Wing will be formed into two Lines, the Continental Forces in the front line, consisting of the following divisions in the following order viz. Muhlenberghs and Hazens Brigades to form The Division on the right under the Command of the Marquis de la Fayette, Waynes and the Maryland Brigade, the Division of the centre for the present to be commanded by Baron de Steuben, Dayton and Clintons Brigades, that on the Left.[38]

Washington included specific instructions for the march that was to commence at 5 a.m. the next day (September 28): "General Muhlenberghs Brigade of Infantry with the Artillery attached to it, preceded by Colonel Lewises Corps of Riflemen and the light Dragoons will form the advanced Guard."[39]

Earlier in the orders Washington had provided instructions on how the army should engage the enemy should Cornwallis be bold enough to meet the allied army on the march: "If the Enemy should be tempted to Meet the Army on its March, the General particularly enjoins the troops to place their principle reliance on the Bayonet, that they may prove the Vanity of the Boast which the British make of their particular prowess in deciding Battles with that Weapon."[40]

Ten

The Siege of Yorktown

W ASHINGTON'S ALLIED ARMY SET OUT FOR YORKTOWN AT DAWN as ordered with Muhlenberg's brigade in advance. The day promised to be hot and humid, and those unaccustomed to such conditions suffered greatly on the twelve-mile march.[1] The American and French forces separated along two different roads about four miles outside Yorktown, the French marching to the left and the Americans to the right to reunite with the militia and supply wagons (which had marched via a different road toward Yorktown).[2] The Americans halted at Great Run Creek to repair a bridge damaged by the British. During this halt, Banastre Tarleton with his British dragoons appeared on the other side of the creek and across a meadow several hundred yards away. Muhlenberg deployed his cannon and riflemen to drive Tarleton off (and cover the pioneers who worked to repair the damaged bridge), and after a few shots from each, Tarleton wisely withdrew.[3]

Muhlenberg's brigade crossed the repaired bridge in the evening and slept on their arms in the meadow where Tarleton had earlier stood.[4] They served as a picket for the rest of Washington's troops, most of whom remained on the other side of the creek until morning. With their tents and baggage well to the rear, all of the troops, including Washington, slept under the stars—like Muhlenberg's men—with their muskets at the ready.

The following day the rest of Washington's army crossed over the creek and advanced farther to the right toward the York River and Wormley Creek, which protected their right flank. Lafayette's division, which was posted on the far right of the American line, was protected by a wide morass created by a mill dam across a section of Wormley Creek. On the high ground overlooking the morass—and across from Muhlenberg, Lafayette, and their troops—were enemy outworks with light cannon and German jaegers. A steady fire occurred between both sides but to little effect.[5] Late in the afternoon, Washington ordered his troops to withdraw out of range of the enemy outworks to set up camp.[6]

The following day passed rather uneventfully. There was sporadic British fire from their outworks, but it was random and ineffective. In the evening Muhlenberg and his brigade served as a reserve for the picket posted, but nothing of consequence occurred so there was no need to respond to any alarm.[7]

Both the Americans and French were shocked and pleasantly surprised to discover the next morning that General Cornwallis had evacuated most of his outworks during the evening to spare his men posted in them. Cornwallis had been assured by Clinton in New York that a large British relief force would arrive soon to break the French naval blockade and allied siege. Cornwallis did not want to needlessly sacrifice his troops in the outworks when relief seemed imminent, so he withdrew his men to the main works in the middle of the night.[8] The allies quickly acted on their good fortune and occupied the abandoned outworks.

Over the next few days neither side made an effort to challenge the other. Patrols in between the lines would occasionally encounter each other at night and a brief skirmish ensued, but they typically ended as quickly as they started and involved few casualties.[9]

Washington was careful to rotate the duties of his men so that no unit was overworked or overextended. While some troops rested in

camp, others worked on earthworks to protect the camp and constructed implements of siege warfare (hundreds of gabions and
fascines) to be used in the trenches once the allies broke ground
against the British. The work parties, as well as the encampment,
were protected by large covering parties that defended against a sudden enemy attack. Muhlenberg's brigade was assigned both work
and guard duty in the first week of October, and once the siege lines
opened up on October 6, Muhlenberg and his men rotated into the
trenches every third day.[10]

To get to the point of opening the first siege line, however, took a
lot of preparation. After a week encamped outside of Yorktown,
Washington described the progress of his army to Edward Rutledge
of South Carolina. "We have been hitherto employed in constructing
some necessary advanced Works, in preparing fascines, Gabions etc.
and bringing our heavy Artillery and Stores from the landing place
on James River. This last has been carried on slowly till within a few
days past, when our Waggons arrived from the Northward. The En-
gineers now think we have a sufficient stock to commence serious
operations, and we open Trenches this Evening."[11]

The time to increase pressure on Cornwallis and his army had arrived, so on the evening of October 6, French and American troops
crept forward to dig the first parallel (trench) that in some spots was
just six hundred yards from the British works.[12] Lieutenant Colonel
Richard Butler in Anthony Wayne's brigade described the process:
"The first parallel and other works being laid out by the engineer; a
body of troops [were] ordered . . . to break ground and form works,
the materials being got ready and brought previously to the spot."[13]

Sergeant Joseph Plum Martin of Connecticut recalled that General
Washington ceremoniously started the trench with a pick ax: "The
troops of the line were there ready with entrenching tools and began
to entrench, after General Washington had struck a few blows with
a pickax, a mere ceremony. . . . The ground was sandy and soft, and
the men employed that night [were not idle], so that by daylight they
had covered themselves from danger from the enemy's shot."[14]

Surgeon James Thacher observed the opening of the parallel and
recalled:

This business was conducted with great silence and secrecy, and we were favored by Providence with a night of extreme darkness, and were not discovered before day-light. The working party carried on their shoulders fascines and intrenching tools, while a large part of the detachment was armed with the implements of death. Horses, drawing cannon and ordnance, and wagons loaded with bags filled with sand for constructing breastworks, flowed in the rear.[15]

The British discovered the new allied works at sunrise and unleashed an intense artillery barrage. Over the course of the next two days, American and French work parties, including Muhlenberg and his troops (who were posted in the trenches on October 7), labored to improve the fortifications and construct battery positions for their cannon, all under a steady, but ineffective, British bombardment.[16]

Up until October 9, the allies had not fired a single cannon at the main British earthworks. The completion of their first artillery batteries in the first parallel, however, allowed them to finally respond to the British, who had been peppering the allies with ineffective artillery fire for nearly two weeks.

The French were first to fire, directing cannon, howitzer, and mortar shot and shell at an isolated redoubt on the right flank of the British works and on British ships in the river.[17] Washington reportedly commenced the American bombardment two hours later, touching off an eighteen-pound cannon whose solid shot smashed through a building with British officers inside, killing one instantly and tearing the leg off another. The rest of the American grand battery (made up of two twenty-four-pound cannon, twelve eighteen-pound cannon, two howitzers, and four mortars) followed suit and pounded two redoubts that sat about three hundred yards in advance of the left side of the British earthworks.[18] Over the next two days, additional allied batteries joined the bombardment, and soon over fifty artillery pieces hurled their deadly ordnance at the redoubts and into Yorktown.[19] American captain James Duncan described the allied bombardment of Yorktown from his perspective in the first parallel: "The whole night was nothing but one continual roar of cannon, mi[xe]d with the bursting of shells and rumbling of houses torn to pieces. As soon as the day approached the enemy withdrew their pieces from their embrazures and retired under cover of their works, and now commenced a still more dreadful cannonade from all our batteries without scarcely any intermission for the whole day."[20]

Captain Johann Ewald described the impact from inside the British works: "Since yesterday the besiegers have fired bombshells incessantly. . . . The greater part of the town lies in ashes, and two [of our] batteries have already been completely dismantled."[21] Stephan Popp, another German soldier, noted, "The heavy fire forced us to throw our tents in the ditches. . . . We could find no refuge in or out of town. The people fled to the waterside and hid in hastily contrived shelters on the banks, but many of them were killed by bursting bombs."[22]

Lieutenant Bartholomew James, a British naval officer detached from his ship to serve on an artillery battery in the British works at Yorktown, described the suffering those trapped in Yorktown experienced during the allied bombardment: "Upwards of a thousand shells were thrown into the works on this night [October 11] and every spot became alike dangerous. The noise and thundering of the cannon, the distressing cries of the wounded, and the lamentable sufferings of the inhabitants, whose dwellings were chiefly in flames, added to the restless fatigues of the duty, must inevitably fill every mind with pity and compassion who are possessed of any feelings for their fellow creatures."[23]

In a letter to the governor of Maryland, Washington provided a more tactical assessment of the siege's impact on the British works: "Our Shells have done considerable damage to the Town, and our fire from the Cannon have been so heavy and well directed against the embrasures [openings in the British works which their cannon fire through] that they have been obliged, during the day, to withdraw their Cannon and place them behind their [earthworks]."[24]

Lieutenant Colonel St. George Tucker observed the allied bombardment from his post with the Virginia militia and made a similar observation about its effectiveness. "A number of shells have been thrown into the Enemy's Works, & the shot so well directed in general that many of the Embrasures of the Enemy's are wholly rendered incapable of offensive Operations—there are but two Cannon now to be seen in their Embrasures."[25]

Cornwallis responded to the bombardment with an urgent message to Clinton emphasizing the desperate situation he and his men faced. Cornwallis added that since the enemy had commenced their bombardment "without intermission with forty pieces of cannon (mostly heavy) and sixteen mortars. . . . We have lost about seventy men, and many of our works are considerably damaged."[26] The besieged British commander at Yorktown closed his letter with a dire assertion: "With such works on disadvantageous ground, against so powerful an attack, we cannot hope to make a long resistance."[27]

Baffled by what he viewed as Cornwallis's "passive beyond conception" response to the siege, Washington ordered allied troops to open a second parallel at point-blank range to the British. On the evening of October 11, American and French troops crept closer to Yorktown and overnight constructed a new parallel within three hundred yards of the British works.[28] Lieutenant William Feltman of Pennsylvania recounted that "Just at dusk we advanced within gunshot of the enemy, then began our work. In one hour's time we had ourselves completely covered, so we disregarded their cannonading; they discharged a number of pieces at our party, but they had but little effect and only wounded one of our men."[29] Feltman and his fellow soldiers were actually more endangered from errant allied cannon fire than fire from the British lines. "We were in the center of two fires, from the enemy and our own, but the latter was very dangerous; we had two men killed and one badly wounded from the French batteries, also a number of shells burst in the air above our heads, which was very dangerous to us. We dug the ditch three and a half feet deep and seven feet in width."[30]

Militiaman Daniel Trabue described the enormous mortar shells that the allies lobbed toward the British, some of which burst prematurely over the allied lines: "The shells were made of pot metal like a jug 1-2 inch thick, without a handle, & with a big mouth. They were filled with powder, and other combustibles in such a manner that the blaze came out of the mouth, and keeps on burning until it gets to the body where the powder is, then it bursts and the pieces fly every way, and wound & kill whoever it hits."[31]

Trabue added that the rapid rate of allied artillery fire, which he described as one "every minute and sometimes 10 or 15 at the same time," wreaked havoc on the enemy:[32] "There were so many [shells] flying and falling in [their] Fort," noted Trabue, "that we had no Doubt but that we were paying them well for their mischief to us."[33]

Dr. James Thacher also acknowledged the intense allied bombardment but added that the British responded with a bombardment of their own:

> From the 10 to the 15, a tremendous and incessant firing from the American and French batteries is kept up, and the enemy return the fire, but with little effect. . . . We have now made further approaches to the town, by throwing up a second parallel line, and batteries within about three hundred yards; this was effected in the night, and at day-light the enemy roused to the greatest exertions; the engines of war have raged with redoubled fury and destruction on both sides, no cessation day or night. . . . The siege is daily becoming more and more formidable and alarming, and his lordship must view his situation as extremely critical, if not desperate.[34]

A French observer also noted the increased intensity of the siege upon the opening of the second parallel and speculated that Cornwallis had been hoarding his ammunition in anticipation of the allied advance. "The day was spent in cannonading and firing bombs at each other in such profusion that we did one another much damage. The enemy seemed to have been saving up their ammunition for the second parallel. It was of very small caliber and very effective, being fired at short range. That night we had six men killed and twenty-eight wounded."[35]

The accuracy of allied gunfire, particularly from the French guns, also played a significant role in suppressing British firepower. Bartholomew James commanded a detachment of thirty-six sailors who were posted in the hornwork section of the British earthworks, less than three hundred yards from the French line and batteries. He recalled, "In fifty-two minutes after my arrival in the hornwork the enemy silenced the three left guns by closing the embrasures, shortly after which they dismounted a twelve pounder, knocked off the muzzles of two eighteens, and for the last hour and a half left me with one eighteen-pounder with a part of its muzzle also shot away, which I kept up a fire till it was also rendered useless."[36]

As he neared the end of his eight-hour shift in the hornwork, James was nearly killed by a shell that burst nearby and gave him a contusion on his face and leg. He was lucky; the losses among his detachment were devastating:

> During my stay in the works [I] had nine men killed, twenty-seven wounded, eight of which died [since] they were removed, and most of the wounded had lost an arm or leg, and some both. In short, myself and the midshipman, both wounded were the only two returned out of thirty-six, having stood a close cannonade with the enemy for eight hours, who had ninety-seven pieces of heavy cannon playing on us all that time.[37]

While British casualties rose steadily due to the allied shelling (as well as rampant illness that raged among the confined troops), allied casualties were rather low in comparison. In the two weeks that had passed since their arrival at Yorktown, the allies had suffered 118 casualties. The French lost nine killed and sixty-seven wounded and the Americans fourteen killed and thirty wounded.[38]

Despite the death and destruction that was inflicted by the constant barrage of artillery, Dr. Thacher found the aerial display over the battlefield fascinating:

> Being in the trenches every other night and day, I have a fine opportunity of witnessing the sublime and stupendous scene which is continually exhibiting. The bomb-shells from the besiegers and the besieged are incessantly crossing each other's path in the air. They are clearly visible in the form of a black ball in the day, but in the night, they appear like a fiery meteor with a blazing tail,

most beautifully brilliant, ascending majestically from the mortar to a certain altitude, and gradually descending to the spot where they are destined to [ex]ecute their work of destruction . . . . When a shell falls, it whirls round, burrows and excavates the earth to a considerable extent, and bursting, makes dreadful havoc around. I have more than once witnessed fragments of the mangled bodies and limbs of the British soldiers thrown into the air by the bursting of our shells.[39]

Completion of the American section of the second parallel was obstructed by the presence of the two British redoubts in advance of the left section of Cornwallis's main line. These outworks, situated near the river about three hundred yards in front of the main British works, protected Cornwallis's left flank and prevented the Americans from extending their second parallel to the river. As a result, Washington determined that the British outworks had to be taken and directed his artillery batteries to blast the two redoubts in preparation for an assault. The French would storm one of the redoubts and the Americans, specifically light infantry troops from Lafayette's division and Muhlenberg's brigade, would storm the other.

In the early evening of October 14, two four-hundred-man detachments, one American and the other French, moved against the British outposts, known today as Redoubts 9 and 10.[40] Originally, Lafayette had placed Lieutenant Colonel Jean Gimat of Muhlenberg's brigade in command of the assault, but Lieutenant Colonel Alexander Hamilton of General Hazen's brigade objected and claimed, as one of the officers of the day, that he was entitled to lead the assault. Hamilton's appeal to Washington, whom he had served as an aide-de-camp for many months, was successful and Washington countermanded Lafayette's orders; Hamilton was thus placed in command of the assault on Redoubt 10.[41] Muhlenberg and Hazen would follow the attack with the remainder of their brigades and Wayne, with two battalions, was positioned to aid either the Americans or French, whichever required assistance.[42]

Redoubt 10 sat on the edge of a bluff overlooking the York River and was defended by approximately seventy British soldiers.[43] The

French, under Colonel de Deux-Ponts, assaulted Redoubt 9, which sat about 225 yards southwest of Redoubt 10. This post was larger and was defended by over 120 German and British soldiers.[44] Both redoubts were protected by earthen walls, a ditch and palisade, and extensive abatis, all of which the allies had to overcome before they reached the enemy.

The American and French detachments approached the redoubts around 7:00 p.m. with unloaded muskets to prevent an accidental discharge. Their bayonets would decide the struggle. Captain Stephen Olney, who commanded a company of Rhode Island light infantry in Lafayette's division, participated in the assault and recalled that "The column marched in silence, with guns unloaded, and in good order. Many, no doubt, thinking, that less than one quarter of a mile would finish the journey of life with them. On the march I had a chance to whisper to several of my men (whom I doubted) and told them that I had full confidence that they would act the part of brave soldiers."[45] Olney continued: "The column . . . moved on, six or eight pioneers [sappers and miners] in front, as many of the forlorn hope next, then Colonel Gimatt with five or six volunteers by his side then my platoon, being the front of the column."[46]

Joseph Plum Martin of Connecticut, who was one of the sappers in the front of the column, recalled,

We . . . moved silently on toward the redoubt we were to attack, with unloaded muskets. Just as we arrived at the abatis, the enemy discovered us and directly opened a sharp fire upon us. . . . Our people began to cry, "The fort's our own!" and "Rush on boys!" The Sappers and Miners soon cleared a passage for the infantry, who entered it rapidly. . . . While passing, [through the abatis] a man at my side received a ball in his head and fell under my feet, crying out bitterly. While crossing the trench, the enemy threw hand grenades into it. As I mounted the breastwork, I met an old associate hitching himself down into the trench. I knew him by the light of the enemy's musketry, it was so vivid.[47]

Olney recorded a similar account of the attack: "When we came near the front of the abatis, the enemy fired a full body of musketry. At this, our men broke silence and huzzaed; and as the order for silence seemed broken by every one, I huzzaed with all my power, saying, 'see how frightened they are, they fire into the air!'"[48]

Struggling through the dense abatis, then into the ditch and over the palisade and parapet, Olney and the Americans engaged in desperate hand-to-hand combat. Olney recalled that when he ascended the parapet he called out in a calm tone, "Captain Olney's company form here!"[49] This attracted the enemy's notice, who pushed "not less than six or eight bayonets at me."[50] Olney continued: "I parried as well as I could with my espontoon, but they broke off the blade part, and their bayonets slid along the handle of my espontoon and scaled my fingers; one bayonet pierced my thigh, another stabbed me in the abdomen just above the hip bone. One fellow fired at me, and I thought the ball took effect in my arm; by the light of the gun I made a thrust with the remains of my espontoon in order to injure the sight of his eyes; but as it happened, I only made a hard stroke to his forehead."[51]

With Americans pouring into the redoubt from all directions, British resistance collapsed. Many fled out the rear of the redoubt in hopes of escaping to the main British works three hundred yards away. A majority made it out, but some were cut off and captured by an American detachment led by Lieutenant Colonel John Laurens of South Carolina. The few remaining British troops still in the redoubt pleaded for mercy and surrendered. About a quarter of the seventy-man British garrison of Redoubt 10 were killed, wounded, or captured. American casualties were higher, with eight killed and thirty-six wounded.[52]

Two hundred yards to the left, the French were still engaged in a bloody struggle for Redoubt 9. Initially unable to penetrate the redoubt's thick abatis, the French suffered a significant number of casualties before they finally broke through. Pouring over the parapet and into the redoubt, a scene of mass confusion and brutality ensued. One of the attacking French regiments wore blue coats instead of the traditional white coats of the French army. In the chaos of the night battle, it was difficult to distinguish between the blue coats of the German defenders and those of the French troops. As a result, a number of French soldiers were cut down by their own men within the redoubt.[53]

Although it took longer and cost more men, Redoubt 9 fell to the French at the loss of approximately eighty soldiers killed and wounded. German and British losses at Redoubt 9 were estimated at between fifty-five to sixty-five troops killed, wounded, or captured.[54] The remainder fled back to the main works, hazarding fire from their comrades who mistook them for the enemy.

The capture of these two outposts allowed the Americans to complete the second parallel. Allied work parties immediately followed the assault and worked feverishly to incorporate the captured redoubts into the second parallel. By daybreak they had succeeded, and the noose tightened once more around the British in Yorktown.

Cornwallis responded to the loss of his outposts with a furious bombardment of the allied lines. Lieutenant William Feltman of Pennsylvania noted that "the enemy threw a number of shells this day and wounded a great number of men, especially militia."[55]

In addition to the intensified bombardment of the allied lines, Cornwallis also sent his first sortie against the allies. In the early morning hours of October 16, Lieutenant Colonel Robert Abercrombie led 350 soldiers into the French and American trenches.[56] They overwhelmed two artillery batteries and spiked a number of cannon before withdrawing in the face of a French counterattack. The assault, although brave, was largely ineffectual, as most of the spiked cannon were repaired and put back in service by that afternoon.

Muhlenberg's brigade was back in the second parallel on October 16, no doubt on edge after Abercrombie's sortie to their left just a few hours earlier.[57] Work on the artillery battery at the second parallel was completed while Muhlenberg and his troops were in the trenches and the American gunners poured deadly shot and shell upon the British from point blank range. Dr. Thacher noted, "Not less than one hundred pieces of heavy ordnance have been in continual operation during the last twenty-four hours. The whole peninsula trembles under the incessant thunderings of our infernal machines;

we have leveled some of their works in ruins and silenced their guns; they have almost ceased firing."[58]

With his ordnance and provisions nearly exhausted, and his force reduced by death, injury, and illness, Cornwallis made one last attempt to forestall disaster. During the evening of October 16, he ferried part of his army across the river to Gloucester Point. He hoped to assemble all those who could march on the north side of the river and break through the allied line at Gloucester. His plan was foiled when a violent storm scattered many of his boats. It was now impossible to complete the movement before daylight, so Cornwallis cancelled the attempt and recalled the troops to Yorktown.

Johann Ewald grimly assessed the British situation on October 17. "All the batteries were dismantled, the works destroyed, munitions and provisions wanting, the wounded and sick lying helpless without medicine, and the army melted away from 7,000 to 3,200, among whom not a thousand men could be called healthy."[59]

In a bitter letter to Clinton written days after the siege, Cornwallis described a similar situation on October 17:

> Our works. . . were going to ruin. And, not having been able to strengthen them by abatis nor in any other manner than by a slight fraising (which the enemy's artillery were demolishing wherever they fired), [I determined that the works] in many parts were very assailable . . . and that by the continuance of the same fire for a few hours longer they would be in such a state as to render it desperate, with our numbers, to attempt to maintain them. We at that time could not fire a single gun: only one eight-inch and little more than one hundred cohorn shells remained. A diversion by the French ships of war that lay at the mouth of York River was to be expected. Our numbers had been diminished by the enemy's fire, but particularly by sickness; and the strength and spirits of those in the works were much exhausted by the fatigue of constant watching and unremitting duty.[60]

With no British relief force in sight, there was only one thing left for Cornwallis to do—surrender. He rationalized his decision to Clin-

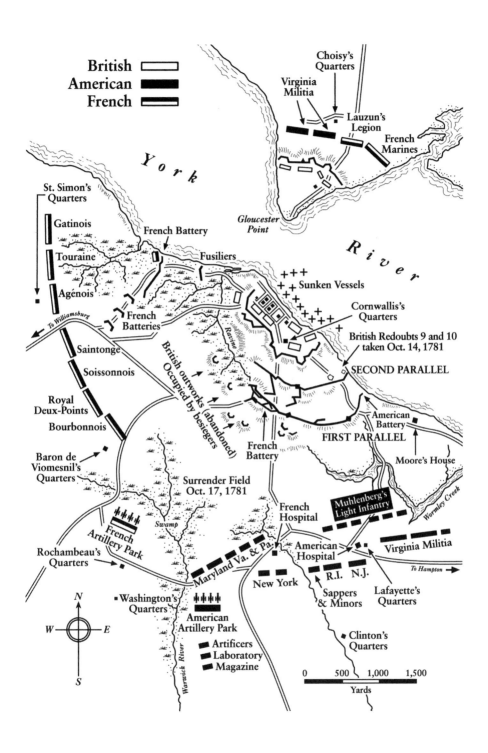

British

American

French

Choisy's
Quarters

Virginia
Militia

Lauzun's
Legion

French
Marines

York

St. Simon's
Quarters

Gatinois

French Battery

*Gloucester
Point*

River

Touraine

Fusiliers

+ + +
+ + Sunken Vessels
+ +
+ + + +
+

Agénois

French
Batteries

Cornwallis's
Quarters

To Williamsburg

Ravine

British Redoubts 9 and 10
taken Oct. 14, 1781

Saintonge

SECOND PARALLEL

Soissonnois

British outworks (abandoned)
Occupied by besiegers

Royal
Deux-Points

American
Battery

Bourbonnois

FIRST PARALLEL

Baron de
Viomesnil's
Quarters

French
Battery

Moore's House

Wormley Creek

Surrender Field
Oct. 17, 1781

Muhlenberg's
Light Infantry

French
Hospital

Swamp

French
Artillery Park

Rochambeau's
Quarters

Maryland Va. & Pa.

American
Hospital

Virginia Militia

To Hampton

New York

R.I. N.J.

N

Washington's
Quarters

American
Artillery Park

Sappers
& Minors

Lafayette's
Quarters

W — *E*

Clinton's
Quarters

Artificers
Laboratory
Magazine

0   500   1,000   1,500

S

Warwick River

Yards

ton a few days after the siege: "Under all these circumstances I thought it would have been wanton and inhuman to the last degree to sacrifice the lives of this small body of gallant soldiers—who had ever behaved with so much fidelity and courage—by exposing them to an assault which, from the numbers and precautions of the enemy, could not fail to succeed. I therefore proposed to capitulate."[61]

At 10:00 a.m. on October 17, 1781, Cornwallis ordered a British drummer to beat a parley upon the parapet of the British earthworks. Alongside the drummer stood a British officer with a white handkerchief. The American gunners opposite the scene could not hear the drummer over the noise of the shelling, but they recognized the meaning of a white flag and ceased their bombardment. A flurry of messages passed between the lines followed by two days of negotiations that resulted in the capitulation of Cornwallis and his army on October 19.

Nearly 7,100 British and German soldiers surrendered at Yorktown. This number swelled to 8,100 when the captured British sailors and camp followers were included.[62] The three-week siege inflicted nearly 500 casualties (156 killed and 326 wounded) on Cornwallis's force.[63] The French reported 60 of their troops killed and 194 wounded. The Americans only lost 28 men killed and 107 wounded.[64]

Washington granted similar terms of surrender to Cornwallis that were granted to the Americans when they surrendered at Charleston in 1780. This meant that most of the British prisoners were not paroled but held as prisoners of war until they could be exchanged for American prisoners.[65] The British and German prisoners were marched to Winchester under militia escort. Cornwallis and a few of his fellow officers avoided this humiliation. They were granted their parole and allowed to return to New York unescorted.

Muhlenberg was also granted a parole of sorts soon after the British surrender. He had come down with a fever just prior to the storming of Redoubt 10 but had remained with his brigade through the duration of the siege. His illness persisted and he received permission from Lafayette to retire to Williamsburg "for the recovery of my health." Muhlenberg now wrote to Washington on October

23 with a request.[66] "A Constant & Violent fever I have had for Ten days past, has not only reduced me very much, but I am afraid if it continues much longer will put it out of my power to remove for some time, I would therefore request Your Excellency's permission to go over the Mountains, as I have at present an Opportunity to make use of a Carriage going that way."[67]

In case Washington was inclined to say no, Muhlenberg reminded him of his thwarted efforts over the last two years to return home to see his family.

> Your Excellency will please remember that I had obtained permission to visit my Family in the Spring of 79, but was prevented by General Woodfords remaining longer in Virga then was expected. In Novr 79 I obtained Your Excellencys permission again but was stopd in Philadelphia By the Board of War, when the Virga Line was ordered to Charleston. Since that I obtained permission from Baron Steuben to go home for a time, but had been there only three days, when I was recalled by Express at the time when Arnold invaded the State.[68]

Washington approved Muhlenberg's request and he finally headed home to his family in Woodstock for a long-overdue reunion with his wife and sons.

EPILOGUE

PETER MUHLENBERG REMAINED IN WOODSTOCK THROUGH THE winter, slowly recovering his health and reconnecting with his family. In February 1782 he wrote to Edward Hand, the adjutant general of the army, to inform him that he was ready to rejoin the army and that he wished to serve in South Carolina under Nathanael Greene.[1] Muhlenberg's request was forwarded to Washington, who informed Muhlenberg directly that, since there was no command available with Greene, he needed to remain in Virginia to once again superintend the recruitment and training of new Continental recruits.[2] Muhlenberg thus spent the remainder of the war in Virginia struggling to raise and equip troops for Greene's army in South Carolina.

With Virginia's government heavily in debt and unable to pay new recruits, providing troops for Greene proved to be a monumental challenge. Fortunately, British efforts to defeat America essentially ended after Yorktown, so the reduced military activity and threat meant a reduced need for troops. Muhlenberg, nonetheless, spent most of 1782 at the appointed rendezvous point at Cumberland Old Court House in command of the few Continental recruits that reported for duty.[3] With military activity winding down in South Carolina, Muhlenberg undoubtedly welcomed the Virginia assembly's decision in November 1782 to move the Continental rendezvous point to Winchester, just twenty miles from his family in Woodstock.[4]

By the spring of 1783 it was clear that an agreement between America and Great Britain to end the war and recognize American independence was forthcoming. Muhlenberg remained on duty at Winchester, but there were few troops to superintend anymore.

On September 30, 1783, Congress approved a gesture of appreciation to all of the Continental officers, including Muhlenberg, who had remained in the army until the end.

> Resolved, that the Secretary of War issue to all Officers in the Army who hold the same rank now that they held in the year 1777, a brevet Commission, one grade higher than their present rank.[5]

This act made Peter Muhlenberg a major general in the Continental army. The action taken by Congress was recommended by Washington. Both agreed that it was an act of justice to the many officers who deserved promotions for their continued service but who had been denied such promotions due to the gradual reduction of the army over time.[6]

The Continental army was formally disbanded less than two months later, allowing Major General Muhlenberg to return to his family in Woodstock for good.

Peter Muhlenberg was heartily welcomed back by his old congregation in Shenandoah (formerly Dunmore) County, but he declined to return to the pulpit, reportedly saying that "it would never do to mount the parson after the soldier."[7] His eight years of service in the army had produced far too many instances and experiences that were incompatible with the life of a minister.

Muhlenberg's long service in the war also came at great financial sacrifice to his family. He decided, therefore, that his best course of action was to return to Pennsylvania to be closer to his extended family and also to enter into the mercantile business.[8]

He and Hanna and their two sons left Virginia in November 1783 and settled permanently in Pennsylvania, first with his father in Trappe and later in Philadelphia.[9]

Muhlenberg's long service in the army earned him approximately thirteen thousand acres of western land, the management of which drew his attention away from the mercantile trade and to the west. In the spring of 1784, at age thirty-eight, he travelled west to view his land and also to administer the distribution of a portion of the western lands (on behalf of Virginia) to former soldiers. He gave an amusing account of what the trip did to his appearance.

> I stand by [incognito] and hear the name of Muhlenberg made use of, sometimes in one way, and sometimes in another; for were I known, I believe no one would have the hardiesse to mention that name with disrespect, and look at me, for I have at present the perfect resemblance of Robinson Crusoe: four belts around me, two brace of pistols, a sword and rifle slung, besides my pouch and tobacco pipe, which is not a small one. Add to this the blackness of my face, which occasions the inhabitants to take me for a travelling Spaniard, and I am sure that my appearance alone ought to protect me from both politics and insult.[10]

His travels took him deep into Ohio and Kentucky, where he observed much evidence of conflict with the Indians. Muhlenberg also suffered several bouts of illness, but he recovered from them all and eventually returned to Pennsylvania.

While Muhlenberg would continue to have much interest in the west, the bulk of his time after the war was spent involved in politics in Pennsylvania. His first biographer noted that Muhlenberg's "frankness and affability of manners seem to have rendered him a favourite with the people," and this was once again demonstrated when he was elected to the office of vice president of Pennsylvania (under President Benjamin Franklin) just a year after returning to Pennsylvania and months after returning from the west.[11] He served several one-year terms, and when the US Constitution was presented for ratification Muhlenberg, like most former officers of the American army, supported it.[12]

Muhlenberg was elected as one of Pennsylvania's first congressmen in 1789.[13] He served three terms in the House of Representatives, but none of the terms were consecutive (1789-91, 1793-95, 1799-1801). Muhlenberg broke from the norm of most former officers and supported the Democratic Republicans of Thomas Jefferson and James Madison.

He was elected to, and briefly served, in the US Senate in 1801-02 but resigned in the summer of 1802 to accept an appointment by President Jefferson as the collector of the port of Philadelphia, a lucrative position in which he served until his death on October 1, 1807, his sixty-first birthday.

An obituary that appeared in newspapers in Pennsylvania and Virginia (and likely many other states) noted that, "General Muhlenberg acted faithfully to his country and honorably to himself. He was brave in the field, and firm in the Cabinet. In private he was strictly just, in his domestic and social attachments he was affectionate and sincere, and in his [conduct] with his friends and fellow citizens, always amiable and unassuming."[14]

Another brief account of Muhlenberg from a Philadelphia newspaper noted that he "Was an active and enterprising officer during our struggle for independence. He lived respected, and died regretted by all good men."[15]

Peter Muhlenberg was buried in Trappe, Pennsylvania, next to his father; the inscription on his marker declares:

Sacred to the Memory of General Peter Muhlenberg . . .
He was Brave in the Field
Faithful in the Cabinet
Honourable in All His Transactions
A Sincere Friend
And
An Honest Man[16]

NOTES

CHAPTER ONE: FINDING A CALLING

1. Henry A. Muhlenberg, *The Life of Major-General Peter Muhlenberg of the Revolutionary Army* (Philadelphia: Cary and Hart, 1849), 17.

2. Ibid.

3. Ibid.

4. Edward W. Hocker, *The Fighting Parson of the American Revolution: A Biography of General Peter Muhlenberg* (Philadelphia, PA, 1936), 18.

5. Muhlenberg, *The Life of Major-General Peter Muhlenberg of the Revolutionary Army*, 26.

6. Rev. William Germann, "The Crisis in the Early Life of General Peter Muhlenberg," *Pennsylvania Magazine of History and Biography*, Vol. 37, (1913), 299-300.

7. Germann, "Peter Muhlenberg to Lector Pasche, January 2, 1766," *Pennsylvania Magazine of History and Biography*, Vol. 37, 306-308.

8. Germann, "Crisis in the Early Life of Gen. Peter Muhlenberg," *Pennsylvania Magazine of History and Biography*, Vol. 37, 300-302.

9. Germann, "Henry Muhlenberg to Lector Pasche, October 14, 1765," *Pennsylvania Magazine of History and Biography*, Vol. 37, 306.

10. Germann, "Peter Muhlenberg to Lector Pasche, January 2, 1766," *Pennsylvania Magazine of History and Biography*, Vol. 37, 307-308.

11. Germann, "Herr Meymann to Herr Fabricius, April 2, 1766," *Pennsylvania Magazine of History and Biography*, Vol. 37, 310.

12. Germann, "Peter Muhlenberg to Herr Fabricius, April 5, 1766," *Pennsylvania Magazine of History and Biography*, Vol. 37, 310-311.

13. Germann, "Peter Muhlenberg to Herr Fabricius, May 8, 1766," *Pennsylvania Magazine of History and Biography*, Vol. 37, 312.

14. Germann, "Peter Muhlenberg to Herr Fabricius, July 20, 1766," *Pennsylvania Magazine of History and Biography*, Vol. 37, 316-317.

15. Germann, "Peter Muhlenberg to Herr Niemeyer, August 14, 1766," *Pennsylvania Magazine of History and Biography*, Vol. 37, 321.

16. Germann, "Madame Neubauer to Herr Fabricius, August 16, 1766," *Pennsylvania Magazine of History and Biography*, Vol. 37, 322.

17. Ibid.

18. Germann, "Herr Niemeyer to G.A. Francke, October 8, 1766, *Pennsylvania Magazine of History and Biography*, Vol. 37, 324.

19. Ibid.

20. Ibid.
21. Ibid.
22. Germann, "Henry Muhlenberg to G.A. Francke, December 9, 1766," *Pennsylvania Magazine of History and Biography,* Vol. 37, 326.
23. Ibid.
24. Paul Wallace, *The Muhlenbergs of Pennsylvania* (Philadelphia: University of Pennsylvania Press, 1950), 71.
25. Ibid.
26. Wallace, "Peter Muhlenberg to Lector Pasche, March 29, 1767," *The Muhlenbergs of Pennsylvania,* 71.
27. Wallace, *The Muhlenbergs of Pennsylvania,* 72.
28. Ibid., 73.
29. Wallace, *The Muhlenbergs of Pennsylvania,* 73.
30. George M. Smith, *The Reverend Peter Muhlenberg: A Symbiotic Adventure in Virginia, 1772-1783* (unpublished report), 55.
31. Henry A. Muhlenberg, *The Life of Major-General Peter Muhlenberg of the Revolutionary Army,* 33.
32. Smith, "James Wood Jr. to Peter Muhlenberg, May 4, 1771," *The Reverend Peter Muhlenberg: A Symbiotic Adventure in Virginia, 1772-1783,* 56.
33. Smith, *The Reverend Peter Muhlenberg: A Symbiotic Adventure in Virginia, 1772-1783,* 57.
34. Wallace, *The Muhlenbergs of Pennsylvania,* 82; and Smith, *The Reverend Peter Muhlenberg: A Symbiotic Adventure in Virginia, 1772-1783,* 58.

CHAPTER TWO: CRISIS IN VIRGINIA

1. John W. Wayland, *A History of Shenandoah County, Virginia* (Baltimore: Regional Publishing Co., 1976), 100-102.
2. Ibid., 217.
3. Ibid., 35.
4. Smith, *The Reverend Peter Muhlenberg: A Symbiotic Adventure in Virginia, 1772-1783,* 58.
5. Ibid., 59.
6. Ibid., 60.
7. Amelia C. Gilreath, ed., "Proceedings of the Dunmore County Court, September 29, 1774," *Order Book, 1772-1774: Shenandoah County, Virginia* (1986), 140.
8. Gilreath, ed., "Proceedings of the Dunmore County Court, May 9, 1774," *Order Book, 1772-1774: Shenandoah County, Virginia,* 185.
9. Robert L. Scribner, ed., "Dunmore County, June 16, 1774," *Revolutionary Virginia: The Road to Independence,* Vol. 1 (Charlottesville: University Press of Virginia, 1973), 122.
10. Ibid.
11. Ibid., 122-123.
12. Ibid.
13. Ibid.
14. Scribner, ed., "The Convention of 1774: A List of Delegates Eligible and of

Those Who Probably Attended," *Revolutionary Virginia: The Road to Independence,* Vol. 1, 219-220.

15. Robert L. Scribner, ed., "Dunmore County Committee January 10, 1775," *Revolutionary Virginia: The Road to Independence*, Vol. 2 (Charlottesville: University Press of Virginia, 1975), 228-229.

16. Muhlenberg, "Extract of Letter from Peter Muhlenberg to his Brother," *The Life of Major-General Peter Muhlenberg of the Revolutionary Army,* 45-46.

17. Scribner, ed., "Dunmore County Committee January 10, 1775," *Revolutionary Virginia: The Road to Independence*, Vol. 2, 228-229.

18. Scribner, ed., "Editorial Note," *Revolutionary Virginia: The Road to Independence*, Vol. 2, 336.

19. Scribner, ed., "Second Virginia Convention, Proceedings of the Fourth Day, March 23, 1775," *Revolutionary Virginia: The Road to Independence*, Vol. 2, 366-367.

20. Robert L. Scribner, ed., *Revolutionary Virginia: The Road to Independence,* Vol. 3 (Charlottesville: University Press of Virginia, 1977), 305.

21. Robert L. Scribner and Brent Tarter, eds., "Dunmore County Committee Meetings on September 26, 1775 and November 11, 1774," *Revolutionary Virginia: The Road to Independence*, Vol. 4 (Charlottesville: University Press of Virginia, 1978), 146, 387.

22. Robert L. Scribner and Brent Tarter, eds., *Revolutionary Virginia: The Road to Independence*, Vol. 5 (Charlottesville: University Press of Virginia, 1979), 27.

23. Scribner and Tarter, eds., "Proceedings of Fourth Virginia Convention, January 12, 1776," *Revolutionary Virginia: The Road to Independence*, Vol. 5, 391.

24. Muhlenberg, *The Life of Major-General Peter Muhlenberg of the Revolutionary Army,* 50.

25. Scribner and Tarter, eds., *Revolutionary Virginia: The Road to Independence,* Vol. 6. (Charlottesville: University Press of Virginia, 1981), 20.

26. William W. Henings, *The Statutes at Large; Being a Collection of all the Laws of Virginia,* Vol. 9 (Richmond, 1821), 76.

27. Henings, 78.

28. Muhlenberg, *The Life of Major-General Peter Muhlenberg of the Revolutionary Army,* 50-54.

29. Ibid., 53-54.

30. Ibid., 52.

31. James Thacher, M.D., *Military Journal of the American Revolution, 1775-1783* (Gansevoort, NY: Corner House Historical Publications, 1998), 154.

32. Scribner and Tarter, "Proceedings of the Committee of Safety, April 3, 1776," *Revolutionary Virginia: The Road to Independence*, Vol. 6, 318.

33. Smith, *The Reverend Peter Muhlenberg: A Symbiotic Adventure in Virginia, 1772-1783"* (unpublished report), 62-63

CHAPTER THREE: TO THE DEFENSE OF CHARLESTON

1. Scribner and Tarter, "Proceedings of the Committee of Safety, March 13, 1776," *Revolutionary Virginia: The Road to Independence,* Vol. 6, 205.

2. Scribner and Tarter, "Proceedings of the Committee of Safety, April 3, 1776," *Revolutionary Virginia: The Road to Independence,* Vol. 6, 318.

3. Philander D. Chase, ed., "General Charles Lee to General George Washington, 5 April, 1776," *The Papers of George Washington, Revolutionary War Series,* Vol. 4 (Charlottesville: University Press of Virginia Press, 1991), 43.

4. Scribner and Tarter, "Proceedings of the Committee of Safety, April 10, 1776," *Revolutionary Virginia: The Road to Independence,* Vol. 6, 369-370.

5. "General Lee to Colonel Muhlenberg, April 11, 1776," *The Lee Papers,* Vol. 1, 410-411.

6. "Major Spotswood to General Lee, April 12, 1776," *The Lee Papers,* Vol. 1, 412-413.

7. "General Lee to Major Spotswood, April 15, 1776," *The Lee Papers,* Vol. 1, 422-423.

8. Ibid.

9. "General Lee to Colonel Muhlenberg, April 23, 1776," *The Lee Papers,* Vol. 1, 444.

10. Ibid.

11. Ibid.

12. "Thomas Burke to General Lee, April 22, 1776," *The Lee Papers,* Vol. 1, 410-411.

13. "General Lee to Thomas Burke, April 24, 1776," *The Lee Papers,* Vol. 1, 410-411.

14. Ibid.

15. Brent Tarter, ed., "Footnote 1: Autograph Diary of Jonathan Clark, entries for May 16 and May 21, 1776," *Revolutionary Virginia: The Road to Independence,* Vol. 7, Part One (Charlottesville: University Press of Virginia, 1983), 248.

16. "General Lee to Congress, May 7, 1776," *The Lee Papers,* Vol. 1, 477-478.

17. "General Lee to Colonel Woodford, May 11, 1776," *The Lee Papers,* Vol. 2, 23-24.

18. Frank E. Grizzard, ed., "Colonel Muhlenberg to General Washington, February 23, 1776," *The Papers of George Washington, Revolutionary War Series,* Vol. 8 (Charlottesville: University Press of Virginia, 1998), 428.

19. Tarter, ed., "General Robert Howe to Edmund Pendleton, May 24, 1776, and Footnote 1: Autograph Diary of Jonathan Clark, entries for May 16 and May 21, 1776," *Revolutionary Virginia: The Road to Independence,* Vol. 7, Part One, 247-248.

20. Tarter, ed., "General Robert Howe to Edmund Pendleton, May 24, 1776," *Revolutionary Virginia: The Road to Independence,* Vol. 7, Part One, 247-248.

21. Tarter, ed., "General Charles Lee to Edmund Pendleton, May 24, 1776," *Revolutionary Virginia: The Road to Independence,* Vol. 7, Part One, 248-249.

22. Ibid.

23. Tarter, ed., "General Charles Lee to Edmund Pendleton, May 24, 1776," *Revolutionary Virginia: The Road to Independence,* Vol. 7, Part One, 248-249.

24. Tarter, ed., "General Charles Lee to Edmund Pendleton, May 24, 1776,"

Revolutionary Virginia: The Road to Independence, Vol. 7, Part One, 248-249.
25. Ibid.
26. "General Lee to Edmund Pendleton, June 1, 1776," *The Lee Papers,* Vol. 2, 51.
27. Edwin C. Bearss, *The Battle of Sullivan's Island and the Capture of Fort Moultrie: A Documented Narrative and Troop Movement Maps* (U.S. Dept. of the Interior, 1968), 139-140.
28. Bearss, 29, 50.
29. Bearss, 29.
30. Ibid., 58-59.
31. Ibid., 59-60.
32. Bearss, 57.
33. "General Lee to Colonel Moultrie, June 23, 1776," *The Lee Papers*, Vol. 2, 81.
34. Bearss, 61.
35. William J. Morgan, ed., "Comments by Major General Henry Clinton Upon the Naval Attack on Sullivan's Island, June 28, 1776," and "Major General Henry Clinton to Lord George Germain, July 8, 1776," *Naval Documents of the American Revolution*, Vol. 5 (Washington, DC: 1970), 802 and 983.
36. Bearss, 58-59.
37. Bearss, 84-85.
38. "General Lee to the President of the Virginia Convention, June 29, 1776, *The Lee Papers*, Vol. 2, 93.
39. Ibid.
40. "General Lee to the President of the Virginia Convention, June 29, 1776," *The Lee Papers*, Vol. 2, 93.
41. Bearss, 86.
42. "General Lee to the President of the Virginia Convention, June 29, 1776," *The Lee Papers,* Vol. 2, 93.
43. Bearss, 102-105.
44. Ibid., 106.
45. Ibid., 107.
46. "General Lee to General Armstrong, July 14, 1776," *The Lee Papers,* Vol. 2, 139-149.
47. "General Lee to President Rutledge, July 22, 1776," *The Lee Papers*, Vol. 2, 159.
48. Charles H. Lesser, ed., "Monthly Return of the Forces in South Carolina, July 1776," *The Sinews of Independence: Monthly Strength Reports of the Continental Army* (Chicago: University of Chicago Press, 1976), 27
49. Lesser, ed., "Monthly Return of the Forces in South Carolina, July 1776," *The Sinews of Independence: Monthly Strength Reports of the Continental Army*, 27.
50. "Colonel Peter Muhlenberg to General Lee, July 31, 1776," *The Lee Papers,* Vol. 2, 183-184.
51. Ibid.

52. Ibid.
53. "General Lee to Colonel Muhlenberg, August 1, 1776," *The Lee Papers,* Vol. 2, 185-186.
54. Ibid.
55. "General Lee to Richard Peters, August 2, 1776," *The Lee Papers,* Vol. 2, 190-192.
56. Worthington C. Ford, ed., "August 13, 1776," *Journals of the Continental Congress,* Vol. 5 (Washington, DC, 1904-1937), 649.
57. "General Lee to Richard Peters, August 2, 1776," *The Lee Papers,* Vol. 2, 188-189.
58. "Orders Issued on the Expedition to Georgia, August 12 and 16, 1776," *The Lee Papers,* Vol. 2, 251- 252.
59. "Orders Issued on the Expedition to Georgia, August 21, 1776," *The Lee Papers,* Vol. 2, 253.
60. Ford, ed., "John Hancock to General Lee, August 8, 1776," *Journals of the Continental Congress,* Vol. 5, 639 and "Orders, September 9, 1776," *The Lee Papers,* Vol. 2, 258-259.
61. "General Lee to General Armstrong, August 15, 1776, *The Lee Papers,* Vol. 2, 230.
62. Ford, ed., "Resolution of Congress, January 21, 1777," *Journals of the Continental Congress,* Vol. 7, 52.
63. Muhlenberg, 69.
64. Muhlenberg, "Peter Muhlenberg to Henry Muhlenberg, December 20, 1776," 69.
65. Ibid.
66. Ford, ed., "Resolution of Congress, January 21, 1777," *Journals of the Continental Congress,* Vol. 7, 52.
67. Grizzard, ed., "Colonel Muhlenberg to General Washington, February 23, 1776," *The Papers of George Washington, Revolutionary War Series,* Vol. 8, 428.
68. Ford, ed., "Resolution of Congress, February 21, 1777," *Journals of the Continental Congress,* Vol. 7, 140.

CHAPTER FOUR: NORTH TO THE BRANDYWINE

1. Grizzard, ed., "George Johnson to Colonel Muhlenberg, March 9, 1777," *The Papers of George Washington, Revolutionary War Series,* Vol. 8, 429.
2. Ibid.
3. Ibid.
4. Henry Melchior Muhlenberg, "May 13, 1777, entry," *The Journals of Henry Melchior Muhlenberg,* Vol. 3, translated by Theodore G. Tappert and John W. Doberstein (Philadelphia: Muhlenberg Press, 1958), 39.
5. Henry Melchior Muhlenberg, "March 31 and April 4, 1777, entries," *The Journals of Henry Melchior Muhlenberg,* Vol. 3, 27, 29.
6. Philander D. Chase, ed., "General Orders, April 11, 1777," *The Papers of George Washington, Revolutionary War Series,* Vol. 9 (Charlottesville: University Press of Virginia, 1999), 123.

7. Chase, ed., "George Johnson to General Muhlenberg, April 13, 1777," *The Papers of George Washington, Revolutionary War Series,* Vol. 9, 124.
8. Chase, ed., "Circular Instruction to the Brigade Commanders, 26. May, 1777," *The Papers of George Washington,* Vol. 9, 532.
9. Chase, "General Orders, May 22, 1776, and Arrangement and Present Strength of the Army in New Jersey, May 20, 1776," *The Papers of General Washington, Revolutionary War Series*, Vol. 9, 495 and 492.
Note: Arendt's German Regiment was originally assigned to General Sullivan's division, but an exchange of units was arranged between General Sullivan and General Greene. Colonel Moses Hazen's Canadian Regiment, which was originally attached to Muhlenberg's brigade, was sent to General Sullivan's division in exchange for Baron de Ardent's German Regiment. See Richard Showman, ed., "General Greene to General Sullivan, May 24, 1777," *The Papers of General Nathanael Greene*, Vol. 2, 90.
10. Chase, "Arrangement and Present Strength of the Army in New Jersey, May 20, 1776," *The Papers of General Washington, Revolutionary War Series*, Vol. 9, 492.
11. Frank E. Grizzard, ed., "Colonel Arendt to General Washington, August 7, 1777," *The Papers of George Washington, Revolutionary War Series*, Vol. 10. (Charlottesville: University Press of Virginia, 2000), 542.
12. Henry Melchior Muhlenberg, "June 26, 1777, entry," *The Journals of Henry Melchior Muhlenberg*, Vol. 3, 54.
13. Henry Melchior Muhlenberg, "July 2, 1777, entry," *The Journals of Henry Melchior Muhlenberg*, Vol. 3, 56.
14. Michael Cecere, "The Diary of Captain John Chilton, July 12-24, 1775,"*They Behaved Like Soldiers, Captain John Chilton and the Third Virginia Regiment, 1775-1778* (Bowie: Heritage Books, 2004), 114-116.
15. Frank E. Gizzard, Jr., ed. "General Washington to General Adam Stephen, July 24, 1777," *The Papers of George Washington, Revolutionary War Series,* Vol. 10, 399.
16. Cecere, "The Diary of Captain John Chilton, July 27, 1777, *They Behaved Like Soldiers*, 117.
17. Philander D. Chase and Edward G. Lengel, eds., "Council of War, August 21, 1777," *The Papers of George Washington, Revolutionary War Series,* Vol. 11 (Charlottesville: University Press of Virginia Press, 2001), 19-20.
18. Michael Harris, *Brandywine: A Military History of the Battle that Lost Philadelphia but Saved America* (El Dorado Hills, CA: Savas Beatie, 2014), 206.
19. Ibid., 206, 210.
20. Ibid., 207-209.
21. Ibid., 209.
22. "General Orders, September 10, 1777," in "Orderly Book of Gen. John Peter Gabriel Muhlenberg, March 26-December 20, 1777," *Pennsylvania Magazine of History and Biography,* Vol. 34, 464.
23. Harris, 253.
24. Thomas McGuire, *The Philadelphia Campaign: Brandywine and the Fall of Philadelphia,* Vol. 1 (Mechanicsburg, PA: Stackpole Books, 2006), 216.

25. Ibid., 224-225.

26. McGuire, 216.

27. Ibid., 238.

28. Otis G. Hammond, ed., "General John Sullivan to Messieurs Powers & Willis Printers in Boston, Oct. 1777," *Letters and Papers of Major-General John Sullivan, Continental Army*, Vol. 1 (Collections of the New Hampshire Historical Society, 1930), 473.

29. Richard Showman, ed., "General Greene to Henry Marchant, July 25, 1778," *The Papers of General Nathanael Greene*, Vol. 2 (Chapel Hill: University of North Carolina Press, 1980), 471.

30. Bob McDonald, ed., "Brigadier General George Weedon's Correspondence Account of the Battle of Brandywine, Sept. 11, 1777," Chicago Historical Society.

31. McGuire, 255.

32. Harris, 354-355.

33. William P. McMichael, contributor, September 11, 1777 entry, Diary of Lieutenant James McMichael, of the Pennsylvania Line, 1776-1778, *Pennsylvania Magazine of History and Biography*, Vol. 16, No. 2, 1892, 150.

34. Ibid.

35. Ira D. Gruber, *John Peebles American War: The Diary of a Scottish Grenadier, 1776-1782* (Mechanicsburg, PA: Stackpole Books, 1998), 133.

36. Joseph Tustin, ed., *Diary of the American War: A Hessian Journal, Captain Johann Ewald, Field Jager Corps* (New Haven, CT: Yale University Press, 1979), 86.

CHAPTER FIVE: GERMANTOWN TO VALLEY FORGE

1. Chase and Lengel, eds., "General Orders, September 12, 1777," *The Papers of George Washington, Revolutionary War Series*, Vol. 11, 204.

2. Chase and Lengel, eds., "General Orders, September 13, 1777," *The Papers of George Washington, Revolutionary War Series*, Vol. 11, 212.

3. Ibid.

4. Chase and Lengel, eds., "General Washington to John Hancock, September 23, 1777," *The Papers of George Washington, Revolutionary Series*, Vol. 11, 301.

5. Ibid.

6. Chase and Lengel, eds., "General Washington to John Hancock, September 18, 1777," *The Papers of George Washington, Revolutionary War Series*, Vol. 11, 262.

7. Henry Melchior Muhlenberg, "September 10, 1777, entry," *The Journals of Henry Melchior Muhlenberg*, Vol. 3, 74.

8. Henry Melchior Muhlenberg, "October 27, 1777, entry," *The Journals of Henry Melchior Muhlenberg*, Vol. 3, 87.
Note: The diary entry for October 27, 1777, describes a letter that Henry Muhlenberg wrote on this date that reports that Hanna is with Friedrich. Another diary entry for October 18, 1777, reports that Peter Muhlenberg and his brigade major and brother-in-law Francis Swaine stopped at Trappe and then rode on

to New Hannover, presumably to see their wives at Friedrich Muhlenberg's home.

9. McGuire, 306.

10. Ibid., 320.

11. McGuire, 322.

12. Chase and Lengel, eds., "General Washington to John Hancock, September 23, 1777," *The Papers of George Washington, Revolutionary Series*, Vol. 11, 301-302.

13. Ibid.

14. Ibid.

15. Chase and Lengel, eds., "Council of War, September 23, 1777," *The Papers of George Washington, Revolutionary War Series*, Vol. 11, 295-296.

16. Chase and Lengel, eds., "Council of War, September 28, 1777," *The Papers of George Washington, Revolutionary War Series*, Vol. 11, 338-339.

17. Thomas J. McGuire, *The Philadelphia Campaign: Germantown and the Roads to Valley Forge,* Vol. 2 (Mechanicsburg, PA: Stackpole Books, 2007), 45-46.

18. Ibid., 47-48.

19. Ibid., 49.

20. Chase and Lengel, eds., "General Orders for Attacking Germantown, Oct. 3, 1777," *The Papers of George Washington*, Vol. 11, 375.

21. Chase and Lengel, eds., "General Orders for Attacking Germantown, Oct. 3, 1777," *The Papers of George Washington, Revolutionary War Series*, Vol. 11, 375.

22. Chase and Lengel, eds., "General Orders, October 3, 1777," *The Papers of George Washington, Revolutionary War Series*, Vol. 11, 373-374.

23. Ibid.

24. "Muhlenberg Brigade Orders, October 3, 1777," in "Orderly Book of Gen. John Peter Gabriel Muhlenberg, March 26-December 20, 1777," *Pennsylvania Magazine of History and Biography*, Vol. 35 (1911), 63.

25. McGuire, *The Philadelphia Campaign: Germantown and the Roads to Valley Forge,* Vol. 2, 52-53.

26. Ibid., 67.

27. McGuire, *The Philadelphia Campaign: Germantown and the Roads to Valley Forge,* Vol. 2, 68, 70, 76-77, 80-81.

28. Ibid., 81, 83, 85.

29. Ibid., 87.

30. Ibid., 88-91.

31. McGuire, *The Philadelphia Campaign: Germantown and the Roads to Valley Forge,* Vol. 2, 94-95.

32. Ibid., 97.

33. Ibid., 99.

34. Ibid.

35. McGuire, *The Philadelphia Campaign: Germantown and the Roads to Valley Forge,* Vol. 2, 101.

36. Joseph Plum Martin, *Private Yankee Doodle: Being a Narrative of Some of the Adventures, Dangers and Sufferings of a Revolutionary Soldier* (Harrisburg, PA: Eastern Acorn Press, 1998), 73.

37. McGuire, *The Philadelphia Campaign: Germantown and the Roads to Valley Forge*, Vol. 2, 114-115.

38. Ibid., 115.

39. Ibid., 115-116.

40. Chase and Lengel, eds., "General Washington to John Augustine Washington, October 18, 1777," *The Papers of George Washington, Revolutionary War Series*, Vol. 11, 551.

41. Ibid.

42. James McMichael, October 4, 1777 entry, Diary of Lieutenant James McMichael, of the Pennsylvania Line, 1776-1778, *Pennsylvania Magazine of History and Biography*, Vol. 16, No. 2, 153.

43. Chase and Lengel, eds., "General Washington to John Hancock, October 7, 1777," *The Papers of George Washington, Revolutionary War Series*, Vol. 11, 417.

44. Chase and Lengel, eds., "General Washington to John Augustine Washington, October 18, 1777," *The Papers of George Washington, Revolutionary War Series*, Vol. 11, 552.

45. Chase and Lengel, eds., "General Orders, October 7, 1777," *The Papers of George Washington, Revolutionary War Series*, Vol. 11, 415.

46. Henings, ed., *Statutes at Large*, Vol. 9, 192-194.

47. Chase and Lengel, eds., "Patrick Henry to General Washington, September 5, 1777, Footnote 3," *The Papers of George Washington, Revolutionary War Series*, Vol. 11, 152.

48. Chase and Lengel, eds., "General Orders, October 9, 1777," *The Papers of George Washington, Revolutionary War Series*, Vol. 11, 452-453.

49. Chase and Lengel, eds., "General Washington to John Hancock, October 13-14, 1777, Enclosed Return," *The Papers of George Washington, Revolutionary War Series*, Vol. 11, 500.

50. Frank E. Grizzard, Jr., ed., "General Orders, November 20, 1777," *The Papers of George Washington, Revolutionary War Series*, Vol. 12 (Charlottesville: University Press of Virginia, 2002), 327-328.

51. McGuire, *The Philadelphia Campaign: Germantown to the Roads and Valley Forge*, Vol. 2, 166.

52. Grizzard, Jr., ed., "Council of War, October 29, 1777," *The Papers of George Washington, Revolutionary War Series*, Vol. 12, 46-48.

53. Ibid.

54. Grizzard, Jr., ed., "General Varnum to General Washington, November 16, 1777," *The Papers of George Washington, Revolutionary War Series*, Vol. 12, 283.

55. Grizzard, Jr., ed., "Colonel Christopher Greene to General Washington, November 17, 1777," *The Papers of George Washington, Revolutionary War Series*, Vol. 12, 288.

56. Grizzard, Jr., ed., "Orders to Major Generals Arthur St. Clair and Johann Kalb and Brigadier General Henry Knox, November 17, 1777," *The Papers of George Washington, Revolutionary War Series,* Vol. 12, 298.

57. Grizzard, Jr., ed., "General Washington to General Varnum, November 19, 1777," *The Papers of George Washington, Revolutionary War Series,* Vol. 12, 322-323.

58. Ibid.

59. Ibid.

60. Grizzard, Jr., ed., "General Varnum to General Washington, November 20, 1777," *The Papers of George Washington, Revolutionary War Series,* Vol. 12, 336.

61. Grizzard, Jr., ed., "General Greene to General Washington, November 21, 1777," *The Papers of George Washington, Revolutionary War Series,* Vol. 12, 340.

62. Grizzard, Jr., ed., "General Greene to General Washington, November 21, 1777," and General Varnum to General Washington, November 21, 1777," *The Papers of George Washington, Revolutionary War Series,* Vol. 12, 340. and 343.

63. Grizzard, Jr., ed., "General Greene to General Washington, November 24, 1777," *The Papers of George Washington, Revolutionary War Series,* Vol. 12, 376-378.

64. Grizzard, Jr., ed., "General Washington to General Greene, November 25, 1777," *The Papers of George Washington, Revolutionary War Series,* Vol. 12, 389.

65. Grizzard, Jr., ed., "General Peter Muhlenberg to General Washington to December 1, 1777", *The Papers of George Washington, Revolutionary War Series,* Vol. 12, 474-475.

66. Ibid.

67. Ibid.

68. Grizzard, Jr., ed., "Circular to the General Officers of the Continental Army, December 3, 1777," *The Papers of George Washington, Revolutionary War Series,* Vol. 12, 506.

69. Grizzard, Jr., ed., "General Peter Muhlenberg to General Washington, December 4, 1777," *The Papers of George Washington, Revolutionary War Series,* Vol. 12, 543-544.

70. Ibid.

71. Ibid.

72. Ibid.

CHAPTER SIX: MONMOUTH COURTHOUSE AND THE BATTLES AROUND NEW YORK

1. Edward Lengel, ed., "General Washington to Henry Laurens, January 1, 1778," *The Papers of George Washington, Revolutionary War Series*, Vol. 14 (Charlottesville: University of Virginia Press, 2003), 103-104.

2. Henry Melchior Muhlenberg, "December 26-27, 1777, entry," *The Journals of Henry Melchior Muhlenberg*, Vol. 3, 116.

3. Henry Melchior Muhlenberg, "February 15, 1778, entry," *The Journals of Henry Melchior Muhlenberg*, Vol. 3, 131.
4. Ibid.
5. "General Orders, March 6, 1778," *Valley Forge Orderly Book of General George Weedon* (New York: New York Times and Arno Press, 1917), 250.
6. Henry Melchior Muhlenberg, "February 19, 1778, entry," *The Journals of Henry Melchior Muhlenberg*, Vol. 3, 132.
7. Lesser, ed., "Return of the Continental Army, January 3, 1778," *The Sinews of Independence: Monthly Strength Reports of the Continental Army*, 58.
8. Lesser, ed., "Return of the Continental Army, February 29, 1778," *The Sinews of Independence: Monthly Strength Reports of the Continental Army*, 59.
9. Ibid.
10. Ibid.
11. Lesser, ed., "Return of the Continental Army, March 30 and May 2, 1778," *The Sinews of Independence: Monthly Strength Reports of the Continental Army*, 60, 65.
12. Ford, ed., "November 12, 1777," *Journal of the Continental Congress*, Vol. 9 (Washington, DC: Government Printing Office, 1907), 896.
13. Grizzard Jr., and Hoth, eds., "General Washington to Henry Laurens, 22 December, 1777," *The Papers of George Washington*, Vol. 12, 668.
14. Ibid.
15. Harry M. Ward, *Duty, Honor or Country: General George Weedon and the American Revolution* (Philadelphia: American Philosophical Society, 1979), 124.
16. Joseph Lee Boyle, ed., "Peter Muhlenberg to the Committee of Congress at Camp, March 7, 1778," *Writings from the Valley Forge Encampment of the Continental Army, December 19, 1777-June 19, 1778* (Bowie: Heritage Books, 2002), 80-81.
17. Ford, ed., "Congressional Resolution, March 19, 1778," *Journal of the Continental Congress*, Vol 10. (Washington, DC: Government Printing Office, 1908), 269.
18. Lengel, ed., "General Muhlenberg to General Washington, April 10, 1778," *The Papers of George Washington, Revolutionary War Series*, Vol. 14, 466.
19. Ibid.
20. Ibid.
21. Lengel, ed., "General Muhlenberg to General Washington, April 10, 1778," *The Papers of George Washington, Revolutionary War Series*, Vol. 14, 466.
22. Lengel, ed., "General Washington to General Muhlenberg, April 10, 1778," *The Papers of George Washington, Revolutionary War Series*, Vol. 14, 467.
23. Ibid.
24. Lengel, ed., "General Washington to Henry Laurens, April 18, 1778," *The Papers of George Washington, Revolutionary War Series*, Vol. 14, 546.
25. Edward G. Lengel, ed., "General Washington to Gouverneur Morris, May 29, 1778," *The Papers of George Washington, Revolutionary War Series*, Vol. 15 (Charlottesville: University of Virginia Press, 2006), 260-261.
26. Lengel, ed., "General Orders, March 22, 1778," *The Papers of George Washington, Revolutionary War Series*, Vol. 14, 265.

27. Lengel, ed., "General Orders, May 7, 1778," *The Papers of George Washington, Revolutionary War Series*, Vol. 15, 68-69.

28. Lesser, ed., "Return of the Continental Army, July 4, 1778," *The Sinews of Independence: Monthly Strength Reports of the Continental Army*, 72.

29. Lengel, ed., "General Orders, May 31, 1778," *The Papers of George Washington, Revolutionary War Series*, Vol. 15, 280.

30. Lengel, ed., "War Council, June 17, 1778," *The Papers of George Washington*, Vol. 15, 415.

31. Lengel, ed., "General Muhlenberg to General Washington, June 18, 1778," *The Papers of George Washington*, Vol. 15, 460-461.

32. Lengel, ed., "War Council, June 17, 1778," *The Papers of George Washington*, Vol. 15, 415; and "General Washington to Henry Laurens, June 18, 1778," *The Papers of George Washington*, Vol. 15, 449. Note: General Charles Lee had been captured in late December 1776 by the British and had spent the last sixteen months on parole in New York City under British supervision. He was allowed to return to active duty upon his exchange for General Richard Prescott, a British general captured by the Americans in Rhode Island in the summer of 1777.

33. Lengel, ed., "General Orders, June 22, 1778," *The Papers of George Washington*, Vol. 15, 493.

34. Ibid.

35. Ibid.

36. Lengel, ed., "War Council, June 24, 1778," *The Papers of George Washington*, Vol. 15, 520-521.

37. Lengel, ed., "General Lafayette to General Washington, June 24, 1778," *The Papers of George Washington*, Vol. 15, 528.

38. Lengel, ed., "War Council, June 24, 1778," *The Papers of George Washington*, Vol. 15, 521; and "General Washington to General Scott, June 24, 1778," *The Papers of George Washington*, Vol. 15, 534.

39. Lengel, ed., "General Orders, June 25, 1778," *The Papers of George Washington*, Vol. 15, 536.

40. Lengel, ed., "General Washington to General Lee, June 26, 1778," *The Papers of George Washington*, Vol. 15, 556.

41. Mark Edward Lender and Garry Wheeler Stone, *Fatal Sunday: George Washington, the Monmouth Campaign, and the Politics of Battle* (Norman: University of Oklahoma Press, 2016), 284.

42. David R. Hoth, ed., "General Washington to Henry Laurens, July 1, 1778," *The Papers of George Washington*, Vol, 16. (Charlottesville: University Press of Virginia, 2006), 4.

43. Lengel, ed., "General Orders, June 29, 1778," *The Papers of George Washington*, Vol. 15, 583.

44. Hoth, ed., "General Orders, July 22, 1778," *The Papers of George Washington*, Vol. 16, 121.

45. Lesser, ed., "Return of the Continental Army, August 1, 1778," *The Sinews of Independence: Monthly Strength Reports of the Continental Army*, 76.

46. Lengel, ed., "General Washington to Timothy Pickering, May 23, 1778, and "General Washington to Lieutenant Colonel Robert Ballard, June 18, 1778," *The Papers of George Washington*, Vol. 15, 204 and 432.

47. Hoth, ed., "General Orders, September 7, 1778," *The Papers of George Washington*, Vol. 16, 534.

48. Philander D. Chase, ed., "General Washington to Henry Laurens, September 23, 1778," *The Papers of George Washington*, Vol. 17 (Charlottesville: University Press of Virginia, 2008), 93.

49. Todd W. Braisted, *Grand Forage, 1778: The Battleground Around New York City* (Yardley, PA: Westholme Publishing, 2016), 115.

50. Chase, ed., "General Washington to General Israel Putnam, September 29, 1778," *The Papers of George Washington*, Vol. 17, 190-191.

51. Chase, ed., "Council of War, October 16, 1778," *The Papers of George Washington*, Vol. 17, 399-340.

52. Chase, ed., "Circular to Seven General Officers, October 14, 1778," *The Papers of George Washington*, Vol. 17, 373.

53. Chase, ed., "Council of War, October 16, 1778," *The Papers of George Washington*, Vol. 17, 399-340.

54. Chase, ed., "General Muhlenberg to General Washington, October 16, 1778," *The Papers of George Washington*, Vol. 17, 408-409.

55. Chase, ed., "General Muhlenberg to General Washington, October 22, 1778," *The Papers of George Washington*, Vol. 17, 527-528.

56. Muhlenberg, "Governor Patrick Henry to General Muhlenberg, September 6, 1778," *The Life of Major-General Peter Muhlenberg of the Revolutionary Army*, 359-360.

57. Ibid.

58. Ibid.

59. Ibid.

60. Chase, ed., "General Washington to General Muhlenberg, October 28, 1778," *The Papers of George Washington*, Vol. 17, 619.

61. Ibid.

62. Note: A November 7, 1778, journal entry in Henry Muhlenberg's journal reported that a short letter from Mr. Swaine (who had recently seen Hanna Muhlenberg in Virginia) noted that she "is nearing the time of her confinement and is quite alone. Without a maid, she is in a deplorable situation." Mother and child appear to have come through fine, for another journal entry for March 1, 1779, noted that Hanna and "her sons are well." Source: Henry Melchior Muhlenberg, "November 7, 1778, and March 1, 1779, entries," *The Journals of Henry Melchior Muhlenberg*, Vol. 3, 193, 219.

63. Edward G. Lengel, ed., "General Washington to General Muhlenberg, November 20, 1777" and "General Washington to Colonel David Henley, November 27, 1778," *The Papers of George Washington, Revolutionary War Series*, Vol. 18 (Charlottesville, University Press of Virginia, 2008), 235 and 309.

64. Lengel, ed., "Circular to the Virginia Brigadier Generals, December 14, 1778," *The Papers of George Washington, Revolutionary War Series*, Vol. 18, 408.

65. Lesser, ed., "Monthly Return of the Continental Troops under Washington. . . for the Month of December 1778," *The Sinews of Independence*, 96.

66. Philander D. Chase and William M. Ferraro, eds., "General Washington to General Muhlenberg, February 17, 1779," *The Papers of George Washington, Revolutionary War Series,* Vol. 19 (Charlottesville: University Press of Virginia, 2009), 223.

67. Edward G. Lengel, ed., "General Orders, May 12, 1779," *The Papers of George Washington*, Vol. 20. (Charlottesville: University Press of Virginia, 2010), 444-445.

68. Lesser, ed., "Monthly Return of the Continental Troops under Washington . . . for the Month of June 1779," *The Sinews of Independence*, 120.

69. Lesser, ed., "Monthly Return of the Continental Troops under Washington . . . for the Month of June 1779," *The Sinews of Independence*, 120.

70. Lengel, ed., "Circular to General Officers, May 28, 1779," *The Papers of George Washington*, Vol. 20, 651-652.

71. Ferraro, ed., "General Orders, June 12, 1779," *The Papers of George Washington*, Vol. 21, 93.

72. Ferraro, ed., "General Wayne to General Washington, July 17, 1779," *The Papers of George Washington*, Vol. 21, 541-543.

73. John W. Hartmann, *The American Partisan: Henry Lee and the Struggle for Independence: 1776-1780.* (Shippensburg, PA: Burd St. Press, 2000), 106-107.

74. Ibid., 107.

75. Frank Moore, ed., "Extract of a letter from an officer at Paramus," *Diary of the American Revolution*, Vol. 2, 207.

76. William B. Reed, "Henry Lee to President Reed, August 27, 1779," *Life and Correspondence of Joseph Reed*, Vol. 2 (Philadelphia: Lindsay and Blakiston, 1847), 126-27.

77. Hartmann, 114-115.

78. Reed, "Levin Handy to George Handy, July 22, 1779," *Life and Correspondence of Joseph Reed*, Vol. 2, 126.

79. Ibid.

80. John C. Fitzgerald, ed., "General Orders, August 22, 1779," *The Writings of George Washington*, Vol. 16. (Washington, DC: U.S Government Printing Office, 1937), 149.

81. Reed, "Henry Lee to President Reed, August 27, 1779," *Life and Correspondence of Joseph Reed*, Vol. 2, 126.

82. Ibid.

83. Ibid., 127.

84. Fitzgerald, ed., "General Orders, September 11, 1779," *The Writings of George Washington*, Vol. 16, 262-265.

85. Fitzgerald, ed., "General Washington to Major Henry Lee, September 1, 1779," *The Writings of George Washington*, Vol. 16, 217-218.

86. Hartmann, 123.

87. Fitzgerald, ed., "General Orders, September 11, 1779," *The Writings of George Washington*, Vol. 16, 262-265.

88. William M. Ferraro, ed., "General Washington to Benjamin Harrison, October 25, 1779," *The Papers of George Washington*, Vol. 23 (Charlottesville: University Press of Virginia, 2015), 33-34.

89. Ferraro, ed., "General Washington to Benjamin Harrison, October 25, 1779," *The Papers of George Washington*, Vol. 23, 34.

90. Ferraro, ed., "General Wayne to General Washington, November 4, 1779," *The Papers of George Washington*, Vol. 23, 154.

91. Ferraro, ed., "Samuel Huntington to General Washington, November 11, 1779," *The Papers of George Washington*, Vol. 23, 243.

92. Ferraro, ed., "General Washington Samuel Huntington, November 20, 1779," *The Papers of George Washington*, Vol. 23, 377.

93. Ferraro, ed., "General Washington to Samuel Huntington, November 29, 1779," *The Papers of George Washington*, Vol. 23, 482.

94. Ferraro, ed., "General Washington to General Woodford, December 8, 1779," *The Papers of George Washington*, Vol. 23, 559.

CHAPTER SEVEN: BENEDICT ARNOLD'S INVASION OF VIRGINIA

1. William M. Ferraro, ed., "General Washington to General Muhlenberg, December 14, 1779," *The Papers of George Washington,* Vol. 23 (Charlottesville: University Press of Virginia, 2015), 613.

2. Ferraro, ed., "General Muhlenberg to Virginia Delegates to Congress, undated," in Footnote 2, *The Papers of George Washington*, Vol. 23, 613.

3. Worthington C. Ford, ed., *Journals of the Continental Congress*, Vol. 15 (Washington, DC: Government Printing Office, 1909), 1418-1419.

4. Ibid.

5. Paul H. Smith, ed., "Samuel Huntington to General Muhlenberg, January 8, 1780," *Letters of Delegates of the Continental Congress*, Vol. 14 (Washington, DC: Library of Congress, 1987), 327.

6. Muhlenberg, *The Life of Major-General Peter Muhlenberg of the Revolutionary Army*, 181.

7. Ibid., 184.

8. Muhlenberg, "General Muhlenberg to the Board of War, April 15, 1780," *The Life of Major-General Peter Muhlenberg of the Revolutionary Army*, 187.

9. Fitzpatrick, ed., "General Washington to Major General Gates or Brigadier General Muhlenberg, July 18, 1780," *The Writings of George Washington*, Vol. 19, 196-197.

10. William W. Henings, ed., *Hening's Virginia Statutes at Large . . .* , Vol. 10. (Richmond, 1822), 257-258.

11. Muhlenberg, *The Life of Major-General Peter Muhlenberg of the Revolutionary Army*, 197.

12. Muhlenberg, ed., "General Muhlenberg to General Washington, Aug ??, 1780," *The Life of Major-General Peter Muhlenberg of the Revolutionary Army*, 200.

13. Muhlenberg, *The Life of Major-General Peter Muhlenberg of the Revolutionary Army*, 198.

14. Muhlenberg, "General Muhlenberg to General Washington, August 26,

1780," *The Life of Major-General Peter Muhlenberg of the Revolutionary Army*, 201.

15. Boyd, ed., "Governor Jefferson to General Gates, September 3, 1780," *The Papers of Thomas Jefferson*, Vol. 3, 588.

16. Muhlenberg, "General Gates to General Muhlenberg, October 12, 1780," *The Life of Major-General Peter Muhlenberg of the Revolutionary Army*, 204.

17. Muhlenberg, "General Muhlenberg to General Gates, October 12, 1780," *The Life of Major-General Peter Muhlenberg of the Revolutionary Army*, 376.

18. Ibid.

19. Davies, ed., "General Leslie to Lord George Germain, November 27, 1780," *Documents of the American Revolution*, Vol. 18, 235.

20. Boyd, ed., "Steps to be Taken to Repel General Leslie's Army, October 22, 1780," *The Papers of Thomas Jefferson*, Vol. 4, 61; and "Governor Jefferson to General Weedon, November 2, 1780," 91.

21. Muhlenberg, "General Muhlenberg to General Gates, November 7, 1780," *The Life of Major-General Peter Muhlenberg of the Revolutionary Army*, 208.

22. Ibid.

23. Boyd, ed., "Governor Jefferson to General Edward Stevens, November 10, 1780," *The Papers of Thomas Jefferson*, Vol. 4, 111.

24. Dennis Conrad, ed., "General Steuben to General Greene, December 4, 1780," *The Papers of General Nathanael Greene*, Vol. 6. (Chapel Hill: University of North Carolina Press, 1991), 525.

25. Conrad, ed., "General Steuben to General Greene, December 15, 1780," *The Papers of General Nathanael Greene*, Vol. 6, 584.

26. Muhlenberg, "General Muhlenberg to the Board of War, December 20, 1780," *The Life of Major-General Peter Muhlenberg of the Revolutionary Army*, 213-215.

27. Ibid.

28. Ibid.

29. Boyd, ed., "Governor Jefferson to Steuben, December 31, 1781," *The Papers of Thomas Jefferson*, Vol. 4, 254.

30. Boyd, ed., "Governor Jefferson to Steuben, January 2, 1781," *The Papers of Thomas Jefferson*, Vol. 4, 298.

31. William B. Wilcox, ed., *The American Rebellion: Sir Henry Clinton's Narrative of His Campaign* (New Haven: Yale University Press, 1954), 235; and K.G. Davies, ed., "General Henry Clinton to General Arnold, December 14, 1780," *Documents of the American Revolution*, Vol. 18 (Shannon: Irish University Press, 1979), 256.

32. Boyd, ed., "Governor Jefferson to Thomas Nelson, January 2, 1781," *The Papers of Thomas Jefferson*, Vol. 4, 297.

33. Muhlenberg, "General Muhlenberg to General Steuben, January 12, 1781," *The Life of Major-General Peter Muhlenberg of the Revolutionary Army*, 222.

34. Muhlenberg, "General Steuben to General Muhlenberg, January 2, 1781," *The Life of Major-General Peter Muhlenberg of the Revolutionary Army*, 221.

35. Muhlenberg, "General Muhlenberg to General Steuben, January 12, 1781," *The Life of Major-General Peter Muhlenberg of the Revolutionary Army*, 222.

36. Muhlenberg, *The Life of Major-General Peter Muhlenberg of the Revolutionary Army*, 223
37. Ibid., 224.
38. Muhlenberg, "General Muhlenberg to General Steuben, January 31," *The Life of Major-General Peter Muhlenberg of the Revolutionary Army*, 381.
39. Ibid.
40. Boyd, ed., "General Lawson to Thomas Jefferson, January 28, 1781," *The Papers of Thomas Jefferson*, Vol. 4, 459-462.
41. Muhlenberg, "General Muhlenberg to General Steuben, January 31," *The Life of Major-General Peter Muhlenberg of the Revolutionary Army*, 381.
42. Boyd, ed., "Governor Jefferson to J.P.G. Muhlenberg, January 31, 1781," *The Papers of Thomas Jefferson*, Vol. 4, 487.
43. Ibid.
44. Ibid.
45. Ibid.
46. Ibid.
47. Ewald, 277.
48. Ibid.
49. Ibid.
50. Ibid.
51. Muhlenberg, "General Muhlenberg to General Steuben, February 18," *The Life of Major-General Peter Muhlenberg of the Revolutionary Army*, 384-385.
52. Ibid.
53. Muhlenberg, "General Muhlenberg to General Steuben, February 18," *The Life of Major-General Peter Muhlenberg of the Revolutionary Army*, 384-385.
54. Robert Friar, *The Militia are Coming out from all Quarters: The Revolution in Virginia's Lower Counties*, (2010), 40.
Note: This is an account of the incident from a participant, William McLaurine, of the Powhatan County militia. The full account is found in the *Virginia Magazine of History and Biography*, Vol. 14, 198.
55. Muhlenberg, "General Isaac Gregory to General Muhlenberg, 23 February, 1781," *The Life of Major-General Peter Muhlenberg*, 386.
56. Muhlenberg, "General Muhlenberg to General Greene, 24 February, 1781," *The Life of Major-General Peter Muhlenberg*, 389-90.
57. Muhlenberg, "General Steuben to General Muhlenberg, February 28, 1781," *The Life of Major-General Peter Muhlenberg*, 391-392.
58. Muhlenberg, "General Muhlenberg to General Steuben, March 4, 1781," *The Life of Major-General Peter Muhlenberg*, 395.
59. Muhlenberg, "Colonel Parker to General Muhlenberg, 2 March, 1781," *The Life of Major-General Peter Muhlenberg*, 394.
60. Ibid.
61. Ibid., 393
62. Muhlenberg, "General Muhlenberg to General Steuben, March 4, 1781," *The Life of Major-General Peter Muhlenberg*, 396-397.
63. Muhlenberg, "General Muhlenberg to General Steuben, March 11, 1781," *The Life of Major-General Peter Muhlenberg*, 398-399.

64. Simcoe, 181.

65. Ibid.

66. Muhlenberg, "General Muhlenberg to General Steuben, March 11, 1781," *The Life of Major-General Peter Muhlenberg*, 398.

67. Muhlenberg, "General Muhlenberg to General Steuben, March 11, 1781," *The Life of Major-General Peter Muhlenberg*, 398.

68. Ewald, 288.

69. Ibid.

70. Ibid., 289.

71. Boyd, ed., "General Weedon to Governor Jefferson, 20 March, 1781," *The Papers of Thomas Jefferson*, Vol. 5, 185-86.

72. Boyd, ed., "James Barron to Governor Jefferson, 21 March, 1781," *The Papers of Thomas Jefferson*, Vol. 5, 187.

73. Boyd, ed., "Richard Barron to Governor Jefferson, 26 March, 1781," *The Papers of Thomas Jefferson*, Vol. 5, 238.

74. Idzerda, ed., "General Lafayette to General Washington, 26 March, 1781," *Lafayette in the Age of the American Revolution*, Vol. 3, 417.

CHAPTER EIGHT: DEFENDING THE OLD DOMINION

1. Muhlenberg, "General Muhlenberg to General Steuben, April 3, 1781," *The Life of Major-General Peter Muhlenberg of the Revolutionary Army*, 401.

2. Muhlenberg, "General Muhlenberg to General Steuben, April 8, 1781," *The Life of Major-General Peter Muhlenberg of the Revolutionary Army*, 244-245.

3. Muhlenberg, "General Muhlenberg to General Steuben, April 13, 1781," *The Life of Major-General Peter Muhlenberg of the Revolutionary Army*, 407.

4. Ibid.

5. Davies, ed., "General Arnold to General Clinton, May 12, 1781," *Documents of the American Revolution*, Vol. 20, 142.

6. Boyd, ed., "James Innes to Governor Jefferson, April 20, 1781," *The Papers of Thomas Jefferson*, Vol. 5, 506.

7. Simcoe, 191.

8. Boyd, ed. "Governor Jefferson to George Weedon, April 23, 1781," *The Papers of Thomas Jefferson,* Vol. 5, 546.

9. Boyd, ed., "John Christian Senf to Steuben, April 20, 1781," *The Papers of Thomas Jefferson*, Vol. 5, 511.

10. Boyd, ed., "General Steuben to General Greene, April 25, 1781," *The Papers of General Nathanael Greene*, Vol. 8 (Chapel Hill: University of North Carolina Press, 147.

11. Ibid.

12. Dennis Conrad, ed., "Steuben to Greene, April 25, 1781," *The Papers of General Nathanael Greene,* Vol. 8 (University of North Carolina Press, 1995), 147.

13. Robert Davis, *The Revolutionary War: The Battle of Petersburg.* E. & R. Davis, 2002, 10.

14. Davis, 11, and Boyd, ed., "Thomas Jefferson to J.P.G. Muhlenberg, April 16, 1781," *The Papers of Thomas Jefferson,* Vol. 5, 475.

15. Davis, 11.

16. Charles Campbell, ed., "Banister to Bland, May 16, 1781" *Bland Papers*, Vol. 2 (Petersburg, VA, 1840), 68.

17. Ibid.

18. Boyd, ed., "Statement of Arms and Men in Service, January 29, 1781," *The Papers of Thomas Jefferson*, Vol. 4, 472.

19. Conrad, ed., "Steuben to Greene, April 25, 1781," *The Papers of General Nathanael Greene*, Vol. 8, 148.

20. Davis, 12.

21. Campbell, ed., "Banister to Bland, May 16, 1781," *Bland Papers*, Vol. 2, 68.

22. Davis, 14.

23. Campbell, ed., "Banister to Bland, May 16, 1781," *Bland Papers*, Vol. 2, 68.

24. Davis, 16, 18.

25. Lillie DuPuy VanCulin Harper, ed., *Colonial Men and Times: Containing the Journal of Col. Daniel Trabue*, 90-91.

26. Davis, 20.

27. Ibid.

28. Lillie DuPuy VanCulin Harper, ed., *Colonial Men and Times: Containing the Journal of Col. Daniel Trabue*, 90-91.

29. Ibid., 90.

30. Muhlenberg, "General Muhlenberg to Frederick Muhlenberg, April 26, 1781," *The Life of Major-General Peter Muhlenberg of the Revolutionary Army*, 249-250.

31. Conrad, ed., "Baron Steuben to General Greene, April 25, 1781," *The Papers of General Nathanael Greene*, Vol. 8, 148.

32. Idzerda, ed., "General Lafayette to General Greene, April 28, 1781," *Lafayette in the Age of the American Revolution*, Vol. 4, 68.

33. Muhlenberg, *The Life of Major-General Peter Muhlenberg*, 250.

34. Boyd, ed., "Thomas Jefferson to General Washington, May 9, 1781," *The Papers of Thomas Jefferson*, Vol. 5, 623.

35. Banastre Tarleton, "General Benedict Arnold to General Henry Clinton, May 12, 1781," *A History of the Campaigns of 1780. and 1781 in the Southern Provinces of North America* (North Stratford, NH: Ayer Co., 1999), 335.

36. Conrad, ed., "Baron Steuben to General Greene, April 25, 1781," *The Papers of General Nathanael Greene*, Vol. 8, 148.

37. Muhlenberg, *The Life of Major-General Peter Muhlenberg*, 250.

38. Conrad, ed., "Steuben to Greene, April 25, 1781," *The Papers of General Nathanael Greene*, Vol. 8, 148.

39. Idzerda, ed., "General Lafayette to General Greene, April 28, 1781," *Lafayette in the Age of the American Revolution*, Vol. 4, 68.

40. Tarleton, "General Arnold to General Clinton, May 12, 1781," 335.

41. Ibid.

42. Ibid.

43. Idzerda, ed., "General Lafayette to General Weedon, May 3, 1781," *Lafayette in the Age of the American Revolution*, Vol. 4, 77.
44. Idzerda, ed., "General Lafayette to General Washington, May 4, 1781," *Lafayette in the Age of the American Revolution*, Vol. 4, 82.
45. Idzerda, ed., "General Lafayette to General Weedon May 3, 1781," *Lafayette in the Age of the American Revolution*, Vol. 4, 78.
46. Boyd, ed., "General Steuben to Governor Jefferson, May 4, 1781," *The Papers of Thomas Jefferson*, Vol. 5, 601.
47. Idzerda, ed., "General Lafayette to General Washington, May 8, 1781," *Lafayette in the Age of the American Revolution*, Vol. 4, 88.
48. Idzerda, ed., "General Lafayette to Jethro Sumner, May 7, 1781," *Lafayette in the Age of the American Revolution*, Vol. 4, 87.
49. Idzerda, ed., "General Lafayette to General Washington, May 8, 1781," *Lafayette in the Age of the American Revolution*, Vol. 4, 88.
50. Idzerda, ed., "General Lafayette to the Chevalier de La Luzerne, May 9, 1781," *Lafayette in the Age of the American Revolution*, Vol. 4, 89.
51. Idzerda, ed., "General Lafayette to General Sumner, May 7, 1781," *Lafayette in the Age of the American Revolution*, Vol. 4, 87; and "Note 5," 125.
52. Idzerda, ed., "General Lafayette to the Vicimte de Noailles, May 22, 1781," *Lafayette in the Age of the American Revolution*, Vol. 4, 123.
53. Idzerda, ed., "General Lafayette to General Steuben, May 10, 1781," *Lafayette in the Age of the American Revolution*, Vol. 4, 91.
54. Tarleton, 292.
55. Idzerda, ed., "General Lafayette to General Weedon, May 15, 1781," *Lafayette in the Age of the American Revolution*, Vol. 4, 104.
56. Idzerda, ed., "General Lafayette to General Greene, May 18, 1781," *Lafayette in the Age of the American Revolution*, Vol. 4, 113.
57. Charles Cornwallis, "State of the Troops that Marched with the Army under the Command of Lieutenant-General Earl Cornwallis, May 1, 1781," *An Answer to that Part of the Narrative of Lieutenant-General Henry Clinton. . .* , (New York: Research Reprints, Inc., 1970), 77.
58. Idzerda, ed., "General Lafayette to the Chevalier de La Luzerne, May 22, 1781," *Lafayette in the Age of the American Revolution*, Vol. 4, 120.
59. Cornwallis, "Earl Cornwallis to Sir Henry Clinton, May 26, 1781" *An Answer to that Part of the Narrative of Lieutenant-General Henry Clinton. . .* , 79.
60. Ibid., 80-81.
61. Idzerda, ed., "General Lafayette to Governor Jefferson, May 28, 1781," *Lafayette in the Age of the American Revolution*, Vol. 4, 136.
62. Ibid.
63. Idzerda, ed., "General Lafayette to Governor Jefferson, May 31, 1781," *Lafayette in the Age of the American Revolution*, Vol. 4, 148-149.
64. Tarleton, "Earl Cornwallis to Sir Henry Clinton, June 30, 1781," 348-49.
65. Michael Kranish, *Flight from Monticello: Thomas Jefferson at War* (New York: Oxford University Press, 2010), 292.

66. Idzerda, ed., "General Lafayette to General Washington, June 18,1781," *Lafayette in the Age of the American Revolution*, Vol. 4, 195; and John Mass, *The Road to Yorktown: Jefferson, Lafayette and the British Invasion of Virginia* (Charleston, SC: History Press, 2015), 114.

67. Idzerda, ed., "General Lafayette to Chevalier de La Luzerne, June 16, 1781," *Lafayette in the Age of the American Revolution*, Vol. 4, 187.

68. Ibid., 186.

69. Idzerda, ed., "General Lafayette to General Greene, June 20, 1781," *Lafayette in the Age of the American Revolution*, Vol. 4, 198.

70. Idzerda, ed., "General Lafayette to General Greene, June 21, 1781," *Lafayette in the Age of the American Revolution*, Vol. 4, 203-204.

71. Idzerda, ed., "General Lafayette to General Steuben, June 22, 1781," *Lafayette in the Age of the American Revolution*, Vol. 4, 206.

72. Idzerda, ed., "General Lafayette to General Wayne, June 22, 1781," *Lafayette in the Age of the American Revolution*, Vol. 4, 207.

73. Conrad, ed., "General Steuben to General Greene, June 19, 1781," *The Papers of General Nathanael Greene*, Vol. 8, 415-416. E. Lee Shepard, ed., "June 24, 1781 Diary Entry," *Marching to Victory: Capt. Benjamin Bartholomew's Diary of the Yorktown Campaign: May 1781 to March 1782* (Richmond, VA: Virginia Historical Society, 2002), 11; and Idzerda, ed., "General Lafayette to General Wayne, June 25, 1781," *Lafayette in the Age of the American Revolution*, Vol. 4, 212.

74. Shepard, ed., "June 24, 1781 Diary Entry," *Marching to Victory: Capt. Benjamin Bartolomew's Diary of the Yorktown Campaign: May 1781 to March 1782*, 11.

75. Idzerda, ed., "General Lafayette to General Greene, June 27, 1781," *Lafayette in the Age of the American Revolution*, Vol. 4, 216.

76. Earl Cornwallis, "General Cornwallis to General Clinton, June 30, 1781, *An Answer to that Part of the Narrative of Lieutenant-General Sir Henry Clinton, Which Relates to the Conduct of Lieutenant-General Earl Cornwallis During the Campaign in North America in the year 1781* (London, 1783), 120.

77. Jared Sparks, ed. "General Wayne to General Washington, 8 July, 1781," *Correspondence of the American Revolution Being Letters of Eminent Men to George Washington* (Boston: Little, Brown, 1853), 348.

78. Tarleton, "Earl Cornwallis to Sir Henry Clinton, July 8, 1781," 400.

79. *Caledonian Mercury*, 10 October, 1781, "Extract of a letter from an officer in the 76. regiment dated on board the Lord Mulgrave transport, Hampton Road, Virginia, July 23, 1781," 3.

80. Gillard Hunt, ed., "Colonel John Francis Mercer, *Eyewitness Accounts of the American Revolution: Fragments of Revolutionary History* (New York Times and Arno Press, reprint, 1971), 48.

81. Sparks, ed., "General Wayne to General Washington, 8 July, 1781," *Correspondence of the American Revolution Being Letters of Eminent Men to George Washington*, 348.

82. Peter Decher, ed., *Journal of Lt. William Feltman of the First Pennsylvania Regiment, 1781-1782* (Samen, NH: Ayer, 1969), 7.

83. Ebenezer Denny, *Military Journal of Major Ebenezer Denny* (Philadelphia: J.B. Lippincott, 1859), 37.

84. Tarleton, 354.

85. "Major William Galvan to Richard Peters, 8 July, 1781," *Gazette of the American Friends of Lafayette* Vol. 1, No. 1 (February, 1942), 4.

86. Ibid.

87. Sparks, ed. "General Wayne to General Washington, 8 July, 1781," *Correspondence of the American Revolution Being Letters of Eminent Men to George Washington*, 348.

88. Henry P. Johnson, *The Yorktown Campaign and the Surrender of Cornwallis: 1781* (Fort Washington, PA: Eastern National, 1997), 190.

CHAPTER NINE: THE FRENCH AND AMERICAN ALLIANCE

1. Tarleton, "General Cornwallis to Tarleton, July 8, 1781," 402.

2. Idzerda, ed., "General Lafayette to Allen Jones, July 10, 1781," *Lafayette in the Age of the American Revolution*, Vol. 4, 241.

3. Idzerda, ed., "General Lafayette to Thomas Nelson, July 13, 1781," *Lafayette in the Age of the American Revolution*, Vol. 4, 244.

4. Ibid.

5. Idzerda, ed., "General Lafayette to General Wayne, July 15, 1781," *Lafayette in the Age of the American Revolution*, Vol. 4, 248.

6. Idzerda, ed., "General Lafayette to General Washington, July 20, 1781," *Lafayette in the Age of the American Revolution*, Vol. 4, 255-256.

7. Ibid.

8. Idzerda, ed., "General Lafayette to General Wayne, July 29, 1781," *Lafayette in the Age of the American Revolution*, Vol. 4, footnote 3, 292.

9. Idzerda, ed., "General Lafayette to General Wayne, August 4, 1781," *Lafayette in the Age of the American Revolution*, Vol. 4, 294.

10. Ibid.

11. Idzerda, ed., "General Lafayette to General Washington, August 11, 1781," *Lafayette in the Age of the American Revolution*, Vol. 4, 312.

12. Ibid.

13. John C. Fitzpatrick, ed. "August 14, 1781," *The Diaries of George Washington*, Vol. 2 (Boston: Houghton Mifflin, 1925), 254.

14. Idzerda, ed., "General Washington to General Lafayette, August 15, 1781," *Lafayette in the Age of the American Revolution*, Vol. 4, 330.

15. Idzerda, ed., "General Lafayette to General Washington, August 21, 1781," *Lafayette in the Age of the American Revolution*, Vol. 4, 338.

16. Ibid.

17. Fitzpatrick, ed. "General Washington to Comte de Grasse, August 17, 1781," *The Writings of George Washington*, Vol. 23, 10-11.

18. John D. Grainger, *The Battle of Yorktown, 1781: A Reassessment*, 63.

19. Idzerda, ed., "General Lafayette to General Greene, August 25, 1781," *Lafayette in the Age of the American Revolution*, Vol. 4, 352-353.

20. Idzerda, ed., "General Lafayette to General Washington, August 25, 1781," *Lafayette in the Age of the American Revolution*, Vol. 4, 360.

21. Idzerda, ed., "General Lafayette to Thomas Nelson, August 26, 1781," *Lafayette in the Age of the American Revolution*, Vol. 4, 361.
22. Idzerda, ed., "General Lafayette to Thomas Nelson, August 29, 1781," *Lafayette in the Age of the American Revolution*, Vol. 4, 365.
23. Ibid.
24. William P. Palmer, ed., "Col. Benj. Blunt to Col. Davies, September 9, 1781," and Col. Benj. Blunt to Brig. Genl. Muhlenberg, September 11, 1781," *Calendar of Virginia State Papers*, Vol. 2 (Richmond, 1881), 407, 413.
25. Idzerda, ed., "General Wayne to General Lafayette, August 31, 1781," *Lafayette in the Age of the American Revolution*, Vol. 4, 380.
26. E. Lee Shepard, ed., "September 4, 1781, Journal Entry," *Marching to Victory: Capt. Benjamin Bartholomew's Diary of the Yorktown Campaign, May 1781 to March 1782* (Richmond: Virginia Historical Society, 2002), 20-21; and Palmer, ed., "Capt. John Pryer to Hon. Wm. Davies, September 5, 1781," *Calendar of Virginia State Papers*, Vol. 2, 390.
27. Shepard, ed., "September 6, 1781, Journal Entry," *Marching to Victory: Capt. Benjamin Bartholomew's Diary of the Yorktown Campaign, May 1781 to March 1782*, 21; and Decher, ed., "September 8, 1781," *Journal of Lieut. Wm. Feltman, 1781-82* (Philadelphia: Historical Society of Pennsylvania, 1853), 13.
28. Idzerda, ed., "General Lafayette to General Washington, September 8, 1781," *Lafayette in the Age of the American Revolution*, Vol. 4, 392.
29. Decher, ed., "September 7, 1781," *Journal of Lieut. Wm. Feltman, 1781-82*, 13.
30. Edward M. Riley, ed., "St. George Tucker's Journal of the Siege of Yorktown," *William and Mary Quarterly*, 3 Series, Vol. 5, No. 3 (July 1948), 377.
31. Shepard, ed., "September 14, 1781, Journal Entry," *Marching to Victory: Capt. Benjamin Bartholomew's Diary of the Yorktown Campaign, May 1781 to March 1782*, 22
32. Ebenezer Denny, "September 15, 1781," *Military Journal of Major Ebenezer Denny* (Philadelphia: J.B. Lippincott, 1859), 39.
33. Riley, ed., "St. George Tucker's Journal of the Siege of Yorktown," *William and Mary Quarterly,* 3 Series, Vol. 5, No. 3, 379.
34. "General Muhlenberg to General Washington, September 23, 1781," *Founders Online, National Archives.*
35. Tarleton, 370-371.
36. Fitzpatrick, ed. "General Orders, September 24, 1781," *The Writings of George Washington*, Vol. 23, 134-135.
37. Lesser, ed., "Return of the Continental and Virginia State Troops . . . Sept. 26, 1781," *The Sinews of Independence, Monthly Strength Reports of the Continental Army*, 208; and Fitzpatrick, ed., "General Orders, September 26, 1781," *The Writings of George Washington*, Vol. 23, 140.
38. Fitzpatrick, ed., "General Orders, September 27, 1781," *The Writings of George Washington*, Vol. 23, 146-147.
39. Ibid., 148.
40. Ibid., 147

CHAPTER TEN: THE SIEGE OF YORKTOWN

1. Jerome A. Greene, *The Guns of Independence: The Siege of Yorktown, 1781* (El Dorado Hills, CA: Savas Beatie, 2005), 90-91.

2. Greene, *The Guns of Independence: The Siege of Yorktown, 1781*, 92.

3. Riley, ed., "St. George Tucker's Journal of the Siege of Yorktown," *William and Mary Quarterly*, 3 Series, Vol. 5, No. 3, 380.

4. Ibid.

5. Greene, *The Guns of Independence: The Siege of Yorktown, 1781*, 96-97.

6. Ibid., 97.

7. Fitzpatrick, ed., "General Orders, September 30, 1781," *The Writings of George Washington*, Vol. 23, 153.

8. Wilcox, ed., "Extract of minutes of a council of war held at New York, September 24, 1781," *The American Crisis*, 574.

9. Greene, *The Guns of Independence: The Siege of Yorktown, 1781*, 117.

10. Fitzpatrick, ed., "General Orders, October 1-3, 7, 10, 13, 16, 1781," *The Writings of George Washington*, Vol. 23, 167, 168, 170, 197, 202, 216, 223.

11. Fitzpatrick, ed., "General Washington to Edward Rutledge, October 6, 1781," *The Writings of George Washington*, Vol. 23, 186.

12. Greene, *The Guns of Independence: The Siege of Yorktown, 1781*, 160.

13. Henry S. Commager and Richard B. Morris, "Journal of Colonel Richard Butler, 6. October, 1781," *The Spirit of Seventy-Six* (Edison, NJ: Castle Books, 2002), 1229.

14. Joseph Plum Martin, *Private Yankee Doodle* (Harrisburg, PA: Eastern Acorn Press, 1962), 232.

15. James Thacher, *Military Journal of the American Revolution*, 281-282.

16. Fitzpatrick, ed., "General Orders, October 7, 1781," *The Writings of George Washington*, Vol. 23, 197.

17. Greene, *The Guns of Independence: The Siege of Yorktown, 1781*, 190.

18. Ewald, 334; Greene, *The Guns of Independence*, 190.

19. John E. Selby, *The Revolution in Virginia: 1775-1783* (Williamsburg, VA: Colonial Williamsburg Foundation, 1988), 306.

20. Egle, ed., "Diary of Captain James Duncan . . ." *Pennsylvania Archives*, 2 Series, Vol. 15, 751.

21. Ewald, 334.

22. Nell Moore Lee, *Patriot Above Profit: A Portrait of Thomas Nelson Jr., Who Supported the American Revolution With His Purse and Sword* (Nashville, TN: Rutledge Hill Press, 1988), 471.

23. John K. Laughton, ed., *The Journal of Rear-Admiral Bartholomew James* (1896), 122.

24. Fitzpatrick, ed., "General Washington to Governor Thomas Sims Lee, October 12, 1781," *The Writings of George Washington*, Vol. 23, 210.

25. Edward M. Riley, ed., "St. George Tucker's Journal of the Siege of Yorktown, 1781, *William and Mary Quarterly*, Vol. 5, No. 3 (July 1948), October 10, 1781 entry, 386.

26. Wilcox, ed., "Copy of a letter from Earl Cornwallis to Sir Henry Clinton, October 11, 1781," *The American Crisis*, 581.

27. Ibid.

28. Fitzpatrick, ed., "General Washington to the President of Congress, October 12, 1781," *The Writings of George Washington,* Vol. 23, 213.

29. Decher, ed., *Journal of Lt. William Feltman of the First Pennsylvania Regiment, 1781-1782,* 19.

30. Ibid.

31. Lillie DuPuy VanCulin Harper, ed., *Colonial Men and Times: Containing the Journal of Col. Daniel Trabue,* 112.

32. Ibid.

33. Ibid.

34. Thacher, 283-284.

35. Howard Rice and Anne Brown, "Clermont, Crevecoeur Journal," *The American Campaigns of Rochambeau's Army,* Vol. 1 (Princeton, NJ: Princeton University Press, 1972), 59.

36. John K. Laughton, ed., *The Journal of Rear-Admiral Bartholomew James* (1896), 124.

37. Ibid.

38. "Return of Killed and Wounded . . ." *Pennsylvania Gazette and Weekly Advertiser,* No. 2681, October 31, 1781, 2.

39. Thacher, 284.

40. Greene, *The Guns of Independence: The Siege of Yorktown, 1781,* 237.

41. Ibid., 238.

42. Ibid., 241.

43. Nell Moore Lee, 476.

44. Ibid.

45. Mrs. Williams, ed., "Life of Captain Stephen Olney of Rhode Island," *Biography of Revolutionary Heroes,* (1839), 276.

46. Ibid.

47. Martin, 235-236.

48. Mrs. Williams, ed., "Life of Captain Stephen Olney of Rhode Island," *Biography of Revolutionary Heroes,* 276

49. Ibid., 277.

50. Ibid.

51. Ibid., 276.

52. Greene, 251; and "Return of Killed and Wounded . . . " *Pennsylvania Gazette and Weekly Advertiser,* No. 2681, October 31, 1781, 2.

53. Greene, 251.

54. Ibid., 252.

55. Decher, ed., *Journal of Lt. William Feltman of the First Pennsylvania Regiment, 1781-1782,* 20

56. Tarleton, 386.

57. Fitzpatrick, ed., "General Orders, October 16, 1781," *The Writings of George Washington,* Vol. 23, 223.

58. Thacher, 286.

59. Ewald, 336.

60. Wilcox, ed., "Extract of a letter from Earl Cornwallis to Sir Henry Clinton, October 20, 1781," *The American Crisis,* 585-586.

61. Ibid.

62. Greene, 308.

63. Ibid., 307.

64. Ibid.

65. Greene, 307.

66. "General Muhlenberg to General Washington, October 23, 1781," *The Washington Papers*, Founders Online: National Archives.

67. Ibid.

68. Ibid.

EPILOGUE

1. Muhlenberg, 278.

2. John C. Fitzpatrick, ed., "General Washington to General Muhlenberg, March 12, 1782," *The Writings of George Washington,* Vol. 24 (Washington, DC: US Government Printing Office, 1938), 60-61.

3. Muhlenberg, 279.

4. Ibid., 286-287.

5. Ford, ed., "September 30, 1783," *Journals of the Continental Congress*, Vol. 25, 633.

6. Ibid.

7. Muhlenberg, 290.

8. Ibid.

9. Ibid.

10. Ibid., 292.

11. Ibid., 311-312.

12. Ibid., 314.

13. Ibid., 315.

14. "Mortuary Notice, October 14, 1807," *The Enquirer*, Richmond, VA.

15. "October 7, 1807," *The Tickler*, Philadelphia, Pennsylvania.

16. Muhlenberg, 333.

BIBLIOGRAPHY

PRIMARY SOURCES

Boyd, Julian P., ed. *The Papers of Thomas Jefferson,* Vol. 3-6. Princeton, NJ: Princeton University Press, 1951-1952.

Boyle, Joseph Lee. *Writings from the Valley Forge Encampment of the Continental Army,* Vol. 1-5. Bowie: Heritage Books, 2000-05.

Campbell, Charles, ed. *The Bland Papers*, Vol. 1-2. Petersburg, VA: E. & J.C. Ruffin, 1840-1843.

Clark, William B. *Naval Documents of the American Revolution*, Vol. 4. Washington, DC, 1969.

Commager, Henry S. and Richard B. Morris. *The Spirit of Seventy-Six,* Edison, NJ: Castle Books, 2002.

Cornwallis, Earl Charles. *An Answer to that Part of the Narrative of Lieutenant-General Sir Henry Clinton, Which Relates to the Conduct of Lieutenant-General Earl Cornwallis During the Campaign in North America in the year 1781.* London, 1783.

Davis, K.G., ed. *Documents of the American Revolution*, Vol. 20. Shannon: Irish University Press, 1979.

Decher, Peter, ed. *Journal of Lt. William Feltman of the First Pennsylvania Regiment, 1781- 1782,* Samen, NH: Ayer Co, 1969.

Egle, William H. ed., "Diary of Captain James Duncan . . ." *Pennsylvania Archives*, 2 Series, Vol. 15, 1893.

Ewald, Johann. *Diary of the American War: A Hessian Journal.* New Haven & London: Yale University Press, 1979. Translated and edited by Joseph P. Tustin.

Force, Peter, ed. *American Archives, Fourth Series,* Vol. 4. Washington, DC, US Congress, 1848-1853.

Ford, Worthington C. ed. *Journals of the Continental Congress: 1774-1789*, Vol. 9-10, 15, 25. Washington, DC: Government Printing Office, 1907-1909.

Galvan, Maj. William. "Major William Galvan to Richard Peters, 8 July, 1781," *Gazette of the American Friends of LaFayette*, Vol. 1, No. 1. February, 1942.

Germann, Rev. William. "The Crisis in the Early Life of General Peter Muhlenberg," *Pennsylvania Magazine of History and Biography*, Vol. 37. 1913.

Gilreath, Amelia C., ed. *Order Book, 1772-1774: Shenandoah County, Virginia*, 1986.

Greene, Jerome A. *The Guns of Independence: the Siege of Yorktown, 1781*. El Dorado Hills, CA: Savas Beatie, 2005.

Greene, Nathanael. *The Papers of General Nathanael Greene*, Vol. 1-9. Chapel Hill: University of North Carolina Press, 1976-1997

Hamilton, Stanislaus M. ed. *Letters to Washington & Accompanying Papers*, Vol. 5. Boston & New York: Houghton Mifflin, 1902.

Hammond, Otis G., ed. *Letters and Papers of Major-General John Sullivan, Continental Army*, Vol. 1. Collections of the New Hampshire Historical Society, 1930.

Hening, William W., ed. *The Statutes at Large Being a Collection of all the Laws of Virginia*, Vol. 9. Richmond: J. & G. Cochran, 1821.

Hunt, Gillard, ed. *Eyewitness Accounts of the American Revolution: Fragments of Revolutionary History*. New York: NY Times & Arno Press, Reprint, 1971.

Idzerda, Stanley J., ed. *LaFayette in the Age of the American Revolution: Selected Letters and Papers*, Vol. 3-4. Ithaca, NY: Cornell University Press, 1980-1981.

Laughton, John K., ed., *The Journal of Rear-Admiral Bartholomew James*. 1896.

Lee, Henry. *Lee Papers*, Vol. 1-2. Collections of the New York Historical Society, 1871, 1873.

Lesser, Charles H., ed. *The Sinews of Independence, Monthly Strength Reports of the Continental Army*. Chicago: University of Chicago Press, 1976.

Martin, Joseph Plum. *Private Yankee Doodle*. Harrisburg, PA: Eastern Acorn Press, 1962.

McMichael, William P. "Diary of Lieutenant James McMichael, of the Pennsylvania Line, 1776-1778," *Pennsylvania Magazine of History and Biography,* Vol. 16, No. 2. 1892.

Moore, Frank, ed. "Extract of a letter from an officer at Paramus," *Diary of the American Revolution*, Vol. 2.

Morgan, William J., ed. *Naval Documents of the American Revolution*, Vol. 5. Washington, DC: 1970.

Muhlenberg, Henry Melchior. *The Journals of Henry Melchior Muhlenberg*, Vol. 3. Translated by Theodore G. Tappert and John W. Doberstein. Philadelphia: Muhlenberg Press, 1958.

"Orderly Book of Gen. John Peter Gabriel Muhlenberg, March 26-December 20, 1777," *Pennsylvania Magazine of History and Biography,* Vol. 34. 1911.

"General Muhlenberg to General Washington, September 23, 1781," *Founders Online, National Archives.*

"General Muhlenberg to General Washington, October 23, 1781," *The Washington Papers.* Founders Online: National Archives.

Palmer, William P., ed. *Calendar of Virginia State Papers*, Vol. 2. Richmond, 1881.

Reed, William B. Reed. *Life and Correspondence of Joseph Reed*, Vol. 2. Philadelphia: Lindsay and Blakiston, 1847.

Rice, Howard and Anne Brown. "Clermont, Crevecoeur Journal," *The American Campaigns of Rochambeau's Army,* Vol. 1. Princeton, NJ: Princeton University Press, 1972.

Riley, Edward M., ed. "St. George Tucker's Journal of the Siege of Yorktown, 1781," *William and Mary Quarterly*, Vol. 5, No. 3. July 1948.

Schreeven, William Van, and Robert L. Scribner, eds. *Revolutionary Virginia: The Road to Independence,* Vol. 1-2. Charlottesville: University Press of Virginia, 1973-75

Scribner, Robert L, ed. *Revolutionary Virginia: The Road to Independence* Vol. 3. Charlottesville: University Press of Virginia, 1977.

Scribner, Robert L. and Brent Tarter, eds. *Revolutionary Virginia: The Road to Independence*, Vol. 4-7. Charlottesville: University Press of Virginia, 1978-83.

Shepard, E. Lee, ed. *Marching to Victory: Capt. Benjamin Bartholomew's Diary of the Yorktown Campaign: May 1781 to March 1782*. Richmond: Virginia Historical Society, 2002.

Smith, Paul H., ed. *Letters of Delegates of the Continental Congress*, Vol. 6-18. Washington, DC: Library of Congress, 1976-2000.

Sparks, Jared, ed. *Correspondence of the American Revolution Being Letters of Eminent Men to George Washington*. Boston: Little, Brown, 1853.

Steuben Papers (Microfilm). Rockefeller Library, Colonial Williamsburg Foundation, Williamsburg, Virginia.

Tarleton, Banastre. *A History of the Campaigns of 1780-1781 in the Southern Provinces of North America*. Samen, NH: Ayer Company, 1999. Originally printed in 1787.

Tarter, Brent, ed. "The Orderly Book of the 2nd Virginia Regiment," *Virginia Magazine of History and Biography*, Vol. 85, No. 2. April 1977.

Thacher, James, M.D. *Military Journal of the American Revolution, 1775-1783*. Gansevoort, NY: Corner House Historical Publications, 1998.

Valley Forge Orderly Book of General George Weedon. New York: New York Times and Arno Press, 1917.

Washington, George. *The Papers of George Washington, Revolutionary War Series,* Vol. 1-24. Charlottesville: University Press of Virginia, 1985-2016.

Washington, George. "A General Return of the 12 Virginia Battalions in Morristown, May 17, 1777," *The Papers of George Washington, Revolutionary War Series*. Library of Congress online.

Washington, George. *Writings of George Washington,* Vols. 1-24. Fitzpatrick, John C., ed. Washington, DC: US Goverment Printing Office, 1931-38.

Weedon, George. "Brigadier General George Weedon's Correspondence Account of the Battle of Brandywine, September 11, 1777," Manuscript in the Chicago Historical Society. Transcribed by Bob McDonald.

Wilcox, William B., ed. *The American Rebellion: Sir Henry Clinton's Narrative of His Campaign*. New Haven: Yale University Press, 1954.

SECONDARY SOURCES

Bearss, Edwin C. *The Battle of Sullivan's Island and the Capture of Fort Moultrie: A Documented Narrative and Troop Movement Maps.* Washington, DC: U.S. Dept. of the Interior, 1968.

Boatner, Mark M. *Encyclopedia of the American Revolution.* New York: David McKay Co., 1966.

Borick, Carl P. *A Gallant Defense: The Siege of Charleston, 1780.* Columbia: University of South Carolina, 2003.

Braisted, Todd W. *Grand Forage, 1778: The Battleground Around New York City.* Yardley, PA: Westholme Publishing, 2016.

Cecere, Michael. *A Good and Valuable Officer: Daniel Morgan in the Revolutionary War.* Bowie: Heritage Books, 2016.

Cecere, Michael. *An Officer of Very Extraordinary Merit: Charles Porterfield and the American War for Independence, 1775-1780.* Bowie: Heritage Books, 2004.

Cecere, Michael. *Captain Thomas Posey and the 7th Virginia Regiment.* Bowie: Heritage Books, 2005

Cecere, Michael. *Cast Off the British Yoke: The Old Dominion and American Independence, 1763-1776.* Bowie: Heritage Books, 2014.

Cecere, Michael. *The Invasion of Virginia 1781.* Yardley, PA: Westholme Publishing, 2017.

Cecere, Michael. *They Are Indeed a Very Useful Corps: American Riflemen in the Revolutionary War.* Bowie: Heritage Books, 2006.

Cecere, Michael. *They Behaved Like Soldiers, Captain John Chilton and the Third Virginia Regiment, 1775-1778.* Bowie: Heritage Books, 2004.

Cecere, Michael. *Wedded to My Sword: The Revolutionary War Service of Light Horse Harry Lee.* Bowie: Heritage Books, 2012

Cunningham, John T. *The Uncertain Revolution: Washington & the Continental Army at Morristown.* Toronto: Cormorant Publishing, 2007.

Davis, Robert. *The Revolutionary War: The Battle of Petersburg.* E. & R. Davis, 2002.

Friar, Robert. *The Militia are Coming out from all Quarters: The Revolution in Virginia's Lower Counties.* 2010.

Golway, Terry. *Washington's General: Nathanael Greene and the Triumph of the American Revolution.* New York: Henry Holt, 2006.

Graham, James. *The Life of General Daniel Morgan of the Virginia Line of the Army of the United States*. Bloomingburg, NY: Zebrowski Historical Services Publishing Company, 1993. Originally published in 1856.

Grainger, John D. *The Battle of Yorktown, 1781: A Reassessment*. Rochester, NY: Boydell Press, 2005.

Gruber, Ira D. *John Peebles American War: The Diary of a Scottish Grenadier, 1776-1782*. Mechanicsburg, PA: Stackpole Books, 1998.

Harris, Michael C. *Brandywine: A Military History of the Battle that Lost Philadelphia but Saved America, September 11, 1777*. El Dorago Hills, CA: Savas Beatie, 2014.

Hartmann, John W. *The American Partisan: Henry Lee and the Struggle for Independence: 1776-1780*. Shippensburg, PA: Burd St. Press, 2000.

Higginbotham, Don. *Daniel Morgan: Revolutionary Rifleman*. Chapel Hill: University of North Carolina Press, 1961.

Hocker, Edward W. *The Fighting Parson of the American Revolution: A Biography of General Peter Muhlenberg*. Philadelphia, 1936.

Jackson, John W. *Valley Forge: Pinnacle of Courage*. Thomas Publications, 1992.

Johnson, Henry P. *The Yorktown. Campaign and the Surrender of Cornwallis: 1781*. Fort Washington, PA: Eastern National, 1997.

Kranish, Michael. *Flight from Monticello: Thomas Jefferson at War*. New York: Oxford University Press, 2010.

Lee, Henry. *The Revolutionary War Memoirs of General Henry Lee*. New York: Da Capo Press, 1979.

Lee, Nell Moore. *Patriot Above Profit: A Portrait of Thomas Nelson Jr., Who Supported the American Revolution With His Purse and Sword*. Nashville, TN: Rutledge Hill Press, 1988.

Lender, Mark Edward and Garry Wheeler Stone. *Fatal Sunday: George Washington, the Monmouth Campaign, and the Politics of Battle*. Norman: University of Oklahoma Press, 2016.

Loprieno, Don. *The Enterprise in Contemplation: The Midnight Assault of Stony Point*. Heritage Books, 2004

Marshall, John. *The Life of George Washington*. Fredericksburg, VA: The Citizens Guild of Washington's Boyhood Home, 1926.

Mass, John. *The Road to Yorktown: Jefferson, LaFayette and the British Invasion of Virginia.* Charleston, SC: History Press, 2015.

McGuire, Thomas. *The Philadelphia Campaign: Brandywine and the Fall of Philadelphia,* Vol. 1. Mechanisburg, PA: Stackpole Books, 2006.

McGuire, Thomas. *The Philadelphia Campaign: Germantown and the Roads to Valley Forge,* Vol. 2. Mechanisburg, PA: Stackpole Books, 2007.

Muhlenberg, Henry A. *The Life of Major-General Peter Muhlenberg of the Revolutionary Army.* Philadelphia: Cary and Hart, 1849.

Reed, John F. *Campaign to Valley Forge: July 1, 1777-December 19, 1777.* Pioneer Press, 1965.

Reed, William B. *Life and Correspondence of Joseph Reed*, Vol. 2. Philadelphia: Lindsay and Blakiston, 1847.

Selby, John. *The Revolution in Virginia, 1775-1783.* Colonial Williamsburg Foundation, 1988.

Smith, George M. *The Reverend Peter Muhlenberg: A Symbiotic Adventure in Virginia, 1772-1783.* Unpublished report.

Stewart, Catesby Willis. *The Life of Brigadier General William Woodford of the American Revolution*, Vol. 1-2. Richmond, VA: Whitten & Shepperson, 1973.

Stryker, William. *The Battle of Monmouth.* Princeton, NJ: Princeton University Press, 1927.

Trussell, John B.B.Jr., *Birthplace of an Army: A Study of the Valley Forge Encampment.* Pennsylvania Historical and Museum Commission, 1998.

Wallace, Paul. *The Muhlenbergs of Pennsylvania.* Philadelphia: University of Pennsylvania Press, 1950.

Ward, Harry M. *Charles Scott: Spirit of '76.* Charlottesville: University Press of Virginia, 1988.

Ward, Harry M. *Duty, Honor or Country: General George Weedon and the American Revolution.* Philadelphia: American Philosophical Society, 1979.

Wayland, John W. *A History of Shenandoah County, Virginia.* Baltimore: Regional Publishing Co., 1976.

NEWSPAPERS

Caledonian Mercury. 10 October 1781, "Extract of a letter from an officer in the 76 regiment dated on board the Lord Mulgrave transport, Hampton Road, Virginia, July 23, 1781."

The Enquirer. "Mortuary Notice, October 14, 1807," Richmond, Virginia.

The Pennsylvania Gazette and Weekly Advertiser. "Return of Killed and Wounded. . . ." October 31, 1781, No. 2681.

The Tickler. "October 7, 1807," Philadelphia, Pennsylvania.

ACKNOWLEDGMENTS

THERE ARE SEVERAL PEOPLE AND INSTITUTIONS THAT I OWE THANKS to for their assistance and encouragement with this book. Bruce H. Franklin at Westholme Publishing and Don N. Hagist at the *Journal of the American Revolution* were immensely supportive and helpful with the book and a pleasure to work with. Copy editor Nate Best and proofreader Mike Kopf thankfully caught and corrected my many mistakes, Tracy Dungan did a fantastic job creating maps for the book, as did Trudi Gershenov with the book cover. I sincerely thank them all for their hard work.

Many of my fellow Revolutionary War reenactors, especially Buzz Deemer, Drummond Ball, Rob Friar, and Jim Gallagher—all of whom share my passion and interest about this period of history— helped with research as well as encouragement. The Rockefeller Library at the Colonial Williamsburg Foundation and the research library at the Jamestown-Yorktown Foundation were both invaluable resources for my research. I want to also thank my friend and former colleague, Marguerite Knickmeyer, whom I had the pleasure to co-teach with for a decade. Her support, encouragement, and editing of many of my earlier works gave me the confidence to keep writing. Lastly, I want to thank my wife Susan, who has indulged me in my interest in the American Revolution to the point that she now happily hosts colonial dances with me at our home in Williamsburg in full colonial attire. Thank you Sue for being a true partner in our wonderful life together.

INDEX